THE BEST SHORT PLAYS 1980

Chilton Book Company

RADNOR, PENNSYLVANIA

THE
BEST
SHORT
PLAYS *1980*

edited and with an introduction by

STANLEY RICHARDS

Best Short Plays Series

*fully protected under the Copyright
Empire, including the Dominion of
l Copyright Union and the Univer-
, wholly or in part, by any method,
agents. (See* CAUTION *notices at the*

Copyright © 1980 by Stanley Richards
All Rights Reserved
Published in Radnor, Pennsylvania, by Chilton Book Company
and simultaneously in Don Mills, Ontario, Canada,
by Thomas Nelson & Sons, Ltd.

Library of Congress Catalog Card No. 38-8006
ISBN 0-8019-6884-4
ISSN 0067-6284

Manufactured in the United States of America

1 2 3 4 5 6 7 8 9 0   9 8 7 6 5 4 3 2 1 0

for Curt Dempster

BOOKS AND PLAYS BY STANLEY RICHARDS

ANTHOLOGIES:

The Best Short Plays, issued annually, 1968–1979
Great Musicals of the American Theatre: Volume One
Great Musicals of the American Theatre: Volume Two
Best Plays of the Seventies
America on Stage: Ten Great Plays of American History
The Tony Winners
Best Plays of the Sixties
Twenty One-Act Plays
Best Mystery and Suspense Plays of the Modern Theatre
10 Classic Mystery and Suspense Plays of the Modern Theatre
The Most Popular Plays of the American Theatre
Great Rock Musicals
Modern Short Comedies from Broadway and London
Best Short Plays of the World Theatre: 1968–1973
Best Short Plays of the World Theatre: 1958–1967
Canada on Stage

PLAYS:

Through a Glass, Darkly
August Heat
Sun Deck
Tunnel of Love
Journey to Bahia
O Distant Land
Mood Piece
Mr. Bell's Creation
The Proud Age
Once to Every Boy
Half-Hour, Please
Know Your Neighbor
Gin and Bitterness
The Hills of Bataan
District of Columbia

CONTENTS

INTRODUCTION

With *The Best Short Plays 1980,* this series steps into a new and, hopefully, significant decade in the theatre. The indications are there if one glances back at the seventies. During an uncommonly turbulent decade that witnessed enormous upheavals and violent social and political changes the theatre, somehow, maintained a relative stability. It perhaps achieved even more, for the American theatre set records in audience attendance and box-office receipts, particularly in the latter half of the decade. For example, in the Broadway theatre alone, the 1978–79 season attracted an attendance of 9.8 million theatregoers which yielded $136 million in ticket sales and was the sixth consecutive season to see continual increases in both totals. Although inflation, which brought higher prices for tickets, played a partial role in the rises of revenues, the attendance figures indicated a steady and appreciable growth in theatregoing.

The heightened interest in the theatre is especially pertinent in view of its two most formidable contemporary competitors for audience attention: television and motion pictures. Yet, more and more theatregoers were lured into legitimate playhouses than ever before in our history. This, of course, is inspiring to those who dedicate themselves to the theatre, especially to our playwrights who are fully aware that no viable theatre can possibly exist without that all-important audience.

A film is completed and shipped off for distribution and exhibition whatever its ultimate fate, a television program is taped and often slips into obscurity after its prime and lesser-time viewing, but for a play to endure there must be a constant flow of audiences, not for a single showing but for many performances and many productions.

The challenge in writing for the theatre, then, is an enormous one, yet there is nothing more rewarding for a writer in the entertainment media than seeing his work performed nightly by live actors before receptive audiences. Perhaps Sir John Gielgud, one of the world's outstanding players, best summed up the enchantment of the stage when he declared: "Nothing can compare with the magic of the real occasion, which is to me the true glory of the art of the theatre—the living actor appearing before the living audience."

During the seventies, *The Best Short Plays* series published 124 plays. It introduced works by many new dramatists as well as by some of our most prominent and established writers. Of the new dramatists represented in these pages during the past decade, at least a dozen have gone on to national and international prominence. This is exceedingly gratifying to the writers, of course, but almost equally so to an editor who feels that his staunch support and confidence have been tangibly substantiated.

From the number of plays published, seventy-two were presented in New York either before or after selection for these annuals. Some were seen on Broadway, others Off and Off-Off-Broadway. Many then traveled far and wide across the nation and often into foreign territories. Thus, more than fifty percent of the plays that appeared in these pages during the seventies were presented in one form or another in New York which still maintains its status as the theatrical capital of the nation. As for the other plays published in this series, I know for certain that a majority were given presentations elsewhere, for most contributors keep me happily informed.

The stages of the seventies, then, were "alive" with plays culled from *The Best Short Plays* series. If this is a harbinger of the years to come, the eighties should be an even more productive and rewarding decade for our dramatists who steadfastly hold that live theatre is still the dwelling place of wonder.

STANLEY RICHARDS
New York, NY

Shirley Lauro

THE COAL DIAMOND

Shirley Lauro

When Shirley Lauro's *The Coal Diamond* was first performed at the Ensemble Studio Theatre in 1979, it was greeted with enthusiasm and considerable praise from the New York press. Mel Gussow reported in *The New York Times* that: "Mrs. Lauro precisely captures a time, a place and a community of characters . . . with humor, affection and a grasp of provincial language." Other theatre journalists were equally impressed, particularly Marilyn Stasio who wrote in the *New York Post:* "This meticulously crafted play deals us in on a hilarious bridge game played by four gossipy women who work in an insurance company in Missouri in 1955. Before long, secrets pop out, and the emotional stakes go up, until the game turns into a cutthroat competition for pride and place . . . *The Coal Diamond* is an unflawed gem."

Born and raised in Des Moines, Iowa, Mrs. Lauro received her B.A. from Northwestern University and her M.A. from the University of Wisconsin. Initial recognition as a literary figure came in 1965 with the publication of her novel, *The Edge.* A harbinger of the Women's Movement, the widely-read novel was described by reviewers as "an absorbing record of one woman's journey into self-awareness . . . a powerful and moving story written with the assurance of an artist and with great sensibility."

Following its publication and the dissolution of an early marriage, Mrs. Lauro spent seven years on her own, "raising my young daughter, earning my own living for the first time—as an instructor at City College of New York and Yeshiva University—and attempting, along with a mainstream of young American women in those years, to 'come of age.' They were painful but important years for me."

When she resumed writing, she turned to the dramatic form. As she explains: "I had majored in theatre and started out to be an actress. Also, my approach as a writer has always been through character exploration, often the exploration of women in conflict—with themselves or other women. The theatre seemed a natural habitat for my work. In addition, the urgency and immediacy of a play make it a very potent literary form for these frenetic times. More so, I feel, than the novel."

Mrs. Lauro's first full-length play, *The Contest,* was written in 1976. Produced originally at the Alley Theatre in Houston,

Texas, it later opened in New York at an Off-Off-Broadway playhouse with the critics concurring that she had found the right milieu for her writing: "Mrs. Lauro, heretofore a novelist, has a natural and unquestionable talent for the theatre."

Her emergence as a dramatist was followed by a second full-length play, *The Story of Margaret/The Story of Kit,* and three inter-related short plays—*I Don't Know Where You're Coming From at All!, Open Admissions* and *Nothing Immediate*—which were produced in New York under the overall title *Lessons.*

Recently cited by *The New York Times* as one of the ten leading women playwrights who are "writing a new chapter in the American theatre of the late seventies," Mrs. Lauro lives and writes in Manhattan. Remarried, she makes her home with her husband, Dr. Louis Lauro, a psychoanalyst, and her daughter, Andrea, in a "large, rambling apartment on Central Park West with wonderful views of the park."

The Coal Diamond appears in an anthology for the first time in *The Best Short Plays 1980.*

Characters:

INEZ, *mid-twenties to mid-thirties. Tall, thin, flat chested. Nothing fits right although she drinks malts to gain weight! Wears a flowered chintz skirt and peasant blouse that won't stay in. Bare-legged, white sandals that she kicks off. She smokes Camels and chews a lot of gum.*

LENA, *middle-aged. Wears girdle, hose, rayon print dress, pumps. Little gold rimmed glasses. Permanent in her hair. "The Boss".*

BETTY JEAN, *nineteen. Peroxide blond, dark at roots, in ponytail with pink ribbon. Noticeably pregnant, wears pink and white polka dot maternity smock, flat white sandals. Toenails and fingernails are painted pink.*

PEARL, *mid-twenties to mid-thirties. Summer dress. Trying hard to look like the office girls here in Valley Center. She's just moved to town and it's a new town and a new job, and she doesn't feel as smart as the other girls. Especially the ones here in Research.*

Scene:

The Insurance Office, Research Department of Southeastern Missouri Farm Insurance Co., Valley Center, Missouri.

August, 1955. The hottest day of the year.

A corner of the Research Office. Where the "smart girls" work.

Lunch time.

Two gray desks with typewriters on them. An old-fashioned ceiling fan, moving only in centimeters. If at all. A water cooler. One desk has been pushed up to the window to get whatever breeze there may be.

Office is deserted except for three typists who are bustling around, getting ready to eat lunch and play bridge—Lena, Inez and Betty Jean.

In the dark we hear Inez typing.

Lights up.

LENA: *(Telling punchline of joke)* And then, he said to her: "I said *bells*, lady, not *balls!*"

(Peals of laughter from Inez, Betty Jean and Lena)

BETTY JEAN: Oh, Lena, that's jist awful!

INEZ: (*Makes mistake on typewriter*) Law! You got me laughin' so, I jist made a mistake.

LENA: You can fix it this afternoon. It's ten after twelve already! And both you girls have put in a terrible hard mornin' as it is.

BETTY JEAN: Isn't that the truth! Land! This hot ole mornin' seemed a thousand hours long.

LENA: Well, come on now, Betty Jean . . . let's us jist all relax our brains—and have us some *fun!* It's "Lunch Time," girls!

(*Pearl enters, carrying her lunch, looking around, not immediately seeing the others, who are now setting up for bridge game and lunch. They put deck of cards and scorepad on desk, and take out brown paper bags with boloney and cheese sandwiches, apples, candy bars and Cokes. Inez puts a pack of Camels on the desk*)

INEZ: Hey, Pearl, honey. You jist come right along over here! We're jist about ready to start.

PEARL: (*Joining the group*) I'm jist terrible sorry to be late and all. I got stuck doin' this report. And I couldn't remember how she said to do it. Finally, I jist give up!

INEZ: (*Rising, encircling Pearl's waist*) Jist never you mind, Pearl, honey. It's okay. Why, we're all so tickled to git us a fourth, we're about to die! Now jist let me name you around. Everyone: this here's my friend, Pearl Brewster, like I said. Jist started to work here Monday. They stuck her in Underwriting.

BETTY JEAN: Oh, Law!

INEZ: This here's Betty Jean McGaffee.

PEARL: Pleased to know you, Betty Jean.

BETTY JEAN: Thanks.

INEZ: Her husband works out to the Firestone Plant. First Shift!

BETTY JEAN: Shoot! Don't have to give her my family tree!

INEZ: (*Patting Betty Jean's stomach*) Somebody already gave you your family tree, girl! (*Everyone laughs*) Anyhow, this little gold-haired honey jist graduated high school a year ago June, and already got herself this good job in Research, a husband on First Shift, and a kid almost due!

PEARL: (*Taking in the black roots on Betty Jean's hair*) Isn't that something now?

(*Betty Jean takes her knitting—booties—from desk drawer*)

INEZ: And finally, . . . this is Lena Travis, Boss of the Research Section. (*Lena shakes Pearl's hand*) Lena is terrible smart at insurance and bridge. Only thing is—she can't get her a man!

(*The other girls smile ever so sweetly at Lena*)

LENA: (*Hitching up her glasses, which she does very often, and then taking a bite out of her apple*) Never you mind what I got or ain't got, Inez Potter!

INEZ: Heck! I was only teasin', Lena! Truth is, Pearl, honey, Lena is jist too dang good for any old man! Why, Betty Jean and me, we never had such a wonderful girl to work for ever in our lives as Lena Travis. And that's a fact!

LENA: (*Touched*) Shoot!

(*Lena sits, motions Pearl to sit. Betty Jean goes to window, opens it wide*)

INEZ: Well, it's the Lord's truth, Lena, and you know it is. Why, we're jist crazy about workin' for you!

BETTY JEAN: She is jist terrible nice, Pearl. Heck! Everytime I get the backache, she give me this pass to the lounge. And she sure has got a swell sense a humor, Lena has. Keeps us in stitches all the time. "I–I said *bells*, lady, not *balls*!"

(*Betty Jean, Lena and Inez laugh. Everyone settles down at table*)

LENA: Aw go on! (*Begins to welcome Pearl, dealing cards as she does*) Now, I mean to tell ya, Pearl, honey, we're proud to have ya come in like this of a Friday to be a fourth. Friday noons is terrible hard to get a fourth. Everybody goes on uptown, see, to make their deposits on account of we git paid about a quarter of. Why it's a positive chore gittin' someone up here of a Friday. Specially since we're the only department hasn't got us our air-conditioner yet. Hot as this weather is . . .

PEARL: (*Kicking off sandals and spreading her toes over the cool linoleum. Opens lunch bag now, eating her jelly doughnut first. It drips on her dress*) Oh, pshaw! Don't bother me none about the air-conditioner. I'm jist glad to git out of Underwriting! All they do is play pinochle! Got this mean ole boss . . .

LENA: Edna?

PEARL: . . . Edna! Always makes me do my reports over again.

INEZ: Well, don't worry. You'll catch on. Pearl just moved to town. From River Falls. You was cashierin' there, weren't ya? Never tried office work before?

PEARL: Mmm. It's double the money. It's gonna be our break.

INEZ: That's where we two met. When I was livin' in River Falls.

PEARL: (*Confused*) It is? I thought we met at that company picnic when our husbands was workin' over at Atlas Movin' Outfit in Cherokee.

INEZ: (*Chuckles, wads up gum wrapper and shoots it at the wastebasket*) Pshaw! Pearl! You got a memory like a frog! It was over to River Falls we met. Before we was ever married. (*Others laugh*) She can't even remember bird one!

PEARL: You're right. I remember it all now. It was at one a them Baptist Fellowship Picnics we met. And they had it right on the river bank . . . and there was these big ole horseflies around. And they bit Inez! And she started yellin' out—so I come over and . . .

INEZ: (*Anxious to get off the topic*) We all set?

(*Cards have been dealt. Lena and Betty Jean are partners, sitting opposite, and Pearl and Inez*)

LENA: Mmm. Let's play cards. Here we go: one heart.

INEZ: Crime 'n Itly! I haven't got anything! Pass!

BETTY JEAN: Two hearts.

PEARL: Two spades.

LENA: Three hearts.

INEZ: I still haven't got piddly: pass.

PEARL: That's okay.

BETTY JEAN: Pass. My land! What a hot ole August day!

PEARL: You got it, Lena. It's yours.

LENA: Ain't that nice now. Three hearts.

(*Inez leads out, Betty Jean lays down hand, gets up and goes around to look over Lena's shoulder at her hand*)

PEARL: (*Taking the first trick*) Hey . . . who's the fourth here the rest of the week?

INEZ: Wanda Sue Turner. Goes to the bank to deposit on Fridays regular. Puts away every cent she gits, I guess!

LENA: (*Slapping her card down to take trick*) I guess! (*Leads out*)

PEARL: Tight, huh?

LENA: (*Taking next trick, winking at Betty Jean*) Tight? Girl, I mean to tell you she puts Jack Benny to shame! Why she lives in a rented room over Ramsey's Auto Parts Store. Hasn't even got a hot plate to her name. She makes a complete diet outa soda crackers and skim milk, and she won't even chip in on the baby showers or birthday cards for the rest of the force!

PEARL: (*Stunned*) She don't chip in?

LENA: Isn't that the limit though? Why, when she first came in here to work and I knew she was a stranger in town, yah know? I tried to find her a place to live. I told her about my apartment . . . the Glenview Arms? Them real swell apartments over by the river?

PEARL: Oh, I seen them . . . they're just awful nice.

LENA: So, anyhow, she says, how much do they cost, and I says I pay sixty dollars a month, and . . .

PEARL: Oh, Law! You pay sixty dollars a month? Jist for yourself?

LENA: Mmm. Sixty-five dollars now. That was three years ago. Anyhow. You shoulda seen ole Wanda's face when I told her. Flabbergasted is the only word to name the state of that girl's face. I figured her out then and there.

(*Betty Jean goes back to the window*)

INEZ: Aw, that ain't nice, Lena! She's not so tight. (*She takes a swig of her Coke*) Truth of it is, Wanda Sue's hopin' to git married. She's savin' for her hope chest. Lena jist don't like her. She's got a chip on her shoulder about poor Wanda Sue.

PEARL: Oh?

LENA: She is too tight! Among other things . . .

(*Betty Jean bursts out laughing at this, and Inez, in spite of better instincts, does too. Betty Jean goes back to look over Lena's shoulder*)

PEARL: Well, jist listen to you all! What is it? What are you savin' it up for, the fourth of July? Tell me before you bust your seams!

LENA: Shoot! Now will you look at her? Miss Curiosity! Honey, you're too young. I don't want to dirty up those lily white ears!

(*Betty Jean finds this incredibly funny; she shrieks with laughter*)

PEARL: Go on! Is she . . . ornery?

LENA: Ornery? Well, I don't know as I'd call it that . . .

exactly. Besides it ain't really her . . . it's that bum she thinks is gonna marry her! (*She trumps the trick*)

PEARL: What's wrong with him?

LENA: Everything! (*She stops game now to devote full attention to telling this*) He has got himself a reputation all over this office, I mean to tell you! He used to work here.

INEZ: 'Til he got himself fired! Lena had to let him go. (*Betty Jean crosses to her own desk to powder face*)

PEARL: Oh . . . he was the one was . . . ornery then?

LENA: Shoot, he was way past ornery. Dirty! That's the word to describe that man. Filthy dirty man!

PEARL: No! Right here in this office?

LENA: Mmm. Why he was always takin' anybody he could git a hold of out behind the candy machine in the hall, and you better believe he wasn't shovin' nickels in a machine for no Hershey bars out there!

PEARL: No!

LENA: Shoot! Once I seen him back that Dago girl, Marie . . . you remember Marie, don't ya, Inez? Worked for Dooley?

INEZ: Married some Hunkie in Chicago?

LENA: Yeah, that's her. Anyhow I seen Wanda's intended back this Dago girl, Marie, up against a wall and about rip her blouse off her, out there by the candy machine. Right from my desk I had a complete view. Poor thing was so scared she didn't know which end was up!

PEARL: All right here in this office? Law!

LENA: Well, don't drop your pants about it, Pearl, honey. I'm tellin' you the man was trash!

PEARL: (*Pouting*) Pshaw! We haven't got nobody like that up in Underwriting. All we got is Mr. Johnson. Lives with his mother in Clive.

INEZ: Well, thank your stars, Pearl, honey, on that account. It was a terrible influence on us havin' him here. Why, he never even went to church Easter Morning!

PEARL: No!

LENA: And the stories he used to pass around! Why . . . he told Betty Jean here . . . and before she was even married, you understand . . . told her how he'd gone to this sideshow out by Hampton and seen some girl performer do something with a stud pony! Well! I don't mean to spell it out for ya, but Law, when Betty Jean here told her Earl Henry about it, didn't he about knock her cuckoo for knowing about such disgustin' things!

BETTY JEAN: (*Coming back from her desk*) He was terrible mad!

PEARL: No! In Hampton they do that?

LENA: Crime 'n Itly! That's jist nothin to how low he was! He came right over to Inez at her desk, right before Inez had her baby, James Orville, and he yells jist as loud as a fire truck, "Hey, Inez." He yells, "Why don't you send that husband of yours up to Merrimack and git that doctor up there to fix him for ya!"

PEARL: The nerve! They do that in Merrimack?

INEZ: Doesn't that beat all? Why the very idea! Could have spoiled the rest of my married life?

LENA: Oh, I don't know as *that's* true. Lola what's-her-name, used to work on the IBM Machine on two? She sent her husband up to that doctor in Merrimack.

PEARL: Really?

INEZ: I didn't know that.

BETTY JEAN: (*Pressing in her back*) Well, she already had five kids.

PEARL: Mmm. This Lola happen to say what happened after her husband got himself fixed?

LENA: Nothin'. . . so she says! Didn't do nothin' but make him worse than he already was! Wasn't anything could hold him down after the operation Lola said. Wasn't ten months later she had her a set a twins. Both boys. A course, all you girls'd know more about that sorta thing than me!

(*Hand of cards is over. Lena crosses to water cooler to get drink*)

INEZ: Pshaw! Lena . . . you gonna go through life like that? Fudge! I'd die of the curiosity. It's just a cryin' shame you can't hook somebody or the other. Law!

(*Betty Jean sits. Inez deals the next hand*)

LENA: Maybe I don't want to. Ever think of that? Maybe there ain't no dang man this side of the Mississippi I'd give the time of day to, let alone have livin' off my good salary the rest of my natural life! And cashin' in on all my insurance if I pass first!

BETTY JEAN: (*Soothingly*) Well, sure! Can't say as I blame

you in the least, Lena, honey. What with the kinda money you make and all the insurance you musta piled up from here for your retirement.

(*Lena comes back and sits. Pearl is watching Lena*)

PEARL: You ever been in River Falls? Visitin' or anything? Or Mountain Point?

LENA: Nope. Why?

PEARL: You . . . you look like I know you from someplace. Only I can't locate where.

INEZ: Isn't she the limit? Shoot! Somebody's always lookin' like somebody else to old Pearl. Every Tom, Dick or Harry on Mulberry Street puts her in mind of someone else!

PEARL: No, but Lena *really* does!

(*Inez finishes the deal. They sort their hands*)

INEZ: Pass.

BETTY JEAN: One club.

PEARL: Pass.

LENA: Pass.

INEZ: You got it Betty Jean for one club.

BETTY JEAN: Hardly worth it. Mangy little ole bid. Well, Pearl, lead out. Law! I'm so hot I'm stickin' to this seat!

(*Pearl leads*)

PEARL: So, they met here . . . ?

INEZ: Who met here?

LENA: He was in the stockroom. Doesn't that take the cake? A forty-year-old man stackin' envelopes at sixty cents per?

PEARL: Tommy Paul gets one-fifty out to John Deere now.

BETTY JEAN: Earl Henry just got raised to two.

LENA: It was the only job I figured he could handle, don't ya know? I was the one hired him to start with and first few years he was okay.

PEARL: But you fired him?

LENA: Had to, finally. After Wanda Sue started workin' here he wasn't the same man. Couldn't even handle his stupid little job. And I had to tell him so in front a everyone and yell at him and everything 'cause he was makin' such a mess of that room.

BETTY JEAN: It was an awful scene the day she let him go. Upset me to me stomach the whole afternoon. And Wanda Sue! Law, she threw up!

PEARL: What she look like? She pretty?

INEZ: Not bad. Big blue eyes. A natural blond. (*She glances at Betty Jean*)

LENA: Ain't her looks that's gittin' us down about her. It's that she's turnin' out to be so blame stupid and ignorant.

BETTY JEAN: Yeah. It's all jist comin' out now. Why, Pearl, 'it takes her a solid morning to type a row of figures down a page.

LENA: She come in here after her junior year of high school. Doesn't have no diploma a course. So she don't make the same as the rest of my Research girls!

INEZ: Not by half!

(*Pearl again has spilled jelly from doughnut on dress. She goes to water cooler to clean it off*)

BETTY JEAN: She is so dumb! Can you believe she's *makin'* her own wedding dress? And after I told her ninety-eleven times about them gorgeous little numbers over at "Three Sisters" where I bought mine. Jist gobs and gobs of lace and tulle for $29.98. She didn't listen. She jist keeps bringin' in her silly old veil to work and sewin' on it here at lunch. Isn't that dumb? She got the mayonnaise on it jist last week!

(*The other girls all laugh*)

PEARL: Hey, she got her an engagement ring?

(*Pause. The others look at each other, begin to smirk and wink*)

INEZ: Uh . . . what'd you say, honey? Has she got her an engagement ring? That's the question you have asked?

PEARL: (*Bewildered. Turns at cooler to look at them*) Yes.

INEZ: (*Winking*) That's what the girl asked, Betty Jean. What do you say to that? Has Wanda Sue got her an engagement ring?

BETTY JEAN: An engagement ring, huh? Well, I don't know. Lena, what'd you say? Does Wanda Sue got her an engagement ring?

LENA: Has she got a ring? Well, I would say . . . she has got her the most unusual ring this side of the Pennsylvania mines! That's what I would say!

(*Betty Jean, Inez and Lena all burst out laughing very loudly, splattering their cards on the table and floor, totally disrupting the game*)

PEARL: Hey, you all! What's goin' on? What is this?

LENA: Honey, she's engaged all right! And she's got a ring! A *coal diamond!* All of her very own!

(*The girls laugh more at this*)

PEARL: A *what?*

LENA: (*Magnanimously*) Oh, let's let Inez tell it. She saw the thing first!

INEZ: (*For the occasion she lights up a Camel, takes a drag, sticks her gum under the desk, tilts back in her chair and clears her throat*) Well! Wanda Sue Turner used to sit next to me. Right side, against the back wall.

LENA: (*Can't keep out of it*) Left side. Against the front wall.

INEZ: (*Giving Lena a look*) As I was sayin'! This Wanda Sue's a close mouth. Never tell ya anythin' you want to know. But, anyhow. In she pops this one morning and announces right outa the blue she's gittin' engaged the very next day and is gittin' a half-carat ring!

PEARL: (*Stunned*) Half-carat? You kiddin' me?

LENA: That's what we all said. We couldn't hardly wait 'til the next day in fact to git a look.

INEZ: Next day, eight-thirty on the nose, in she pops. And sure enough there she is wavin' her hand around with this great big ring. And . . .

LENA: (*Can't restrain herself*) And, it was a half-carat all right. But, honey . . . it had a black spot in the center big as a dime. A chunk a coal nobody could polish into diamond and so they left it stickin' in there, black as the ace of spades!

PEARL: What?

LENA: And she went around like she didn't even see that big black blob in the center. She was jist flashin' the thing around!

INEZ: And we didn't want to say nothin' on accounta its bein' the first day she'd got herself ingaged. We never did say nothin'.

LENA: Only it is the sorriest lookin' ring you'll ever see in this world.

(*A pause*)

PEARL: Seems like I seen her in that ring. In the wash-room, I bet.

LENA: Mmm. Probably. She's still wearin' it. Won't take it off for love nor money. She thinks he's comin' back to her.

PEARL: He left? What's he doin'?

LENA: Sittin' on his dinghy somewhere! (*The girls laugh at this*)

INEZ: Crime 'n Itly, Lena, don't tease Pearl so much! He joined the Navy this week . . . took Wanda out to dance to Pee Wee Hunt's band at the Bel-Air . . .

PEARL: Law! I can't abide Pee Wee Hunt!

INEZ: Well, he sprung it on her out there about how he couldn't git another job in town because Lena kept dis-recommendin' him every place called her up. So Red joined the Navy and is gonna save up and sail home to her in two years with a genuine kimono from Tokyo, Japan. He says!

BETTY JEAN: And she believes it! The rest a these are mine . . . (*Betty Jean shows her cards; others concede the game, laying down their cards*) Sits here all week typin' him mushy letters on company time. Sewin' away on that sorry lookin' veil, draggin' around with that coal diamond on her hand! And doin' her reports wrong so Lena has to make her do 'em again.

LENA: Law, I jist don't know how long I can put up with it all before I have to let ole Wanda Sue go, too. 'Cause I think she's gonna be actin' like that 'til Judgement Day!

INEZ: Same day you git you a man, huh?

LENA: Inez, you ever let up on that? Here . . . I got to go to the john. Deal out, Betty Jean, and I'll be right back . . . we haven't got much time left. (*She gets up, starts out*) Don't none of ya cheat on me, hear? (*She exits*)

PEARL: (*The minute Lena's gone, rising, very conspiratorially*) Hey! What was that guy's name?

BETTY JEAN: Huh? Who? What guy?

PEARL: *That* guy . . . that guy you was all jist talkin' about.

INEZ: Who?

PEARL: The guy with Wanda Sue!

INEZ: Oh, Red.

BETTY JEAN: Red.

INEZ: Red Haner.

PEARL: Red?

INEZ: Mm. Had this big bushy mess a red hair and freck-les. Why? What's eatin' you?

PEARL: (*Triumphant*) That's jist what I thought!

INEZ: What do you mean that's jist what you thought?

PEARL: Boy, have I got a story for you all! Thank the Lord Lena left!

BETTY JEAN: Why?

PEARL: You know how I said Lena looked familiar to me?

INEZ: Oh, everybody looks familiar to you. What's that got to do with the price of eggs?

PEARL: I kept thinkin' all hour I knew Lena from before only I couldn't locate where. Then jist a few minutes ago right outa the blue, I commenced to think on my Aunt Fannie! Used to run this boardinghouse in Clearview. And I used to go visit summers when I was a little kid. Nineteen, twenty years ago.

INEZ: Well, who cares what you did twenty years ago?

PEARL: (*Getting very excited*) But that's when I seen Lena. The summer I graduated grade school and went to visit Aunt Fannie. Lena was rentin' a room off her and had a job in some dinky little hicktown office in Clearview. And Lena was young then, ole Lena was—real young—

BETTY JEAN: Yeah?

PEARL: Mmm. But jist as sorry lookin' then as she is now. An old maid in her youth!

BETTY JEAN: Well—feature that!

PEARL: Never did have any boyfriends like the rest of the girls in the roomin' house, you know? Jist her job. That's all Lena ever did talk about was that dumb ole hicktown office job a hers!

INEZ: Oh, Law!

PEARL: Other girls kept on goin' out on their Saturday night dates while Lena jist sat there with me and Aunt Fannie on the front porch. All the nights of August she jist sat. Until this one night we seen her comin' down Willow Street, runnin', shoutin' at us and wavin' her left hand. And then she come up on the porch and sticks it in our faces and shows us this big ole half-carat engagement ring!

BETTY JEAN: What?

PEARL: And tells us she has met someone on the job and has got engaged and is gonna git married!

BETTY JEAN: Oh, Land!

PEARL: Only thing of it was that ring had a chunk of coal in the middle of it big as a dime!

INEZ: What do you mean?

PEARL: (*Exultant*) That Lena was engaged to Red, too! And wore that coal diamond jist like Wanda Sue! I knew I seen that ring before!

(*A long pause. The revelation has stunned Inez and Betty Jean*)

BETTY JEAN: Crime 'n Itly girl, you mean it?

PEARL: Mmm. And to beat all she pretended there wasn't no coal in the middle of it either. That it was the most perfect ring ever existed in the world of God!

(*Betty Jean and Inez are very excited now, laughing and giggling*)

INEZ: I can hardly believe it at all.

PEARL: Well, it's the Lord's truth. Didn't last more 'n two, three months. After I left, Aunt Fannie said she used to sneak him up to her room, and then he started eatin' in the roomin' house and she footed his bill. But by the time I went back to Clearview for Christmas vacation, it was over. Lena said he had to "support his mother" so had to postpone the wedding and take back the ring because he loved Lena "so dearly" and didn't want to spoil Lena's chances with all the other men! 'Course we knew Red'd jist give Lena that ring to git himself that job!

BETTY JEAN: And then Lena got her *this* job here in Valley Center and moved here and hired him again? Thinkin' she'd git him in the end I bet!

PEARL: Mmm. And then along comes Wanda Sue! Well! How's that for a story, girls? Guess that takes the cake about that swell boss you all keep braggin' on! (*In triumph, Pearl chuckles, takes a big bite out of her apple, tilts back in her chair*)

BETTY JEAN: My Land! How many years was it he was—

(*Lena enters*)

LENA: Well, now, nobody cheated on me, did they?

(*The girls laugh, thinly*)

INEZ: Cheated? Shoot, Lena, not on you!

BETTY JEAN: We were jist killin' time . . .

INEZ: (*Busying herself with cards*) Tryin' to keep cool . . .

BETTY JEAN: Shootin' the breeze . . .

INEZ: Jist waitin' on ya, Lena . . . to come back . . .

LENA: (*Putting her purse away*) Well, I bumped into ole Mavis Jones in the washroom. From Claims on four? And you know how that girl goes on!

BETTY JEAN: (*Busying herself, too*) Oh, Law!

LENA: Mmm. She told me they're hirin' two more Claims Investigators for over there at Boone Ridge.

BETTY JEAN: Two more?

LENA: Pshaw! They could use eight more over there. And that's a fact!

(*Pause. Lena sits down again to continue game. The girls are trying to supress giggles. There is much tension—then Inez blurts out mischievously:*)

INEZ: Mmm. We got ole Pearl here talkin' . . . about her past . . .

BETTY JEAN: (*Laughing lightly*) Which she kin hardly remember . . .

INEZ: 'Cause she got a memory like a frog . . . although she did remember as how she'd visited in Clearview . . . when she was a kid? Came to visit her Aunt Fannie. Ran a roomin' house in town . . . for girls . . . isn't that what you said, Pearl, honey?

(*A long pause. Pearl looks at Inez, terrified. Lena looks at Pearl. Finally:*)

LENA: That a fact, Pearl?

PEARL: Oh, but it was so long ago I disremember everything about it. I can't remember a thing! Not a thing! (*She smiles weakly*)

INEZ: That's ole Pearl for you! Always did have a memory like a sieve!

(*Pause. Lena is shaken. Arranges her hand, regaining her composure. Finally:*)

LENA: Well, now, let's see can we finish the rubber off. Betty Jean? Your bid!

BETTY JEAN: (*Looking at Inez, then Lena*) I pass . . .

LENA: Pearl?

PEARL: Pass.

LENA: One spade. Inez?

INEZ: Pass.

BETTY JEAN: Two spades.

PEARL: Pass.

LENA: Pass.

INEZ: Pass.

PEARL: You got it, Lena. For two spades.

LENA: Well. Then it's ours, Betty Jean. Inez, lead out! (*Inez leads. Lena becomes very dictatorial now, ordering everyone*) Betty

Jean, lay down your hand! (*Betty Jean does*) Uh-huh. Put the eight on the three! Pearl, what you gonna do?

PEARL: The King . . . I got no choice . . .

LENA: That's a shame! Here comes the Ace! Put down that King! (*Lena takes the trick*)

BETTY JEAN: Oh, my! Lena, that's good! (*She crosses and stands looking over Lena's shoulder*)

LENA: Okay, here we go! There's mine. Inez, put down yours! (*She leads, Inez plays*) So, Pearl, you're in Underwriting, huh?

PEARL: Yes . . . yes, ma'am, I am . . . I . . .

LENA: Me and Edna a course are such good old girlfriends . . . we go back must be fifteen years . . .

PEARL: Oh, Edna's just a wonderful boss to work for, I can tell you that.

LENA: Thought you said she was mean?

PEARL: Edna? Oh, no, I didn't . . .

LENA: Oh, well . . . it don't matter.

PEARL: Leastways, I . . . I disremember . . .

LENA: *Memory* matters though. Memory's just a terrible important asset for the insurance business. A person would have trouble doin' a good job on their work without a good memory. Don't you think so, girls?

(*A short pause*)

INEZ: Why, I think memory's the most important thing to have of all!

LENA: Betty Jean?

BETTY JEAN: Oh, definitely the most important thing of all. Why everytime I have to type a report I have to remember all them things in my head . . .

LENA: Mmm. In my experience you can't hardly handle the work without it. Most of the girls who stay on and advance theirselves have superior memories. Without that a girl could be a downright detriment to the firm. I think all the bosses of the sections feel exactly the same way . . . in point a fact, I'm sure they do . . . at least the ones I know . . . (*Lena has been taking trick after trick*) 'Course I'm a little more lenient than some. I say, sometimes people *do* forget some things that aren't important to them at all . . . (*Lena looks at Betty Jean and Inez*)

INEZ: Shoot, I'm like that!

BETTY JEAN: Me, too.

LENA: Other people have a more general problem . . . (*A bell rings*) That's it! End a lunch!

BETTY JEAN: And we didn't even finish the rubber off. Fudge!

PEARL: (*Jumping up*) I . . . I got to go. I got to finish my report . . . I . . . I'll see you all . . . I . . . (*She is terrified. She starts hurrying out*)

LENA: Pearl?! (*Pearl stops*) You come on back next Friday, hear? We'll make it permanent on Fridays. At least for a while . . . see how everything goes . . . 'Cause you're jist like us Pearl, honey, you hear? You play one mean hand of bridge!

(*A pause. Pearl exits quickly as Inez and Betty Jean begin to set up office desks for the afternoon work. As they move around her, Lena sits staring after Pearl*)

The lights dim to black

Romulus Linney

TENNESSEE

Romulus Linney

Romulus Linney's *Tennessee,* which appears in print for the first time in *The Best Short Plays 1980,* was presented in New York in 1979 at the Ensemble Studio Theatre. As part of the Theatre's *The Invitational,* "a celebration of the short play," the work was one of six plays, either new, revised, or written especially for the occasion, by Mr. Linney, Tennessee Williams, David Mamet, Murray Schisgal, Marsha Norman and Christopher Durang. All had their premieres during the month-long festival that attracted capacity audiences and some of New York's major reviewers.

Marilyn Stasio of the *New York Post* described *Tennessee* as "A wonderfully comic play. Romulus Linney writes with thrilling lyric intensity of the lives of his mountain people. Beyond capturing the plain-tongued poetry of their idiom, he celebrates the uncompromising character of these Appalachian mountaineers, who lived *with,* not *off* the land."

The *Village Voice's* correspondent, Terry Curtis Fox, acclaimed it as "A gem. . . . What Linney has done in the telling of this story is extraordinary. Each bit of narration is textured with rich detail so that an entire world emerges, in which land is important not only as property but a ground for sustenance, independence, and family continuity." Others were in accord, terming it "a marvelous backwoods tale . . . handsomely crafted . . . with superb character portraits."

Romulus Linney was born in Philadelphia, Pennsylvania, in 1930. He grew up in Madison, Tennessee, with summers spent in North Carolina. He was educated at Oberlin College where he received his B.A. in 1953, and the Yale School of Drama, earning an M.F.A. in 1958.

Mr. Linney is the author of two highly regarded novels, *Heathen Valley* and *Slowly, by Thy Hand Unfurled,* and many plays, including *The Love Suicide at Schofield Barracks,* which was produced on Broadway in 1972; *Democracy; Holy Ghosts;* and *Old Man Joseph and His Family.*

His best known play perhaps is *The Sorrows of Frederick,* a psychological drama about Frederick the Great. Its many stage incarnations include the 1967 premiere at the Mark Taper Forum in Los Angeles with Fritz Weaver in the title role, and subsequent productions in New York with Austin Pendleton, in Canada with Donald Davis, in Great Britain with John Wood and, later, Tom Conti. It also was performed at the Dusseldorf Schauspielhaus in Germany and at the Burgtheater in Vienna, where it successfully played in classical repertory through the season of 1969–70 in a production that won two Austrian theatre awards.

The noted critic Martin Gottfried has written of the author: "Romulus Linney is one of the best kept secrets in the American theatre, a playwright of true literacy and one with a unique vision. Linney is a writer in the grand tradition, using the techniques of high theatre to deal with great ideas. His plays achieve size without pageantry through the heroism of their thoughts, the substance of their passions, and the striking quality of their stylizations."

Mr. Linney also has written extensively for television, had an opera made from a short play, *The Death of King Phillip,* and has published a number of short plays and fiction in numerous literary magazines. He received two fellowships from the National Endowment for the Arts, and from 1976 until 1979 served on its literary panel. He also has been an Adjunct Professor at many schools, including Columbia University, Brooklyn College, the University of Pennsylvania and Connecticut College. His most recent works are a play about Lord Byron, *Childe Byron,* and three short plays about the South, *Choir Practice,* from which *Tennessee* is taken.

Note: Romulus Linney's *Tennessee* won a 1980 Obie Award for Outstanding Achievement in the Off and Off-Off-Broadway theatre.

Characters:

HERSHEL
MARY, *his wife*
CARDELL, *his son*
THE OLD WOMAN
GRISWOLD PLANKMAN
NEIGHBOR

Time:

1870.

Place:

The Appalachian Mountains of North Carolina.

The porch of a log house, facing us. A young woman in a homespun dress stands nursing a baby and gazing out over the slopes. She sees someone, and waves.

MARY: Whoo—oo!
VOICES: (*Off*) Whoo—oo!
(*Mary nurses her baby, sings to it. She makes a face, wincing as the baby's gums pinch her nipple, then she smiles again. Enter Hershel, her husband, and Cardell, her son, carrying axes. They are hot and tired*)
MARY: Well, it's about time.
HERSHEL: We're here, ain't we?
(*They drop their axes, stretch, and go to a bucket sitting on the porch. They reach in it and throw water on their faces. Hershel mops his face with a kerchief. His son does the same*)
MARY: Oh, goodness me. Just so tired and all wore out. I bet you both been laying on the creek bank thinking about supper.
HERSHEL: See, Cardell, what you got to look forward to? You go out into the world. You get yourself some land, a house and a wife. Then you keep careful note of ever' minute

in the day, because you're going to account for ever' damn one. Yes, m'am. That's it. We been laying on the creek bank, counting clouds.

MARY: I ain't surprised.

HERSHEL: How about you? We going to watch you feed that baby all night, or do we get something to eat, too?

MARY: There might be something in the pot for you, if you don't ask for it too often. Ouch. Ow-ee! Baby, go easy on me! Ow!

HERSHEL: Eating you up, is he? Well, why not?

MARY: You'd know why not, you had him pulling on you. There now. Shoo! That's better. All right, supper's ready. Come on.

HERSHEL: Hold it. Take a seat.

MARY: What?

HERSHEL: Take a seat, I said. Cardell, you, too. I want to sit here and watch the sun go down. Supper can wait.

MARY: I never heard you say that before. Cardell, what's wrong with your father?

CARDELL: I don't know. Feeling good, I reckon.

HERSHEL: That's it. I'm feeling good. Sit. (*They sit in slat chairs. Hershel props his feet on a crate, fills a pipe. He is suddenly relaxed, expansive, thinking about something that is important to him. They sit for awhile*) So tell your mother what we did today.

CARDELL: We girdled a stand of them tulip trees. I still say we didn't notch them deep enough, though.

HERSHEL: Oh, yes, we did. Just so the bark's cut through, they'll die. And come down dry wood. We'll have us a new porch and a whole new floor, with boards that won't warp. What about that, Mary?

MARY: That'll be all right.

HERSHEL: Yes, by God, it shore will. We're coming along. Four years a-groaning and sweating on another man's land, and now we got our own. This here is our estate, you know that? Be yours, Cardell, one day, if you want it. And the baby's. 'Cept it'll look different then. I aim to build out this porch half again as wide. How about that?

MARY: That'll be nice.

HERSHEL: I aim to cut into that brush yonder and add it to my slope field. Then we can look out over fifty damn acres. All of it cleared. All of it ours. How about that, by God?

MARY: Ain't you hungry yet?

HERSHEL: Yeah, I'm hungry! Hungry for what's mine! And I got it, too! It cost me, but I got it.

MARY: Hush! Cost you what?

HERSHEL: The getting of it. Not so easy. Your son here can tell you about that. He's commencing to want his own in this life. He's commencing to think on that, worry about it. He'll pay for it, just like I have. Yes, you will, Cardell. Son, you're getting about the age now where you and me are looking slant-wise at each other. I notch a tulip tree, and you stand there thinking how much better you could do it yourself. That right?

CARDELL: I didn't mean nothing about them trees.

HERSHEL: The hell you didn't!

MARY: Hershel. Don't swear at the children.

HERSHEL: But that's all right, son. That's the way it ought to be. That's the way you'll get *your* estate. Pretty soon here, you'll get fed up with the way I do things. Turn red about to bust wanting them your own way. You'll say no, and I'll say yes, and I'll say yes, and you'll say no, and then you won't give a damn what I say. And that's the way it ought to be. That's good. When you can go, Cardell, you can go. Understand?

MARY: All right, wise grandpa. Enough of this. Supper's ready.

HERSHEL: Stay right where you are! Look at this estate! Drop a penny in that ground, and grow yourself half a dollar. North Carolina bottom land! Whoo-pee!

MARY: I declare, Hershel. What's got into you?

HERSHEL: Satisfaction's got into me! I'm taking time to think about it! House, land, a new baby, a son standing up to me like he should, a wife with sore tits but otherwise all right—

MARY: I certainly am glad I'm otherwise all right, Hershel. You took a big load off my mind.

HERSHEL: Yeah. I growed up crawling over a dirt floor in a shack, like a goddamned ant. Going to work with my Daddy, Cardell, for a man lived in a big white house on a hill. People up there in the shade, eternally fanning theirselves, and yelling at my old man, do this and fetch that, me getting hauled about and swore at. Then, when I got just big enough to tell my Daddy, enough of this, having to go serve in the goddamned Confederate Army. So I crawled some more and got hauled around and swore at some more. Ended up lying in a pine forest watching shells set them pines on fire. Men scared to death, running ever' which way, and me, lying there waiting to fry like a piece of bacon, thinking, I'll never get out, never.

MARY: But you did.

HERSHEL: Yeah, I did.

(A cowbell is heard, ringing not far away)

I ain't there no more. I'm where I dreamed I'd be, someday.

(The cowbell is heard again)

On my estate, by God! I got it! And it's mine!

(The cowbell rings again, closer)

MARY: Well, you can enjoy it on an empty stomach, if you have to keep on bragging. *(She points offstage)* Cardell, split me some more wood. I got to heat everything up again.

HERSHEL: Never mind, son. You just sit there and think about what you want in this life, too. I'll go get the damn wood. How about that?

MARY: Hershel, that will be right nice.

(Exit Hershel in the yard, and Mary into the house. Cardell sits dreaming, thinking about his father. The cowbell is heard again, much closer. Cardell looks up.

A light flashes in his face, making him blink. It plays about him, a strange reflection of the afternoon sun, jumping about. He covers his face, blinks. He shades his eyes, stands, and looks out into the brush.

Enter the bent figure of an Old Woman. Her dress is ragged and torn. Her white hair, unbound, is stringy and wild. She carries a cowbell in one hand, ringing it. In the other hand, she carries a piece of shattered mirror glass, holding it up, reflecting the sunlight into Cardell's astonished eyes.

She stares at Cardell)

OLD WOMAN: Didn't expect to see me. Did you?

CARDELL: Who're you?

OLD WOMAN: What?

CARDELL: I said, who are you?

OLD WOMAN: Where's everybody else? Where'd they go to?

CARDELL: What?

OLD WOMAN: Wait. Hold on. Let me figure something out. You're just a boy. Do you live here?

CARDELL: Yes, I do.

OLD WOMAN: Since when?

CARDELL: Since a year ago. My Daddy bought this place a year ago.

OLD WOMAN: Who from?

CARDELL: Nobody. From the county, I think. There was some old man living here, but he died. He didn't have nobody to leave it to, so it was for sale.

OLD WOMAN: What was his name?

CARDELL: Larman.

OLD WOMAN: I know that. I mean his first name.

CARDELL: Abner, I think it was. Wait a minute, you can ask my Daddy. (*He exits, running*)

(*The Old Woman rings her cowbell. She looks at the house. She gazes into the piece of mirror. She laughs. She drops the piece of mirror on the ground. She looks at the house again, studies it. She rings her cowbell.*

Enter Mary, carrying the baby)

MARY: Listen now. Enough of this. Put that cowbell down and come on in to supper—(*She sees the Old Woman*) Oh.

OLD WOMAN: Well, I guess that's that.

(*She laughs. Enter Hershel, with wood, and Cardell with him*)

HERSHEL: Don't get so excited, son. Where—

(*He sees the Old Woman. They stand staring at her. She chuckles and rings her bell and stares right back at them*)

OLD WOMAN: Heh, heh. Heh, heh.

MARY: Hershel, say something to her.

(*Hershel puts down his load of wood, approaches her cautiously*)

HERSHEL: How do you do?

OLD WOMAN: Hidy.

HERSHEL: What can we do for you?

OLD WOMAN: Nothing. You can't do nothing for me at all.

HERSHEL: Well, I'm sorry, then. Uh—

OLD WOMAN: This here your boy?

HERSHEL: Yes.

OLD WOMAN: He says you bought this place from a man named Abner Larman. That right?

HERSHEL: I bought this house, and fifty acres, yes. But I bought it from the county. Mr. Larman died here all alone.

OLD WOMAN: All alone, you say? That figures. Fifty acres, you say?

HERSHEL: Right.

OLD WOMAN: You got cheated. There was over seventy.

HERSHEL: How do you know that?

OLD WOMAN: Never mind. It has been pleasant talking to you. (*She rings her cowbell and starts off*)

MARY: Hershel, she's so old. It's getting dark, and she ain't got no light. She'll fall down. Ought'n we to do something?

HERSHEL: Yeah. Let me see. (*He catches up with her*) M'am! Just a minute!

OLD WOMAN: Yes?

HERSHEL: Don't you want to come sit with us a minute? It's a piece from here to the roads. You live near here?

OLD WOMAN: (*Laughing*) Oh, yes! Oh, yes! I live near here. About seven miles, over the mountain. That's close. Oh, yes!

HERSHEL: You got somebody waiting on you hereabouts?

OLD WOMAN: Nobody's waiting for me nowhere, Mister.

MARY: Come sit with us, then. Please.

HERSHEL: You look tired out.

OLD WOMAN: I do feel a mite puny. All right.

(*Hershel leads the Old Woman up onto the porch and seats her in his chair. She holds onto her cowbell*)

HERSHEL: Like something to eat? Mary?

MARY: I got some spoonbread you might like.

OLD WOMAN: Sounds good. Got any tea?

MARY: I brew boneset tea. Want some of that?

OLD WOMAN: Boneset. I made it myself, once. Here. I'll help you. (*She tries to get up, but slips back in the chair*)

MARY: Stay right there. I'll bring it out to you. Cardell, take the baby, and come on with me.

(*Exit Mary, Cardell and the baby. The Old Woman smiles, nods, and rocks in the chair. Pause*)

OLD WOMAN: So.

HERSHEL: You say you live seven miles from here?

OLD WOMAN: (*Nodding and thinking*) In Tennessee.

HERSHEL: Oh. (*Pause*) You know, I thought the Tennessee border was a good eighty miles over the mountains there.

OLD WOMAN: So did I.

HERSHEL: You sure you live in Tennessee?

OLD WOMAN: That is the only thing in this world I am sure of, Mister. I live in Tennessee, all right.

HERSHEL: No wonder you're tired, then, walking all the way from Tennessee.

OLD WOMAN: Only seven miles. (*Laughs*) Figure it out. I can't.

HERSHEL: Where'd you stay last night?

OLD WOMAN: Well, let me see. Oh, I found a stand of pines, and went in and lay down. Pulled the needles up around me. Dry, mostly. I was cold, but I slept. No, wait. That was the first night. Last night, there was this stream I knowed from a long time ago, it seemed. Comes down the mountain undercutting the rock. Sand underneath. Dry again. Slept there. Made me a gig out of a hickory stick. Had frog legs for breakfast.

HERSHEL: You're on a trip of some kind?

OLD WOMAN: That's right.

HERSHEL: Where you heading?

OLD WOMAN: Back to Tennessee, now.

HERSHEL: I mean, where were you heading?

OLD WOMAN: Here, Mister. Right here.

(*Enter Mary, with a bowl of spoonbread, and a jug of tea*)

MARY: You see if this don't do you some good.

OLD WOMAN: Nice people. Nice people.

(*She eats and drinks. Hershel and Mary move aside to talk. Cardell, holding the baby, comes onto the porch and watches the Old Woman*)

MARY: Hershel, what are we going to do with her? She's too old just to let walk out into the night.

HERSHEL: I know. She can stay with us tonight.

MARY: You think she's a mite crazy?

HERSHEL: She's a mite something. I almost got her to say who she is and all, but not quite. She slept on the ground last night, and the night before that. She gigs frogs.

MARY: How old you think she is?

HERSHEL: Hard to say. I suspect she was a handsome woman once.

MARY: When Cardell seen her, he said she had some kind of a flashing thing in her hand.

HERSHEL: Flashing thing?

MARY: Said she was grinning at him, and it was like she was holding a star in one hand.

HERSHEL: Yeah. Well, she's something else, all right.

(The Old Woman finishes her meal. She seems stronger)

OLD WOMAN: Listen, that was good. You ought not to boil the boneset so much, but it was good anyhow.

MARY: I'm glad you liked it.

HERSHEL: You feel better?

OLD WOMAN: Well, of course. I had me a good meal, on this porch. Sure I feel better.

HERSHEL: Did you tell me awhile ago that you were coming here, to this house? All the way from Tennessee?

OLD WOMAN: That's what I said. I see you put in new post beams. Some of this flooring is all different. Not much of a job, though. You do it?

HERSHEL: Did the beams, not the flooring. I reckon Abner Larman did that.

OLD WOMAN: No. Ab wouldn't bother. It must have been Billy. I suppose he's dead, too.

HERSHEL: Billy?

OLD WOMAN: Poppa's joy. He was always the one. It would have been him. He put the first floor in with Poppa, when we built this place. Ab cared about the farm, not the house. And I guess lasted longest, died last of all, in the house. Well, all except me. You know, Mister, this here estate of yours, it ain't rightfully yours at all. It's mine.

HERSHEL: What? I got the deed, lady!

OLD WOMAN: Look at him jump. Men! Fuss and fume. Think ever'body wants what you got. Sit still, I ain't no bandit. You're welcome to it, this here estate of yours.

HERSHEL: Goddamn right it's mine!

MARY: Hershel.

OLD WOMAN: Men! How old you think I am? Come on. Guess.

MARY: We were wondering. I can't tell. Sometimes you look right young.

OLD WOMAN: Nice people. Sometimes a pea will shrink so tight it's smooth. I'm the same age as my tongue, and a little older than my teeth. Comfort me. Guess. Mister?

HERSHEL: Sixty-five?

OLD WOMAN: I'll never see that again. Way off. Son?

CARDELL: Two hundred.

OLD WOMAN: Whoa now. Don't kill me. I got a little time left. *(To Mary)* How about you?

MARY: I would say you are either nineteen or ninety.

OLD WOMAN: Nineteen or ninety! That's comfort. You hit it. Nineteen or ninety. That's me! Yes, sir. (*She steps off the porch, stands in the yard, facing out, speaking to the family on the porch directly behind her*) When I was nineteen, I stood right here. Right where I'm standing now. And I wasn't no shriveled up pea then. I was a choice item. The best looking woman in these mountains. And the meanest. Mean and proud. Damn men! I didn't like 'em. Said so. Drove Momma crazy. You're wild, she said. Settle down. Like you? I said. Marry when you're a child. Work and slave for men who don't care one spit what you think or how you feel. Who never listen. Don't talk like that, Momma said, but I did. I give men hell. They'd come, and I'd spit, and they'd go. You didn't like it, either. You, you up there. You didn't. (*She is speaking to the family without looking at them, as if, now, they are her own*) Ab and Billy. Rachael and Poppa. Momma. You don't know what to do, do you? You just sit there, shake your heads. Watch me fight. Damn men! (*She stands straighter. She strokes her white hair*) Heavy-footed, tongue-tied, bug-eyed horsefaces, coming here looking for a slave. Wanting to lie on top of me one minute, and work me to death the next. And take me away from you. And you hoping one of them would. Clucking your tongues, saying, Lands sakes, what will become of her, treating men like this? Wanting me to go. Well, I won't! I won't leave this house, and you, to be plowed under like dirt by some sweating, groaning, bone-headed man! Hell, no! (*She stares offstage. She sees someone coming*) And then, he came by. Griswold Plankman, the joke of the world. He came my way.

(*Enter Griswold*)

GRISWOLD: (*Slowly*) Mr. Larman. Mrs. Larman. Billy. (*Pause*) Miss Larman.

OLD WOMAN: Hello, Griswold. You out of debt yet?

GRISWOLD: Well—

OLD WOMAN: You going to say: getting there, getting there.

GRISWOLD: Well—

OLD WOMAN: And what fine land it is, all eight acres of it.

GRISWOLD: Well—

OLD WOMAN: Now if I wait here a few days, you'll wonder

how come I know so much about you. I know enough, Griswold Plankman. You're too poor to paint, and too proud to whitewash.

GRISWOLD: Well—

OLD WOMAN: I'd sure like to buy you for what you're worth, and sell you for what you think you're worth. I can look right through you, and a little piece on the other side.

GRISWOLD: Well—

OLD WOMAN: Get it straight, Griswold. We are as different as cheese from chalk. To speak plainly, as far as I am concerned, you are as ugly as homemade sin, and as welcome here as the bastard at the family reunion!

(Griswold smiles and shakes his head)

GRISWOLD: You know what made the river angry? It got crossed so many times. *(He laughs)*

OLD WOMAN: Huh?

GRISWOLD: You know why lightning shocks people? It don't know how to conduct itself. *(He laughs)*

OLD WOMAN: Oh, my God!

GRISWOLD: When is a door not a door? When it's ajar. *(He laughs)*

OLD WOMAN: Man, this is pitiful. Will you just shut up?

GRISWOLD: Why is a pig the strangest of all animals?

OLD WOMAN: I don't know, Griswold! I don't care!

GRISWOLD: Because a pig gets killed before he gets cured.

OLD WOMAN: I wouldn't have you, man, off a Christmas tree! Go home!

GRISWOLD: Know why life is the hardest riddle?

OLD WOMAN: Home!

GRISWOLD: Everybody has to give it up. *(Pause)* What is this I hear about you wanting to be took to Tennessee?

(Pause)

OLD WOMAN: Who told you that?

GRISWOLD: Hensley Edwards.

OLD WOMAN: Hensley Edwards is a fool!

GRISWOLD: I know that. But you told him the only man you'd marry was the man who would sell his farm and take you all the way to Tennessee. How come you want to go to Tennessee?

OLD WOMAN: Never you mind.

GRISWOLD: But you did say it?

OLD WOMAN: All right. I said it. It's my word, and I mean it.

GRISWOLD: Long trip. Awful hard country. Eighty-odd miles, here to the Tennessee border. Just mountains. How come you want a man to take you there?

OLD WOMAN: Griswold, stop going around your elbow to get to your thumb. What business is it of yours?

GRISWOLD: This. Come with me. I will take you there.

OLD WOMAN: What?

GRISWOLD: I will sell my land, and take you to Tennessee.

OLD WOMAN: Griswold, you don't know what you're saying. You ain't got the sense God promised a billy goat!

GRISWOLD: If you think marriage is necessary, all right. If not, all right.

OLD WOMAN: You think I'm fool enough to go somewhere with a man, and *not* be married to him?

GRISWOLD: Then we can get married.

OLD WOMAN: Oh, Griswold. You are so green, when it rains, you'll sprout.

GRISWOLD: I'm taking you at your word. You're the one who said the thing.

OLD WOMAN: And what's wrong with my word? It's just as good as any damn man's. But that don't mean you get to put your shoes under my bed.

GRISWOLD: You want to go to Tennessee. I will take you there. I'm not asking you why. No questions. Hard country. Dangerous and powerful lonely. No dances, no parties. And I give up my bottom land. But if that is what you want, we'll go. Think it over.

(Exit Griswold. The Old Woman speaks to the family)

OLD WOMAN: Oh, hell! I didn't care nothing about no Tennessee. I only said that to keep off that fool Hensley Edwards. Cross all them mountains? Great God Almighty! But I did say it. My word. Well, I'm safe enough. Not even Griswold Plankman is dumb enough to sell off North Carolina bottom land and go farm a wild Tennessee mountain. *(Pause)* Yes. I know. You want me gone. Have done with this eternal squabbling over men. Well, I won't! I won't go!

HERSHEL: *(Very softly)* But you said you would. You'd marry the man who'd take you to Tennessee.

OLD WOMAN: And I will! No man's idiot enough to do that, never mind try to marry me.

(Enter Griswold. He puts some flowers in her hands. He turns her gently but firmly so she stands beside him, facing out. Pause)

OLD WOMAN: Well, go ahead and say it.

HERSHEL: I now pronounce you man and wife.

OLD WOMAN: Goddamn!

GRISWOLD: I'll put your boxes in the wagon. Say goodbye.

(Griswold stacks several wooden boxes together, making a sort of wagon seat)

OLD WOMAN: Well, Poppa. Billy, Ab. Rachael. Momma. There's more to say. I don't know about Tennessee.

HERSHEL: You will get there all right.

OLD WOMAN: Yes, I know. But it seems like there was something else I had to say. Listen—

GRISWOLD: Honey. It's time.

(Griswold takes her to the wagon seat, sits her there. He sits beside her, flicks imaginary reins)

OLD WOMAN: Poppa!

(She resigns herself. They travel. Pause)

OLD WOMAN: Can't you drive this thing no faster than this?

GRISWOLD: In a hurry, are you?

OLD WOMAN: I'd like to get to Tennessee before I die. Who sold you this wagon? Did you look at it at all before you bought it? Don't expect me to fix it when it breaks down. When are we going to stop, and spend the night?

GRISWOLD: Anytime.

OLD WOMAN: What do you mean, anytime? Griswold, where are we going to spend our wedding night?

GRISWOLD: Right here.

OLD WOMAN: You mean *in the wagon?*

GRISWOLD: I don't mean no boarding house.

OLD WOMAN: Oh, God! I've married a miser. Go through the thicket, then pick a crooked stick. He's so tight, when he walks, he'll squeak.

GRISWOLD: I don't want to be shut up in a tiny little room, with neighbors, and a good-looking bride like you. I figure we'll want to make some noise about it.

OLD WOMAN: Oh, you do, do you? You goddamn man! You coarse, dumb, stupid, goddamn man! You wouldn't give a lady air in a jug! I'm going home! They should have buried you, Griswold, and raised the afterbirth! (*She starts to get out of the wagon. He grabs her, and holds her*)

GRISWOLD: And you are as hot as a hen in a wool blanket.

OLD WOMAN: *What?* (*She beats at Griswold with her fists. There is a considerable scuffle*) Man! Man! Goddamn man! (*He holds her until she is tired, and a little frightened*) All right. You can let go of me now.

GRISWOLD: Honey, I ain't never letting you go. How about that?

OLD WOMAN: It is what's happened to me. I confess it, Lord save me. Let go, I won't hit you again.

GRISWOLD: You can if you want to. I think I like it.

OLD WOMAN: Stop! Wait! Stop the wagon!

GRISWOLD: Now what? You aim to run off again?

OLD WOMAN: No, you fool! We knocked over a box. It fell off in the road. Stop the wagon, and I'll go get it.

GRISWOLD: All right. Don't run off.

OLD WOMAN: Just shut up about that, and will you stop the wagon?

(*He stops the wagon. The Old Woman gets down and stoops over an imaginary box, fallen from the wagon, and broken open*)

GRISWOLD: Yours or mine?

OLD WOMAN: Mine. My box of dressing things. Oh, Lord, look here! My mirror's busted. (*She picks up a piece of shattered glass. It is the piece she herself brought with her and dropped. She holds it now in one hand, looking into it sorrowfully*) My mirror. My good mirror. Busted. Oh, me!

(*Griswold puts the imaginary box back onto the wagon*)

GRISWOLD: Come on, honey. You ain't going to need many mirrors in Tennessee.

OLD WOMAN: Oh, me.

GRISWOLD: All right, I'll get you another one, somewhere. Now, come on.

OLD WOMAN: Just wait a minute! My hair's messed up.

GRISWOLD: It wouldn't be noticed on a galloping horse.

OLD WOMAN: Just wait one damn minute!

GRISWOLD: All right! A minute! (*The Old Woman holds the mirror, looking about for a place to prop it, so she can look into it with her hands free*) Stick it in the burl of that tree there.

OLD WOMAN: What?

(*Griswold takes the mirror and sticks it into a burl on the tree stump in the yard, or into one of the logs Hershel brought on and set down.*)

The Old Woman kneels before it, touching up her hair. Griswold gets back into the wagon. The Old Woman does too, looking back at the mirror in the tree)

OLD WOMAN: Look at it shine in the sun. Like a star in the daytime. Well, goodbye. Let's go, Griswold.

(They travel. Time passes. They travel. Griswold is placid. The Old Woman gets more and more oppressed. She looks about, frightened. She holds it in. She can't stand it. She lets it out)

OLD WOMAN: Yiiiiiiiii!

GRISWOLD: What's the matter?

OLD WOMAN: Mountains. Nothing but mountains. My Lord! Nobody nowhere. No cleared land. Nothing. Just mountains.

GRISWOLD: And more to come. It's eighty miles to the Tennessee border, up and down. You should have thought about that.

OLD WOMAN: If I had, I might not be no Mrs. Plankman.

GRISWOLD: That's possible.

OLD WOMAN: Oh, me.

GRISWOLD: *(Pointing)* Sourwood. That gold is birch poplar.

OLD WOMAN: Don't nobody live in these mountains at all?

GRISWOLD: Not many now. Maybe some later, but not so many. It's wild up here. Steep. Worse in Tennessee. Not much water on the slopes. You got to look hard for decent land. But come fall, when the slopes turn, Tennessee is beautiful. Like a big fire a-burning, all your own. Red and orange and silver leaves, too, and gold and green, and God knows what all.

OLD WOMAN: Oh, shut up, Griswold! You ain't never been to Tennessee, no more than I have. What do you know about it?

GRISWOLD: Let's say I understand the nature of Tennessee. I've heard people talk about it. I've thought about it. A lot.

OLD WOMAN: You're crazy.

GRISWOLD: Maybe.

(They travel. They travel. The Old Woman looks about, more and more frightened. She squirms, hold her hands in front of her eyes. She explodes again)

OLD WOMAN: Yiiiiiiiii!!

GRISWOLD: Now what?

OLD WOMAN: How long is this going to last? I can't stand it no more! We been on these godforsaken trails past six weeks now. Ain't we done eighty miles yet? When are we going to get there?

GRISWOLD: Eighty miles, but up and down. Mountains. Yes, it's a hell of a trip we're taking, you and me. A long ways from your Momma and Daddy's house. Wilderness. But not so long now. Pretty soon.

OLD WOMAN: Better be pretty soon. (*Pause*) You know why?

GRISWOLD: Why?

OLD WOMAN: Guess.

GRISWOLD: Just tell me.

OLD WOMAN: You best get me there sometime inside the next eight months. I just say that.

GRISWOLD: Well, hoo-pee! Then I sure will. We ain't wasted the time, have we?

OLD WOMAN: No, we didn't. Part way to Tennessee, and a baby all ready. Oh, me.

GRISWOLD: (*Happy*) Yeah.

(*He whistles. They travel, they travel. Then, looking about, Griswold stops the wagon*)

OLD WOMAN: Well, what now?

GRISWOLD: We're in Tennessee. Look.

OLD WOMAN: But it's just the same. Mountains and mountains and nobody here but us.

GRISWOLD: All three of us.

OLD WOMAN: Oh, me.

GRISWOLD: But it's open land. I can clear about over there. Hush, hear the water?

OLD WOMAN: (*Listening*) It's over there.

GRISWOLD: No, over there. But it's water. Might near a creek.

OLD WOMAN: Well, build next to it.

GRISWOLD: And get flooded out in the spring? No, you'll have to walk for it. But here we are, honey. You get the pot. I'll get the wood. We'll go down to that creek tonight, and gig us some frogs, for breakfast.

OLD WOMAN: Oh, me.

GRISWOLD: It's where you wanted to go, and here we are. Hop, honey! (*Exit Griswold, whistling*)

OLD WOMAN: I hopped, all right. Hopped while you built the house. Hopped while you sat aching and sweating, waiting for your supper. Then you hopped while I had Sally, and we lost Malcolm, and again when Sarah came. And we lived there, alone. At least I did. There was a store, finally, eight miles off. I didn't get to go much. When I did, I knowed Griswold didn't want me saying nothing. We lived, like a man and woman can, sometimes speaking, sometimes not. Oh, I took the skin off him now and then. (*Smiles*) He come home once saying there was this girl Polly something working at the store, and it was unfortunate, the girl was pregnant. (*Pause*) And they were trying to blame it on us. (*Laughs*) Us. Men. Well, I made him pay for that. (*She looks at the mountains around her*) And it went by. Slow. Fast. Fast. Slow. My God! (*She smiles at the family*) Alone in the mountains. Maybe I saw fifty people all my days there. Three families only we saw more than once a year. I'd sweep my dirt yard smooth as the palm of my hand, they'd come sit, and the shadows danced. Tennessee. Them neighbors we had, oh, they all loved the place. Never stopped saying how lucky we were to be there. Griswold smiling, saying, well it's where she wanted to go. Everybody nodding, good, good. I wondered why they always did that, but they just always did. Days went by. (*She looks about, fearfully. She stoops. She ages*) Griswold.

(*Enter Griswold, aged now, too. He stands partly in shadow*)

GRISWOLD: What's on your mind?

OLD WOMAN: It's hard without the girls. I miss my children.

GRISWOLD: They got good men. They had to go off, too, like you did.

OLD WOMAN: If Malcolm had lived, he'd be farming for you now.

GRISWOLD: But he didn't.

OLD WOMAN: No. (*Pause*) Sarah. Sally. What's left?

GRISWOLD: I'm left. Tennessee's left.

OLD WOMAN: Then they will have to do.

GRISWOLD: Think we will?

OLD WOMAN: Well, I got my complaints.

GRISWOLD: About me or Tennessee?

OLD WOMAN: Tennessee's all right. And you did bring me here.

GRISWOLD: (*Smiling*) That's right. I did. (*He whistles. Exit Griswold*)

OLD WOMAN: Smiling at me. Saying, "That's right. I did bring you here." (*Griswold's whistling stops*) We both outlived our children. They died young, worn out wives. Their children melted away into other kin's families, and after awhile, we didn't hear of them no more. (*She sits on the edge of the porch*) Griswold was eighty-nine when he fell and cut hisself on his sickle. I did what I could, but he'd lost too much blood. So I got him to a bench he'd made, and sitting there, he looked at me sideways—a funny sort of look—and then closed his eyes. I couldn't hold him up no more, so I let him slide off. There was some linen left in my mother's wedding present box. I made Griswold a winding sheet of some quality, and I buried him there in Tennessee. (*She stands. Thinks*) That was—a few days ago. I think it was. Can't tell, exactly. When my neighbor come, she stayed a few days, that's right. Then she commenced to leave, and something was bothering me. Something I didn't feel bad about. But I didn't know what it was. (*Enter, slowly, Neighbor, a woman her age*) I tried to tell my neighbor about it, when she was going back home.

NEIGHBOR: You sure you're all right now?

OLD WOMAN: Oh, yes. (*Pause*) Yes.

NEIGHBOR: No. (*Pause*) Something. What?

OLD WOMAN: You're my only friend now. And you live four miles off. Nobody else is left. Something is just not right.

NEIGHBOR: Natural feeling.

OLD WOMAN: Not Griswold dead. Something else. Not plumbline straight. I'm powerful uneasy.

NEIGHBOR: You're a-grieving.

OLD WOMAN: Yes, but why does it seem nothing's level? I want to move. Walk. Got the fidgets bad. Go where? Why now? I don't know.

(*The Neighbor puts a hand on the Old Woman's arm*)

NEIGHBOR: Listen. You stay here. Don't try to leave Tennessee.

OLD WOMAN: Why not? What's to hold me?

NEIGHBOR: Nothing, but don't leave. Don't think about it.

OLD WOMAN: What could happen?

NEIGHBOR: You could get lost.

OLD WOMAN: What difference would that make. Something is eating in me never was there before. Says go. Do it. Move.

NEIGHBOR: And I say, don't. Stay. You've had a good life here.

OLD WOMAN: Sometimes

NEIGHBOR: No woman can ask for more. (*She backs away*) Listen to me now. Don't leave. Stay here. In Tennessee. (*She is gone*)

OLD WOMAN: But it kept eating in me. I still don't know what, or why. I commenced taking little walks. Ever'day a little further. Then I didn't go back. I was loose, in country like country I'd never seen before, that I *had* seen before. I kept on. Slept in my pine needles. Gigged my frogs. Didn't know nothing, except I know this now: I was coming here.

HERSHEL: Wait a minute. Here, from Tennessee? You know yourself, Tennessee is eighty miles—

(The Old Woman rings her cowbell)

OLD WOMAN: I heard this, see? And it seemed like they was all around me, in the woods. I couldn't see quite through the brush, but I knew they were there, Momma, Poppa, Rachael, Billy, Ab. And Griswold. All of them talking about me. I'd try to hear but couldn't, no more than their whisperings, and I'd find myself standing in places of powerful remembrance, places I'd stood before. Two days of that walking, when I heard this. (*She rings her cowbell*) I'd follow Poppa to the barn, a little girl as pleasant as the flowers are made. Hearing this. I heard it again, and went for it again, and what do you think I found?

HERSHEL: Lady, I sure don't know.

OLD WOMAN: Guess.

CARDELL: A cow?

OLD WOMAN: One for you, sonny! Big jersey.

CARDELL: I thought that was our cowbell, Daddy. You missed that.

HERSHEL: So I missed it. (*To Old Woman*) You found our cowbell. Then what?

OLD WOMAN: *Your* cowbell? (*Rings it, then suddenly throws it to him*) Look inside! What do you see?

(Hershell does)

HERSHEL: You see a ringer, that's what you see.

OLD WOMAN: What else? Damn man.

CARDELL: Daddy, that's the cowbell was lying on the ground when we come here. There's a big L cut on the inside of it.

HERSHEL: Oh, yeah.

CARDELL: You missed that, too, didn't you?

HERSHEL: All right! I missed that, too!

OLD WOMAN: L! You damn right L! Larman! I took this bell off your cow. Only one bell in the world sounds like this one. I rang it and rang it, and I found the road, and came walking, not understanding nothing. Poppa's cowbell, on some cow two day's walk, not hardly seven miles, from my yard in Tennessee? What about this, I thought. What about this? Am I dead, or what? Is this heaven? What's going on? (*She moves about the yard, ringing the bell*) Then, on the road, I seen the bend again, and came round it. There it was again. I seen it almost buried in the tree, but not quite. Enough left sticking out of the burl so's it could flash at me. Just one little wink in the sun, but I seen it. (*She goes to her mirror again, where Griswold stuck it. She pulls it loose*) I pulled open the growth of the burl, and there hidden was my star in the daytime. I pulled it loose, my mirror, where I'd left it on the way to Tennessee. (*She looks at herself in the mirror*) There I was. Old woman. Two flashes of a mirror. Little girl, old woman. Good God Almighty, I thought, when I took my bridal mirror out of the tree where he put it, broken, on my wedding day.

HERSHEL: Whew!

MARY: Hershel, she's crazy. None of this makes sense.

OLD WOMAN: It makes sense, all right. I can see it! Why, that man. That damn man! I left the road, took the trail, light-headed and dizzy. One day in Tennessee, the next day Poppa's cowbell, and my mirror? Then I come out of the brush, into the clearing, and I seen the house. A boy on the porch. And you. You nice people. (*Pause*) And I am still not sure, not even now while I'm a-talking to you. Are you the strangers give me spoonbread and tea? Or are you Poppa? Are you Rachael, Billy, and Ab? Is my mother back in the house, making me my wedding dress?

HERSHEL: (*Gently*) I am afeared we're the strangers give you spoonbread.

OLD WOMAN: Ah, I know it! Oh, that man! Griswold, you damn man! What did you do to me?

HERSHEL: Listen, you best come inside and lie down now. You must be awful tired.

OLD WOMAN: Oh, my God! Don't you understand? What's

wrong with you? Don't you see it yet? I do! I do! Good God! Great God A-mighty! (*The family stands watching her, alarmed. The Old Woman shakes her head, swings her arms. Wheezing, coughing, hopping up and down, ringing her cowbell and flashing her mirror, she stamps out a sort of dance in front of them*) That man! That bloody scoundrel! He never took me to Tennessee at all! He put me in a wagon, and he drove me around these mountains over a month! These same mountains! Around, in circles! Then he settled where he'd meant to all along, in a valley *seven miles off!* And I thought I was in Tennessee! Oh! My God! All them people, my neighbors, they was in on it! Oh! My children, my own children, *they* was in on it! And—oh, no. To get me gone, was it? Poppa? Momma? You, too? Oh, Griswold! You never told me. You never would have told me. By God, you *died* without telling me! What kind of a joke was that? Griswold! My whole life! You damn man! (*She rages. Her passion pours out of her. She hacks and coughs and stamps her feet. Slowly, her convulsion subsides. She gets her breath*) Whew! Shoo! Well, that's that. Think you lived your life in Tennessee. Find out you didn't. You, up there. Nice people, with your fine estate. House, land, yard and porch. It's all yours—for awhile. Good luck. (*She looks at the cowbell and the mirror*) Poppa. Griswold. (*She drops them both*) Bye. (*To the family*) So long.

MARY: Wait! Don't go now. It's dark.

OLD WOMAN: I know it.

MARY: Hershel! Stop her.

HERSHEL: Wait, now. Where you going?

OLD WOMAN: Back to Tennessee. Where else? That man. That damn man!

(*She is gone*)

MARY: Hershel?

HERSHEL: Let her go. (*Hershel and Mary look at each other. They shiver. Hershel looks out at his land, then back to the house*) I'm hungry. Let's go and eat now. Give me the baby.

(*He takes the baby from Cardell, holds it tightly, then pushes his wife ahead of him, in to supper.*

Cardell stares off after the Old Woman. He picks up her mirror, and sees his face in it)

Curtain

Jack Heifner

PATIO
and
PORCH

Jack Heifner

A native of Corsicana, Texas, Jack Heifner was educated at Southern Methodist University and, upon graduating from the theatre department, came to New York to begin a career as an actor. After several brief appearances, he and Garland Wright formed an Off-Off-Broadway group, the Lion Theatre Company, with Heifner as actor and Wright as director.

During this period, he wrote his first play, *Casserole*, a black comedy staged at Playwrights Horizons in 1975. The audience reaction was a turning point for Mr. Heifner: "I couldn't believe that what I thought was funny made other people laugh, too." The surprising response (and critical reaction) encouraged him to "pack away his leotards and make-up box" and invest in an electric typewriter. The next script he wrote (in two days) was *Vanities* and, thereupon, a theatrical legend was born.

Dealing with the lives of three Texas cheerleaders, it was first staged by Garland Wright in 1975 at the Lion at a production cost of $200, with sets hammered together by the playwright and costumes straight from the actresses' own closets at home. ("In the Los Angeles production, which starred Sandy Dennis, Lucie Arnaz and Stockard Channing, the clothes alone cost $10,000," the author recently observed. "By the time we got to Chicago, with Elizabeth Ashley, the set cost $30,000.")

Following a four-week run, the play moved to Long Island for five more weeks, then returned to New York's Chelsea Westside Theatre on March 22, 1976. An immediate success, the play presently is in its fourth year and on September 9, 1979 became the longest-running play in Off-Broadway history.

Shortly after *Vanities'* New York opening, several other companies were formed for presentation in more than a dozen major cities. Since 1976 it has spawned over two hundred additional regional, repertory and stock productions in the United States and abroad, and in the last two years (when performance rights were more generally released) it received more professional productions in this country than any other play.

On April 13, 1978, Mr. Heifner's *Patio* and *Porch*, two short plays set in a small Texas town, opened on Broadway at the

Century Theatre with Fannie Flagg and Ronnie Claire Edwards as the leads in both plays. Subsequently, *Patio* and *Porch* were presented in Dallas and settled down to a lengthy run. This editor has chosen to include both plays in *The Best Short Plays 1980* for they complement each other and customarily are performed together as a full evening in the theatre.

In the autumn of 1978, the author was reunited with the Lion Theatre Company in the presentation of a play with music based on Colette's *Music Hall Sidelights*. Early in 1980, the Lion offered the premiere of his newest stage work, *Star Treatment*.

At present, Mr. Heifner is working on an original screenplay and developing a television project for CBS and Columbia Pictures.

PATIO

Characters:

JEWEL, *a woman in her mid-thirties. She wears slacks, a blouse and plenty of jewelry. Her hair is ratted high upon her head.*
PEARL, *a woman in her mid-thirties. She wears a sundress and sensible shoes.*

Both characters speak with Texas accents.

Scene:

The concrete patio of a pre-fabricated, modern brick house. There is a patio table, a barbeque pit, a cyclone fence, and a few tiny trees. The backyard is decorated for a party. Paper garlands, Oriental lanterns, paper party items are scattered about. Despite the decorations, the setting looks very dry and hot. A sliding glass door leads from the patio into the house.

PEARL: Would you look? (*She is inside the house*)

JEWEL: At what? (*She is up on a ladder on the patio*)

PEARL: Come here and look.

JEWEL: Honey, I can't. I'm trying to put up these lanterns of yours.

PEARL: You should see this.

JEWEL: Sweetheart, I'm half way up this ladder with an armload of Oriental shades. Where am I supposed to put them? On the roof?

PEARL: In my fruit trees.

JEWEL: Oh, for Pete's sake . . .(*To herself*) I didn't need a ladder to put these in her fruit trees. (*She comes down and starts putting them in the two tiny trees by the patio*) I'll have to bend over to put them in her fruit trees.

PEARL: (*Finally entering from the sliding door*) Oh, I could just scream.

JEWEL: What is it? What's wrong?

PEARL: Do you know there's not a cube of ice in my freezing compartment? Not a cube? Come look!

JEWEL: I can't come look. You've got me doing this.

PEARL: Is it too much to ask for a few cubes of ice when I want to make limeade? Huh?

JEWEL: I don't think so.

PEARL: I tell you, one of these days I'm gonna get a new ice box . . . a big one . . . with one of those automatic ice machines. It's gonna turn out cubes faster than I can use them. I'm gonna have to throw away ice! In the future, when I decide to make limeade, I'm not going to have to go through all this worry. (*She exits back into the house*)

JEWEL: Well, I hope not. (*To herself*) Lord, there ain't enough places for all these. (*Shouting to Pearl*) Pearl, you bought too many lanterns!

PEARL: There should be just enough.

JEWEL: Just enough for what? (*She throws the lanterns over the fence*)

PEARL: (*Entering again with more party things*) You know, I may have goofed. May have put the hot dogs on too early. Jumped the gun on them. (*She crosses to the barbeque*)

JEWEL: So?

PEARL: So, I've got to get them off before they burn. Oh . . . by the time we want to eat, they'll be like ice. We're going to have hot limeade and cold wienies. It's all backwards and isn't that always the way things turn out when you try and plan something pretty?

JEWEL: Well, it does look pretty. It all looks real nice.

PEARL: And . . . I must apologize for the table setting.

JEWEL: Apologize? What for?

PEARL: For the napkins.

JEWEL: You got napkins.

PEARL: Not the right ones . . . not the ones that match. You'd think if they were gonna carry the centerpiece and the paper cups and plates they'd have the good sense to know a person would want the napkins. I mean, it's all part of a set and I like things to be finished. Don't you?

JEWEL: Well, I don't miss those napkins. I took one look at your decorations and the fact that your napkins don't go with your plates did not enter my mind.

PEARL: You wouldn't kid me, would you?

JEWEL: Girl, I don't care one way or the other whether you have those *Snoopy* napkins.

PEARL: Are you sure? Don't just humor me.

JEWEL: Sure, I'm sure.

PEARL: I'm just doing this for you, you know?

JEWEL: Sure, I know. Now you just sit down and relax. You've been running around like a chicken with her head cut off. Sit down, Pearl. (*She does*) It all looks finished. See, I finally got all the lanterns in place. Don't they look nice? I tell you, Pearl, when it comes to decorations you wrote the book.

PEARL: I'll rearrange those lanterns in a minute. (*She is up and moving around again*) First, I'd better put this centerpiece over the hole in the table. Cover up the hole.

JEWEL: What's wrong with the way I did the lanterns?

PEARL: I wish I had gotten the umbrella for this. That's what the hole is for and somehow it looks sort of silly without it. It's an umbrella table!

JEWEL: I want you to know I've hung a lantern on every twig in this yard.

PEARL: I could have used a little shade out here all these years.

JEWEL: You could have used some bigger trees.

PEARL: You know, I always thought I'd get back down there and get that umbrella. I always thought that.

JEWEL: Well, you thought wrong.

PEARL: Well, I didn't get enough stamps.

JEWEL: How many books?

PEARL: Sixteen.

JEWEL: That seems like a lot of books to waste on an umbrella.

PEARL: Not if you need the shade.

JEWEL: Besides, I thought you were saving up for a concrete bird bath.

PEARL: I was, but I changed my mind.

JEWEL: Was it too many books?

PEARL: No . . . no, it was only eight. But I just decided I didn't care to have all those little birds bathing in my backyard. Nasty pooh.

JEWEL: Well, that makes some sense.

PEARL: For a long time I thought getting that umbrella was the most important thing. They say people aren't supposed to sit in the sun too much.

JEWEL: Well, you know, rich people do . . . sunbathe, suntan.

PEARL: And you know, they are just asking for trouble . . . sunburn, sunstroke. I don't know why some people want to burn themselves up? Do you?

JEWEL: No, you've got me stumped.

PEARL: However, I never had much choice except to sit in the sun, because I never got the stamps together to get that umbrella.

JEWEL: Get your mind off the umbrella. You'll drive yourself crazy.

PEARL: What if they discontinue it? What if, by the time I buy enough groceries and gas to get my sixteen books together . . . what if, I go down there and they tell me there's no way to get it? Do I have to live the rest of my life with a table with a hole in the middle and nothing to put in it?

JEWEL: Well, there are other things you could put in that hole.

PEARL: Other things? Like what?

JEWEL: Well . . . well . . . you could run yourself up a flagpole.

PEARL: Oh, don't be silly. What would I want with a flagpole? Then I'd have to get a flag.

JEWEL: I guess one thing leads to another, doesn't it?

PEARL: Sure it does. Besides, I think a flagpole would just look silly in the middle of a picnic table. It's not proper.

JEWEL: I guess you're right.

PEARL: Can you see me running out here day and night running a flag up and down a pole? I'd go crazy.

JEWEL: Let's just drop it.

PEARL: Not to mention rain. You couldn't leave an American flag out in the rain. I'd have to worry about that. What if I was downtown and it started to rain and my flag was up?

JEWEL: Well, I guess it would just get wet.

PEARL: Well, sure it would and I'm not about to have a wet American flag on my conscience. I've got enough to worry about.

JEWEL: You sure do. Now you just forget about that silly hole and sit. Who knows, you just might decide you want to get rid of this table completely. Just begin again with all new patio things.

PEARL: I just might cover up this entire patio with Astroturf.

JEWEL: That sounds great. Up to date. Just sit down, Pearl.

PEARL: I will, I will . . . but I just have to redo those lanterns and I've gotta put the candles in these holders. Now what has happened to the tapers?

JEWEL: What do we need candles for? It's broad daylight out here.

PEARL: *Better Homes and Gardens* says, "Any hostess knows a properly appointed party table includes tapers."

JEWEL: If it's dark.

PEARL: No, not "if it's dark." One *must* have tapers to offset . . . to balance the centerpiece on a fancy table. Haven't you ever been to a party?

JEWEL: You know I've been to parties . . . plenty. I just never knew of anyone who burned candles in the daytime.

(Pearl is looking all over the yard for the tapers)

PEARL: You don't burn them, dumbo. They're for looks. Oh, don't you remember when you went to Esther's wedding and she had candles on her reception table?

JEWEL: I didn't notice.

PEARL: Well, that's always been the difference between you and me. I see everything. Old eagle eyes. And, I tell you, Esther had two tapers on each side of her centerpiece. Yes sir, she had blue candles on each side of that arrangement of blue carnations in the white swan.

JEWEL: She used a swan?

PEARL: She sure did. And, confidentially, I didn't think it was all that clever. I didn't see what a swan had to do with getting married.

JEWEL: Maybe it meant marriage is for the birds! Ha, ha, ha! *(Jewel has broken herself up, Pearl is not laughing)*

PEARL: I think, if I had been Esther, I would have put those carnations inside a wedding bell or coming out of the top of a church steeple. That makes more sense than using a bird.

JEWEL: HA! HA! HA!

PEARL: I can't figure out for what occasion I would use a swan.

JEWEL: HA! HA! HA!

PEARL: What's wrong with you?

JEWEL: Nothing . . . nothing. I just got the giggles.

PEARL: I'm glad you're having a good time . . . "a successful party means people had a good time."

JEWEL: Well, I am . . . ha, ha, ha!

PEARL: Are any of your friends gonna come see you off or have I just worked myself silly for nothing?

JEWEL: Now don't get mad, but I had to invite Mary Louise and Minnie Beth.

PEARL: I'm not mad.

JEWEL: You know I've worked along side them every day for years.

PEARL: I'm not mad.

JEWEL: It seemed rude not to let them come!

PEARL: *I'm not mad!* Even though I suppose it slipped your mind that Minnie Beth drinks?

JEWEL: So what?

PEARL: And I hope she knows that I have not included any alcohol in my party plans.

JEWEL: Now don't you worry about that. Minnie Beth always travels with her own six pack.

PEARL: And did I tell you that the last time I saw Mary Louise, she didn't even bother to say "hello"?

JEWEL: Maybe she didn't see you.

PEARL: She saw me. I was standing right in front of her in the checkout line and all I said was, "Mary Louise, you look thirty years younger." And she just turned up her nose and rolled her cart into another lane.

JEWEL: Well, I think that was the wrong thing to say, Pearl. She's very touchy. Besides . . . she just turned twenty-seven.

PEARL: I like Mary Louise. She's done wonders after her tragedy.

JEWEL: You said it. I couldn't lose my mind and pop back that fast.

PEARL: They say for three days in that sanitarium she didn't remember a thing. Not even her name. Then on the fourth day, she woke up, remembered who she was . . . and broke down and cried like a baby.

JEWEL: I'd cry too if I woke up and found out I was Mary Louise.

PEARL: Isn't that the truth? But I like Mary Louise. So . . . with Wanita, Katherine . . .

JEWEL: And Sylvia and Faith.

PEARL: And us . . . are we talking about eight?

JEWEL: Ten's about right.

PEARL: Well, two of them may not get to eat. At this point, I figure I've got about eight wienies that haven't been reduced to ashes.

JEWEL: Don't you worry. Sylvia said she'd bring a pie of some sort. My bet would be apple. And you know Wanita always brings that congealed salad you love.

PEARL: And I guess Katherine will bring her usual "surprise" dish.

JEWEL: The surprise always remains even after you've eaten it. Everyone wondering . . . "what was that?"

PEARL and JEWEL: (*Together*) Surprise!

PEARL: Now . . . let me get the picture. Come here. (*She gets a magazine*) So what do you think? (*Showing Jewel the picture*)

JEWEL: It's perfect, Pearl. The very thing. You've lifted that party right out of *Better Homes and Gardens* and into your backyard. Good for you, girl!

PEARL: Oh, I don't know. I mean, I got all they called for . . . the *Snoopy* decor, with the exception of those napkins . . . and the tapers. Same menu. The same . . . all the same. But it doesn't look the same. Maybe what's off is the way you did those lanterns.

JEWEL: Actually, Pearl, what's out of whack is your backyard. See here in the photo? All those shade trees and leafy bushes? If you'll notice what you've got back here, honey, it's tiny twigs and scrawny shrubs.

PEARL: Well, that's not my fault.

JEWEL: I didn't say it was.

PEARL: I can't help it if the soil is so poor nothing will grow. I tried for years to get Buddy to put some more fertilizer out, but he was too gal darned lazy. Finally I bought a bag of store-bought manure and spread it around, but it didn't help. I've done my best to get things to grow, so don't blame me if the backyard's bare.

JEWEL: I'm casting no blame, honey. All I'm saying is that you created the same lovely decorations they have right in this magazine, but you just don't have nature on your side. It still looks pretty. Childish, but pretty.

PEARL: Childish? How can you say that? This article is about, "How To Throw A Summer Garden Party." It's about that and that's just what I've done.

JEWEL: But down here at the bottom it says, "Suitable for children ages three to ten."

PEARL: Where?

JEWEL: Down here. (*Pointing to the magazine*)

PEARL: Well, I didn't see that.

JEWEL: And I thought you saw everything.

PEARL: The print's too fine. They should have made it bigger if they intended me to read it.

JEWEL: Now see, here . . . here on the next page? Here we have your adult garden party. See? It's got a South Sea Island theme.

PEARL: (*Getting angry*) I don't happen to like the South Seas.

JEWEL: See? You got your fishnet and flamingoes . . . a luau decor. It's Hawaiian. And it's appropriate for ages fifteen and up. That's our group. The one we're in. *Snoopy's* for children.

PEARL: Well, I happen to love *Snoopy*. Just look how cute he is.

JEWEL: I didn't say he wasn't cute.

PEARL: I only read *Peanuts* for *Snoopy*. Don't you?

JEWEL: I have nothing against the dog.

PEARL: So, I'm sorry to say, when it comes to figuring out who likes what at which age, *Better Homes and Gardens* is dead wrong. Right?

JEWEL: All right. Okay. You win, Pearl. I'm sorry that I even brought it up. I guess that's why they call it *Better Homes and Gardens*, not *GREAT Homes and Gardens*.

PEARL: (*She picks up the centerpiece and screams*) Oh, heck! I could just have a hissy fit! Look!

JEWEL: What is it? What's wrong?

PEARL: LOOK! (*She is indicating the centerpiece*) The candles were under the centerpiece and they've done melted all over *Snoopy*. He's got this red mess all over his tail.

JEWEL: It looks okay . . . just pull them off.

PEARL: It does not look "okay." It looks awful!

JEWEL: It looks okay, I tell you.

PEARL: (*Furious*) And I tell you it does not look okay for *Snoopy* to have two candles stuck to his little butt.

JEWEL: Just pull them off.

PEARL: Oh! How could you think of messing him up? How dare you attack my decorations!

JEWEL: Just listen to me! (*She grabs the* Snoopy, *pulls the candles off, and the tail, too . . . Pearl goes hysterical and Jewel is equally shocked*)

PEARL: Oh! Oh! You've ruined him! You . . . you murderer!

JEWEL: (*She grabs Pearl by the shoulder and shakes her*) Now you just pull yourself together! Pull yourself together, baby sister, and listen to me! No one cares if you have candles, no one cares if you have paper lanterns, no one gives a damn if *Snoopy* loses his tail! Do you hear me? No one cares!

PEARL: I try so hard to do things right. *I* care!

JEWEL: I know you do.

PEARL: And you tell me no one gives a damn?

JEWEL: That's right, Pearl. Nobody does. That's what's the matter with people, but that sure is the way it is. No one gives a damn, darling.

PEARL: But I do.

JEWEL: Well it won't get you anywhere.

PEARL: I don't understand you, Jewel. You used to care. Care as much as I do. How can you be so hard? What's happened to you?

JEWEL: Oh, yes, honey . . . I used to care. I spent my time working and working trying to make people happy, worrying about how they were going to like my work, worrying about "doing it right" . . . and they didn't care. When I enrolled in the Lady Linda School of Beauty, I wanted to be the best damn hairdresser on the face of this earth. Curling, coloring, stripping, frosting, dyeing, waving . . . I did it all. I learned every aspect of the scalp. When you pour a bottle of peroxide on a woman's head you gotta know what you're doing. Leave a bleach job on one second too long and do you know what you've got? Huh?

PEARL: No!

JEWEL: A handful of blonde hairs that ain't attached to nothing!

PEARL: Oh, my God!

JEWEL: It's tricky, Pearl . . . doin' hair is a dangerous business.

PEARL: Are you scared?

JEWEL: Oh, I used to be . . . used to be when some woman would come in, I'd practically faint. I'd always be scared.

What if I push an orange stick too far into the cuticle when I'm giving a manicure? It would be like having bamboo shoots under the finger nail. What if I put a black rinse on someone's hair and the next day the woman calls me and says she's gotta black pillow case . . . that the rinse didn't take, that her husband reached over and touched her hair and ended up with a handful of soot!

PEARL: Oh, no!

JEWEL: Oh, yes! Those, Pearl, are the hazards of hairdressing.

PEARL: So what do you do? How do you face it?

JEWEL: Confidence, Pearl, confidence. First, I learned that hairdressing is no art. It is a science. When you put bleach on someone's hair . . . you set a timer. When the timer goes off . . . you wash her off. No guessing. When someone calls up and says her rinse rubbed off, you blame it on her. Tell her she's had so many dye jobs that she abused her hair . . . make her feel guilty . . . make another five dollars by giving her a hot oil treatment. And you know what a hot oil treatment does to her hair?

PEARL: No.

JEWEL: It fries it. Then you recommend a "conditioning treatment" and charge her another two-fifty. Then you throw an eyelash and eyebrow dye into the bargain and you've got her hooked. Ruin a woman's hair and you've got a customer for life. She's dependent on you . . . I mean, what does a woman want when it comes to her hair?

PEARL: I don't know.

JEWEL: No .   . and she don't know . . . she just wants it to be there . . . no trouble . . . no worry. She wants it to sit on her head like a monument. She doesn't know the first thing about making it look the way I can make it look. All she cares is that it sits there . . . shining . . . colorful . . . and immovable like a giant cow patty. She doesn't want it to be easy to take care of, because she wants me to take care of it. She doesn't care what I have to do, as long as she has to do nothing. And you know what? I don't care if she don't care. I could put my life's work, all the knowledge I know onto a woman's head . . . work myself silly . . . and she'll go out, jump into the lake, get it all wet, come back and want me to fix it.

PEARL: Doesn't that break your heart?

JEWEL: It used to . . . I used to sit down and cry when somebody would come in ruined after I'd spent three hours on the most perfect sausage curls you ever laid eyes on. Broke my heart. How could she ruin my masterpiece? But then, I got hard . . . bitter about it. Now . . . I don't give a damn . . . I look at her . . . she's hysterical . . . needs it all fixed up before the husband comes home and sees her at her worst . . . she's at my mercy . . . I control her hair . . . and I look at her and say, "I don't have time . . . I'm booked up." She goes into a fit . . . pleads for my help . . . and I eventually work her in and charge her double. I take five minutes . . . sweep her whole messed up head into a hairstyle . . . rat it, spray it . . . laugh to myself about how silly she looks and she pays me, tips me, and goes out thanking me for her life. She doesn't care about her hair . . . not how healthy it is, not if it's dying from all the dye, not if her scalp is rotted . . . she just wants to look nice when she faces her man. Caring, Pearl, is a thing of the past . . . just like my customers don't care about the life of their hair, nobody cares whether your centerpiece has its tail. (*She has been on a sermon and doesn't realize it*)

PEARL: No matter what you say, Jewel . . . I care . . . I care about doing things right . . . and if my napkins don't match, and the food is a mess, and *Snoopy's* missing his tail . . . there's no way I'm going to say, "To hell with it!" That has always been the difference between you and me, me and Buddy, me and everybody else. I care. For instance, Buddy used to complain all the time . . . he couldn't understand why I could spend five hours cleaning the bathroom, why I would scrub every tile until it sparkled . . . he couldn't understand that.

JEWEL: I'm with him.

PEARL: He used to say he felt guilty about using the bathroom . . . that I had taken away its function and turned it into a showplace.

JEWEL: You'll have to admit, Pearl, that you are a fanatic when it comes to the bathroom.

PEARL: I am not . . . I don't care if someone messes it up as long as they understand that I will always feel the urge to clean it after they finish. It's no reflection on them. It applies to everyone.

JEWEL: It is, however, a bit off-putting that you stand out-side the door with your sponge and Ajax in hand waiting for people to finish. Always asking, "When will you be through?"

PEARL: I can't live in a dirty house.

JEWEL: Nobody's ever been in your house. When people ring the front doorbell, you always holler for them to come around here to the back.

PEARL: I don't want people tracking dirt into the living room.

JEWEL: Has anyone ever been in the living room? I can't remember a time when guests haven't been "off limits" in there.

PEARL: Do you know how many years I've worked to get that room just right . . . how long it's taken to reach perfec-tion?

JEWEL: No . . . I don't know . . . all I do know is that you might as well put some velvet ropes across the doorways . . . you've turned it into a museum. Why have a living room, if not to live in it?

PEARL: Doing that living room was the highpoint of my life . . . you don't understand that, Buddy never could. I always wanted a pink velvet sofa, so I saved and saved and finally I got it. It took all my married years to get that and the end tables and the swag lamps. Buddy used to say, "Why don't you just get something else for that room?" And I would always say, "I'd rather do without than have crap." It applies to everything. It's my philosophy of life. Finally, Buddy said, "Would you rather do without me?" And I said, "I guess so, Buddy, because you are crap." I didn't want a bad marriage anymore than I want bad furniture.

JEWEL: You know, I think he built this patio as some sort of oasis. Some place where he could relax, get his hands dirty, drink his can of beer in peace. I think Buddy understood you very well.

PEARL: I can't look at this patio without thinking of him. I've tried to make it my own. I've put plastic flowers in the beds . . . they're easy to wash off . . . and nothing will grow. I've hosed it down several times a day . . . but this patio remains slightly dirty and therefore will always be just like Buddy.

JEWEL: You know I've always liked Buddy.

PEARL: Well, you should have married him then . . . or marry him now if you like him so much.

JEWEL: And I think Buddy always liked me.

PEARL: Maybe more than he liked me.

JEWEL: Lord, he was a good-looking man. Football hero. He'd drive that convertible of his up and down the street and the two of us would just die . . . collapse in ecstasy. He had that sort of attraction a man has when he comes from a broken home . . . from the wrong side of the tracks. Like a Marlon Brando or a James Dean. Sort of tough and trashy. You'll have to admit that Buddy was one damn good-looking punk.

PEARL: Yeah, well, I certainly *did* marry him for his looks. I picked out my crystal, my silver and my husband all at the same time. But, you know, tastes change. What's attractive to a seventeen year old girl . . . torn T-shirts and dirty jeans . . . begins to turn off a thirty-five year old woman.

JEWEL: But you've got to admit Buddy had a great sense of humor. Lordy, that man could make me laugh . . . one joke after another.

PEARL: He had a filthy mouth.

JEWEL: His jokes weren't dirty.

PEARL: Filthy.

JEWEL: (*Remembering*) Yes . . . filthy.

PEARL: Buddy had me to clean and cook, and you to joke with. I used to be in the house and hear the two of you out here just hooting. I always wondered what was so funny? Everytime I came out here the two of you would stop laughing. What would our lives have been like if you hadn't dropped by all the time?

JEWEL: Not as much fun, I expect.

PEARL: Maybe I would have tried harder. I never had to be entertaining. You always provided the floor show. You and Buddy would laugh and laugh, have some beers, run off to the bowling alley. I'd stay here and clean the oven or do something constructive. Then he'd come home after being out all night with you and climb in the bed with me. It didn't make much sense. Why did you hang around so much?

JEWEL: I thought you liked having me here.

PEARL: I never said that.

JEWEL: Well, you never said you didn't.

PEARL: There were a lot of things I never said. I think after Buddy and I got married, I never said I loved him. Isn't it funny how when you're going together or engaged, how many times you say, "I love you." All the time . . . *"I love you."* Then I got married and I got busy with the house; and he got busy with his job . . . and I think I forgot to tell him I loved him anymore. I guess it slipped my mind. Or else I took it for granted. Then one morning, I woke up and realized I was no longer a wife. I didn't have a husband, so I was no longer a wife. So . . . all I was left with, then and now, at the end of a bad marriage is the perfect furniture I always wanted and a house and this patio, which I've always hated. I should have said more . . . done more.

JEWEL: There's all the time in the world, Pearl, to get over it.

PEARL: All the time in the world? What does that mean?

JEWEL: You've got your whole life ahead of you.

PEARL: I'll have my whole life ahead of me when I'm eighty.

JEWEL: I guess you're right.

PEARL: Maybe I've got my whole life behind me. I never wanted a career. You did. I never wanted to run around with a new guy each night. You did. I only wanted Buddy. So did you. I got him. You didn't. Or did you? I lost him. Where am I now?

JEWEL: I guess Buddy was the only man either one of us ever loved. But I'm glad you got him.

PEARL: Oh, I wish you had. Things might be different today. Or it might have been different with Buddy if I'd taken time off from cleaning and decorating to have a child or something. But childbearing just seemed sort of messy. And now, you're moving off and I'm just sort of stuck here in my museum. It'll be a lonely old life and I'll miss you. Miss you dropping by for coffee on your way to work . . . miss showing you my new recipe or dress pattern. Who will I show things to?

JEWEL: Pearl, honey, why don't you get out now and then? Have some fun? Go on a date?

PEARL: A what?

JEWEL: A date . . . you know, dates? With men? Girl, you've got a good setup here. Any man would consider you a prime target for marriage.

PEARL: Oh, Lord, I sure don't want another man. It's not so nice to have a man around my house.

JEWEL: Oh, but I'll bet you get you one. Someday soon some good-looking son of a gun is going to come along, fall head over heels for you . . .

PEARL: And mess up my living room. I don't want it messed up.

JEWEL: Are you scared to take a second chance?

PEARL: Do I have to remind you that I have been married? That you're the one who never tied the knot? Talk about afraid. What are you scared of?

JEWEL: Well, it's certainly not of getting my living room dirty. I don't care what people do on my sofa.

PEARL: You're the next one in line to be a bride.

JEWEL: Listen, honey, I may be a Miss, but I'm sure not missing anything. I'm foot-loose and fancy-free. And that's why I'm going away. I've spent my whole life in this hick town. Gone as far as I can go here. You know, there's a great calling for hairdressers in this world. I can pretty well name my price anywhere. I'll bet you as soon as I get moved and walk into Neiman-Marcus or Vidal Sassoon's shop . . . with my experience, my expertise . . . he'll offer me a job on the spot. Vidal'll fall all over me. If I was hooked up with some man, I couldn't do that . . . I'd be tied down. And I don't want to spend the rest of my life in this dead place. I want to live.

PEARL: And you think I don't?

JEWEL: So I'm taking off. I got too much to do. I worry all the time that I'm not going to get it all done before I die or before something worse happens.

PEARL: Something worse?

JEWEL: And you know what I hate most? When you think of something you want to do . . . like something real fun and with it and today; and people say, "Oh, you're too old for that. You should have done that when you were young." The problem is, when I was young, I didn't know what was fun or with it or today.

PEARL: Oh, Jewel, face it . . . you were always wild. Always, as they call it, "doing your thing."

JEWEL: Well, I'm doing it better now. When I get my new apartment set up with my waterbed and the posters of the *Fonz* all over the walls . . .

PEARL: That's just awful.

JEWEL: When I get my pad set up and get on my work schedule at Neiman's or Vidal's . . . I'm going back to school . . . be a coed.

PEARL: A coed? To school? What for?

JEWEL: To study the one thing that's going to put me over the top of this world.

PEARL: What's that?

JEWEL: Facials.

PEARL: What?

JEWEL: A woman's face is her fortune and there's a fortune to be made on facials. Then, with all the money I'm making, I'll buy me a big red Thunderbird and drive up and down dressed up real pretty. I'll take trips . . . to New York and Hollywood. I might even move to Hollywood and go to work for Max Factor. Do up the star's hair and faces. You've seen pictures of that big sign on the side of mountain that spells out "HOLLYWOOD"? Well, I just might live there! Buy me a trailer house and park it smack dab in the middle of the "O"! The sky's the limit! The world's my oyster! Now how do you like them apples? *End .*

PEARL: We are so different.

JEWEL: Isn't that the truth.

PEARL: Were we ever alike?

JEWEL: Well, you copied me. When I went out for Baton Twirler in high school, so did you. We both had those felt skirts with poodles on them. Of course mine was blue and yours was pink.

PEARL: Yeah, well, I've always been stuck on pink.

JEWEL: With me left-handed and you right . . . me tall and you short . . . I guess we never really were alike, but we like each other and Lord knows we've had plenty of good times together.

PEARL: Especially when we were young. You were always getting me into trouble and Mama was always threatening to send us both off to an orphanage.

JEWEL: We weren't at all what Mama intended . . . two gems, a Jewel and a Pearl.

PEARL: If Mama could see us now . . . two big, old, grown-up girls.

JEWEL: She still wouldn't like us much. She used to say, "I

see more of their daddy in those two everyday. It makes me sick." (*They both laugh. The following is a shared recall*)

PEARL: Remember when Mama hung that sign in front of the house, "Beware! There's one word that will make this dog attack." And she never would tell anybody what the word was.

JEWEL: Strangers wouldn't open their mouths for fear they'd be ripped apart.

PEARL: And we didn't even have a dog! (*Laughter*) Oh, Jewel, I'll never forget when we were about sixteen and you were out parking with Chester Herrod . . . parking down there in the cemetery. Buddy and I climbed up in a tree, shook all the branches, went "woooooo," and scared the two of you to death. Whatever made you two park in the cemetery?

JEWEL: Well, what were you doing there?

PEARL: Parking, too. That was some crazy idea of fun.

JEWEL: And we'd take the bus up to Dallas to the State Fair . . . go to the midway, ride the rides, eat ourselves silly on cotton candy and corny dogs. You and me and Cousin Gladys.

PEARL: Poor Gladys . . . to this day they've never found out what made her drive over the side of that bridge. She never drank. Never drove fast. I guess she just lost control and went off. I don't think she meant to. She just, for a second, lost control . . . went off and there was no coming back.

JEWEL: They never found her. I guess she floated out of the car, down the river and out into the Gulf of Mexico.

PEARL: Broke her daddy's heart. After Gladys left him he just went out into the garage, turned on the table saw, ran it across his neck . . . chopped his head off.

JEWEL: Nothing like that ever happened in this town before or since.

PEARL: Nope. That was the most excitement we ever had growing up.

JEWEL: Yep. Those sure were the good old days.

(*A moment of silence as the recall ends . . . Pearl looks over and studies Jewel for a moment*)

PEARL: Well, it's almost four o'clock. I guess the girls will be here soon. About time for us to get this over with so you can get on your way . . . leave the past behind you . . . leave me behind you. First, Buddy . . . now, you.

JEWEL: I'll be back soon.

PEARL: No, you won't. Not soon. Take it from me . . .

people don't come rushing back to something they were dying to leave. I know.

JEWEL: Pearl, I wish you'd at least think about starting over.

PEARL: Start over and do what?

JEWEL: Well, whatever you want.

PEARL: I did what I wanted. I've had what I want.

JEWEL: All you want?

PEARL: Everything but a patio umbrella.

JEWEL: You talk like life is about complete.

PEARL: Well, about.

JEWEL: Don't you dream of anything beyond getting your house in order?

PEARL: I don't think so. No.

JEWEL: Well, then what?

PEARL: Well, maybe I'll never get that umbrella. Never really go down and trade those stamps. Then I'll still have a dream . . . something to look forward to. Don't you worry about me.

JEWEL: Oh, but I will. And just for the record . . . just so you'll know . . . (*She grabs Pearl in an embrace*) Oh, hell, honey . . . I'm gonna be lost without my Pearl.

PEARL: So promise you'll take care.

JEWEL: I will.

PEARL: And write me.

JEWEL: I will.

PEARL: And you won't end up marrying Buddy.

JEWEL: I won't. Like I said, darling, you always copied me. I have never copied you. (*They both laugh*) I'd better run inside and freshen my face. This may be the last time any of you are going to see it for awhile. I'm going to the little girl's room. Don't you follow me with that Ajax!

(*They both laugh and Jewel exits*)

PEARL: (*Yelling*) And, Jewel, on your way back see if that old refrigerator's made any ice.

JEWEL: (*From inside the house*) Okey-doke.

PEARL: (*She wanders around the patio, finishing up the party decorations*) Oh, heavens, I hate this patio. Even all decorated . . . I still hate it. Just dirt and dust and pitiful little fruit trees. Probably never will bear fruit. Can barely bear the weight of a paper lantern. (*Pause and she continues to wander about*) Hot. Could use some shade. Yeah, I sure could use that umbrella. (*Pause*) No, I will do without. I've got to learn to do without. (*She goes to the table and picks up the centerpiece*) Poor little *Snoopy*. Little tail all off. Poor little thing. Don't you look behind, 'cause if you do you'll just look back and find there's nothing there. (*Pause . . . she puts the centerpiece down . . . then looks down at it and straight at the audience with a shock of recognition*)

Curtain

PORCH

Characters:

DOT, *a woman about seventy. She sits in a wheelchair and fans herself with a paper fan, the type one used to get from funeral parlors. She wears an old housedress and bedroom slippers.*

LUCILLE, *a woman about forty-five. She wears a two-piece swimsuit, the kind that Esther Williams would have worn. She also has on plastic jewelry and rubber thong sandals. Lucille has red hair. She reads the newspaper continuously.*

Both characters speak with Texas accents.

Scene:

The porch of an old, Victorian house. The steps are broken and the house is in need of a paint job. The porch has a rocking chair surrounded by magazines and newspapers. There is a wheelchair and lots of junk scattered about. The yard around the porch is dry and hot looking, with a few weeds and flowers growing. A screen door leads from the porch into the house.

The sound of the ice cream truck is heard playing "Pop Goes The Weasel."

DOT: *(In her wheelchair)* Lucille! Lucille! Get back out here! It's the *Good Humor!*

LUCILLE: *(From inside the house)* What'd you want?

DOT: Ice cream.

LUCILLE: What?

DOT: Hurry! Throw something on and run get me an ice cream! Oh, Lucille, you're so slow. He's done gone. Turned the corner. You made me miss it.

LUCILLE: *(Coming out onto the porch)* Miss what? What's to miss?

DOT: Forget it! You're too late.

LUCILLE: I had to go in the house for a minute.

DOT: What for? To admire your figure?

LUCILLE: *(Sitting)* I forgot my newspaper.

DOT: Your newspaper. So you're just gonna rock in your rocker and read?

LUCILLE: Yes. *(She begins to read the paper)*

DOT: Well, I sure don't want to read. I'm burning up. (*Lucille pays no attention to Dot*) Oh, Lord, it's hot. Do you ever remember it being so hot? (*Short pause*) Hot as a firecracker! Aren't you just burning up? (*Short pause*) I'm just dripping wet. Every part of me. Aren't you wet? (*Short pause*) I don't know how you can read when it's so hot. I can't do a thing, I tell you. My energy is sapped.

LUCILLE: Don't think about it.

DOT: I'm not thinking about it . . . I'm just about to die, that's all.

LUCILLE: You want to go in and wash your face or have a Coca-Cola or something?

DOT: I wanted an ice cream. That would have cooled me off. (*Short pause*) You've been reading that all afternoon while I sit here suffering. It must be good.

LUCILLE: What?

DOT: I said, it must be good! You've had your head buried in that paper half the day.

LUCILLE: What?

DOT: I take it the news is good? God, good God . . . it's hot as Hades.

LUCILLE: You want some ice? All chipped up, like a snow-cone?

DOT: Like a snowcone?

LUCILLE: (*Irritated*) Like a cone.

DOT: Oh . . . ooh . . . remember when old man Hayes used to come by selling those cones? Every day? I'd be out on the porch, 'cause Daddy wouldn't let me go outside in the sun. He'd say, "Stay up on the porch, Dottie. You've got fair skin. If you go out you'll get burned." He'd say that. Wouldn't even let me go out to the curb and buy a snowcone from old man Hayes. He was afraid I'd turn red. That's because I used to be a redhead, like you. So let that be a lesson to you, Lucy.

LUCILLE: Who's old man Hayes?

DOT: Oh, you knew old man Hayes. Think, Lucy! You knew him.

LUCILLE: I did?

DOT: Marion's daddy. Marion Hayes . . . that gal I went to school with. Marion Hayes . . . everybody called her "mayonnaise." What ever happened to her?

LUCILLE: She's probably dead.

DOT: I wonder. I really do.

LUCILLE: I don't remember her either.

DOT: Oh, you do.

LUCILLE: Marion Hayes?

DOT: God, she was skinny. Marion Hayes. Her daddy sold snowcones in the summer and hot tamales in the winter. He had that tamale cart. Used to push it up to the corner by the Continental Bus Station. It was red and he rolled those tamales in newspapers. Well, not the tamales themselves . . . they were in corn shucks. But your order of tamales came to you in a newspaper. Like the one you're reading. Whatever happened to him?

LUCILLE: How should I know?

DOT: Whatever happened to her?

LUCILLE: (*Very irritated*) I said, I don't know her. (*She goes back to reading*)

DOT: Poor Marion . . . skinny little thing. But tall. Wore glasses. We used to ride by the tamale stand and hang our heads out the car window and scream at old man Hayes. We'd scream, "Where's my cat?" or "dog." "Where's my dog?" We were accusing him of making those tamales out of catmeat. Dogmeat. Poor old Marion didn't have a chance with her daddy selling snowcones in the summer and tamales in the winter. Nobody liked her because of it. I guess she just up and moved when she had the chance. Went somewhere where nobody knew her past. I guess she just did. Didn't she?

LUCILLE: Huh?

DOT: Didn't she move?

LUCILLE: I guess.

DOT: Well, I guess she'd just have to . . . wouldn't she? Well?

LUCILLE: Well, what? (*She slams the paper down*)

DOT: Well . . . it didn't seem to make much difference if your daddy ran the chili factory. That didn't hurt the kids in that family. They are well thought of. Nobody went around screaming, "Where's my dog," to them. But then, they used to drive that truck around . . . it was shaped like a chili can and had two beavers in the back . . . for Beaver Brand. Beaver Brand Chili. They used to have two stuffed beavers in the pick-up truck in a cage. Nobody questioned whether it was beef or beaver. Did they? (*Short pause*) Isn't it odd?

LUCILLE: What?

DOT: Odd?

LUCILLE: I guess. (*She goes back to reading*)

DOT: Well, of course, it's odd. God . . . I could drop dead or melt. Can people melt?

LUCILLE: What?

DOT: Melt? Like *Little Black Sambo* . . . melt? Turn into butter?

LUCILLE: Beats me.

DOT: Why butter?

LUCILLE: What?

DOT: Why did the tigers turn into butter? Why? What for?

LUCILLE: I don't know.

DOT: It doesn't make any sense. They ran round and round until they turned into butter?

LUCILLE: Yes.

DOT: Why? How? Tigers turning into butter. What would Sambo do with it? What would a little colored boy want with all that butter?

LUCILLE: I don't know.

DOT: It makes no sense to me. It's one of the wonders of the world. (*Short pause*) Hot, hot, hot, hot, hot! (*Short pause*) About finished?

LUCILLE: What?

DOT: With your paper?

LUCILLE: About.

DOT: About time.

LUCILLE: It gets my mind off the heat.

DOT: Hot. Whew it's hot!

LUCILLE: Wish it would rain.

DOT: Wouldn't help. Would just turn into steam. Humidity. If you got to be hot, dry heat is less hot. Not that I want *any* heat . . . just if we've got to be hot, then it's better not wet. Whew wee! Drip, drip, drip! Sweat's running out like sap out of a maple. Whew ooh! (*Pause*) And . . . (*Short pause*) there's not a soul on the street.

LUCILLE: No.

DOT: Yes, I saw one person pass by this morning. Want to know who? Well?

LUCILLE: Well, what?

DOT: Guess who?

LUCILLE: Who?

DOT: Guess! Guess! Oh, Lucille, play a guessing game. Guess who? Guess who?

LUCILLE: I haven't any idea, who?

DOT: Edna Baggett! That's who.

LUCILLE: Oh?

DOT: So Edna came out of her house, crossed the street, got in front of the Christian Church, then just turned around and went back home. I said, "Edna, is it hot enough for you?" And she said, "Girl, you can fry an egg on the sidewalk out here." Could you do that? Fry an egg on the sidewalk?

LUCILLE: I've heard of it.

DOT: Without any grease? How? It would stick and you couldn't eat it, but I guess it would prove how hot it is. Wouldn't it? If you wanted to waste an egg. Would you?

LUCILLE: What?

DOT: Waste an egg to prove a point?

LUCILLE: What?

DOT: Oh, read your paper! Just read on. Me, myself, well . . . I'm getting a wrist ache. Fan, fan, fan, fan, fan. If I was skinny, like you, I wouldn't be so hot. Aren't skinny people cooler? Isn't that what they say? Fat makes you hot?

LUCILLE: So they say.

DOT: I just don't know why it won't melt. Fat melts. I could turn into butter then I'd be as cool as a cucumber. Why are cucumbers cool? (*Short pause*) Because they're skinny?

LUCILLE: (*She screams*) I guess!

DOT: Oh, just read your paper! Just loll around and read! I'm trying to figure out what makes people cool.

LUCILLE: I thought you decided it was because of thinness.

DOT: Well, that theory, Lucille, just won't hold water. Because Edna is skinny and she was hot. Marion Hayes was always hot. Always had some sort of perspiration problem. So thinness making people cool isn't always right. Right?

LUCILLE: I guess not.

DOT: You guess? You guess? I know not. That Marion Hayes never gained an ounce in spite of all those tamales. But, then, maybe she didn't eat them? Maybe she knew for sure what they were made of? Edna, however, lost all her weight . . . got thin . . . when she swallowed that pin. I wonder where everyone is? There's nobody down at the corner that way and there's nobody in the cemetery.

LUCILLE: What pin? (*She lowers the newspaper*)

DOT: Aha! So you *are* listening?

LUCILLE: What pin?

DOT: You really want to know?

LUCILLE: What pin?

DOT: Well . . . oh, you're not really interested. I'll just keep my mouth shut. Read. Read! I'll keep on the lookout for another human being wandering about. Someone to talk to. Read on, Lucy, read on!

LUCILLE: Okay. (*She goes back to reading the newspaper*)

DOT: (*After a pause*) Nothing. No one. Not a soul. Whole place is empty. Ah, well . . .(*She pauses, then slaps the newspaper with her fan. Lucille slams the paper down and listens*) When Edna was selling dresses, she was trying to fit someone one day, unpinned something, put the pin in her mouth, and next thing she knew it was gone. There! I said it!

LUCILLE: Gone?

DOT: Honey, they looked and looked for that pin. They looked through everything she passed. But she never let it out. To this day that pin is somewhere in Edna's body. Either that or she never swallowed it, but she swears she did. At times she'll sit down and can feel it stick her! But it only happens when she sits and only sometimes. She says that must prove the pin is somewhere in her behind. Shall I go on?

LUCILLE: Go on.

DOT: Well, I saw it happen one day, when I was at her house . . . that was several years ago, of course. I saw her sit, heard her carry on, and I think it's actually that chair she's got in her den. I sat on it, the chair, and I felt the pin, too. Must be a spring sticking up. Naturally, I didn't let on to Edna. It would break her heart to know she's suffered ten years over that pin and the pain is actually caused by her furniture. If she ever had that chair recovered she'd probably feel okay, but how could that make up for ten years of pain?

LUCILLE: I don't know. (*She goes back to reading*)

DOT: Well, I don't either.

LUCILLE: No.

DOT: Oh, well . . . it's one of life's mysteries. (*She sings*)
   "Ah, sweet mystery of life at last . . ." (*Pause, she sings again*)
   "Ah, sweet mystery of life at last I've found you,
   Ah, . . ."

(*Lucille slams the paper down and stares at Dot*) Well, I won't sing. I'll just fan myself. Fan, a fan, a fan! (*The sound of hot rods is heard as they scream by on the street*) Oh! Oh! Oh! Lucille, I wish those hot rodders would stay off the street. Shut up! Get lost . . . you beatniks!

LUCILLE: They cut through here on their way to the Dairy Queen. (*She goes back to reading*)

DOT: I know. I know. This used to be a residential neighborhood. Quiet. Relaxed. All American. Just people and their dogs. Now they've put that old Dairy Queen down at the end of the block. Right down practically in the cemetery. And down the other way they got a "do-it-yourself" carwash and a Taco Bell. They tore down the loveliest homes to build that junk. The whole block is a slum, Lucille. We just live in a shanty in old shanty town. And there ain't nothin' I can do about it. Just sit and watch the whole place go straight to hell. Ain't nothin' I can do, except fan. Fan, fan, fan! (*Pause*) Is it interesting?

LUCILLE: What?

DOT: The news?

LUCILLE: I can't tell yet.

DOT: When will you know?

LUCILLE: When I finish, I guess.

DOT: Well, you just let me know.

LUCILLE: I will.

DOT: I sure don't want to waste my time reading if it's not interesting. Why be hot and bored at the same time? I'm already hot, so why be bored?

LUCILLE: It's not boring.

DOT: But it's not interesting.

LUCILLE: But it's not boring.

DOT: Wouldn't you hate to get all the way to the end and hate all the news? Every bit of it? Isn't it awful you have to get to the end before you know? I hate for the news to disappoint me. It's almost always bad. I just hate it! You hear me? I hate it!

LUCILLE: I hear you. You're screaming.

DOT: Well, I'm making a point. Bad news is for the birds! For the birds, Lucille! And that's my point! I made it. That's it. (*Short pause*) Oh, Lord, I've done worked myself into a lather. I'm an excitable person, Lucille, and you've got me all worked up.

LUCILLE: Well, simmer down.

DOT: I'm trying, I'm trying. But you made me lose my temper. I'm too hot now. Hot and bothered. I just might die. I might kick the bucket. What would you do if I did, Lucy? You'd probably just read your newspaper wouldn't you? Huh?

LUCILLE: (*Still reading the paper*) Hey, remember old lady Thigpin?

DOT: Well, sure I do. I've got a good memory. Is she in the paper?

LUCILLE: The old woman with that little shop featuring fried pies?

DOT: Yes . . . that's her. God, those little pies are good. Nobody makes a fried pie like Mrs. Thigpin does.

LUCILLE: Did. She died.

DOT: She did?

LUCILLE: Dead.

DOT: Was she cooking when she croaked? Cooking pies?

LUCILLE: How should I know?

DOT: Well, what does the paper say?

LUCILLE: She died.

DOT: But how? Why? That's incomplete! I want to know it all! The full story. Don't just tell me she's dead!

LUCILLE: And remember Betsy Withrow? That cute little girl that had the Shetland pony?

DOT: Yes. No . . . did she die?

LUCILLE: No. But the pony did. And that woman who took in ironing? Mrs. O'Neal?

DOT: Oh, no.

LUCILLE: (*Looking Dot right in the eye*) Died. Dead. Had a stroke.

DOT: I don't doubt it. With all this heat, it's too hot to iron. Stop reading all that bad news, Lucy. You'll get depressed. I want you to listen to me.

LUCILLE: What? (*She puts down the paper*)

DOT: Listen to me. Do you know that my hair's all stuck to the back of my neck? All stuck up in little ringlets? Hot! Whew! Why don't you give me a shampoo? Whew! Why don't you do up my hair real pretty?

LUCILLE: What for?

DOT: It'll get your mind off your troubles. All those deaths. Busy hands are happy hands, Lucille.

LUCILLE: My hands are happy enough. *I* may be miserable, but my hands are happy.

DOT: Ah, ha, ha, ha! Lucy, you are a scream!

LUCILLE: Am I?

DOT: A regular comedian! Ha, ha, ha! Oh, don't make me laugh so hard. Stop cracking jokes, Lucille.

LUCILLE: I didn't say anything funny.

DOT: You did! You did! Lucille, you are a monkey! A baboon!

LUCILLE: Oh, calm down. You'll bust a gut. Just calm down.

DOT: All right! All right! I'm getting myself under control. Okay. Now see? I'm calm.

LUCILLE: Good. Control yourself.

DOT: I will. (*Lucille waits for Dot to calm down . . . then goes back to reading her newspaper. Dot is quiet for a moment . . . then screams again. Looking offstage*) Oh! Lookee! Look! There's that little Vickery boy! Shoo! Shoo! Tom Vickery, you get out of my rose bushes! Lucille, run out there and shoo him out of my rose bushes! Out! Get out! If you don't move, I'll call your mommy, Tom Vickery! (*Dot suddenly stops screaming and rolls her wheelchair close to Lucille. She speaks quietly*) Oh, for God's sake, Lucille did you hear what I just said? I forgot Mrs. Vickery has passed on. Poor little orphan. What a shame. What an unfortunate thing for me to say. Still . . . (*A short pause*) It doesn't make any sense that he should be stealing my roses. Does it? Just because he's an orphan? Besides, he takes my roses, goes home, makes corsages out of them, and sells them. My roses!

LUCILLE: Maybe he's putting your flowers on his mamma's grave?

DOT: Don't be silly, he sells them! Sold me one . . . back when I used to go downtown. There he was, in front of the Woolworth's peddling corsages, so I bought one from the boy, came home and found my bushes stripped bare! I bought my own flowers, Lucille. Twenty-five cents for my own roses! Don't that beat all? Don't that just make you sick? Huh? Poor little orphan probably needs the quarter, but that don't make it right. Does it?

LUCILLE: What?

DOT: Stealing! Swiping my flowers so the child can play like he's a florist?

LUCILLE: No.

DOT: No. Having no mamma don't make it right. (*Yelling*)
"Thou shalt not steal," Tom Vickery! Get out of my rose bed!
Shoo! Shoo! (*To Lucille*) That's what children do when they
don't have a mamma. Isn't that right, Lucille?

LUCILLE: What?

DOT: Isn't that how children go wrong?

LUCILLE: It's not his fault. He didn't kill his own mamma,
did he?

DOT: Well, of course not. She was killed by that elephant.
I'll bet she'd be sick to death if she could see how her son's
turned out.

LUCILLE: Any way you look at it she's dead. What
elephant?

DOT: Poor woman's probably turning over in her grave
right now. Every time her son steals my flowers, I'll bet she
turns right over. Does a flip.

(*Lucille puts her paper down and really asks the following question*)

LUCILLE: What elephant?

DOT: (*Ignoring the question*) I'll tell you, I learned my lesson
about stealing when I was a little girl. Yes, I did. I went into
the five and dime and lifted a lip rouge. I was only about six
and didn't have any sense. My daddy whipped me. When I
came home wearing lip rouge, he knew I'd stole it. What's a
six year old doing owning a lip rouge? I should have known to
steal something more in my age range. But me, I never liked
toys, I just wanted to be pretty. The only thing *you* were ever
caught stealing was a pair of black panties that had red letter-
ing across the front. They said, "Saturday Night." You were
never interested in make-up. You stole undies. (*Lucille has gone
back to her newspaper . . . bored with Dot's story*) Lucille, you are a
peculiar thing. Ha, Ha! Funny, now that I'm old enough to
wear lipstick every day there are times I just go without it. Of
course, I wouldn't do that if we had company. But just sitting
here on the porch, I think it's okay not to wear it. I think on
my own porch I can sit with a natural face. Well?

LUCILLE: Well, what?

DOT: I don't have to get all done up, do I?

LUCILLE: Not for me. Not if you don't want to.

DOT: I'm not talking about what I want, I'm referring to
what's proper. Would Jackie Onassis sit on her screened-in
porch without her face on?

LUCILLE: I don't know. Find out from her.

DOT: How can I? I don't even know her. Never met the gal. I don't know where to turn.

LUCILLE: Pray, I guess.

DOT: Pray? To who? What am I going to do, ask the Lord Jesus for make-up advice? Don't be silly. (*She laughs*) Lucille, you're a card.

LUCILLE: A what?

DOT: A card! A card! Oh, never mind. Read your paper. Me . . . I'll just fan. Fan, fan, fan. Ha, ha! Hum . . . well, it's dead outside. No one's out and about. Dead as a doornail. What's a doornail? Hum-hum-hum. (*A pause. Suddenly*) Black Diamond!

LUCILLE: What?

DOT: His name was Black Diamond.

(*Lucille, confused, again puts the newspaper in her lap*)

LUCILLE: Who?

DOT: The elephant.

LUCILLE: What?

DOT: The beast that killed that little boy's mommy.

LUCILLE: Yes?

DOT: Yes, what?

LUCILLE: Is that all?

DOT: That's it, honey.

LUCILLE: He killed her?

DOT: Like a doornail.

LUCILLE: Why?

DOT: Because she drove up in her convertible. Drove right up to where that elephant was getting a drink of water. Can you imagine? Getting that close to an elephant? I guess when you're looking for a parking place and need it bad enough, you'll park anywhere.

LUCILLE: So?

DOT: So what?

LUCILLE: How did parking there get her killed?

DOT: Simple. The elephant reached over, picked Mrs. Vickery up out of her convertible and slammed her against the side of the sidewalk.

LUCILLE: Why?

DOT: How would I know why? Because she had the top down, I guess.

LUCILLE: Why would an elephant pick a woman up out of a car and kill her?

DOT: Don't ask me. Why did the chicken cross the road? I don't know.

LUCILLE: So what happened?

DOT: They buried Mrs. Vickery.

LUCILLE: To the elephant? What was an elephant doing downtown anyway?

DOT: Well, what do you think he was doing, Lucille? Shopping? Ha, ha! He was in a circus. Why else would an elephant hang around Main Street? Use your head, Lucy!

LUCILLE: So what happened?

DOT: The elephant was buried, too.

LUCILLE: Where?

DOT: I don't know, Lucille. Where do you bury an elephant? Who cares? My point is till this very day, you'll never catch me feeding peanuts to them at the zoo.

LUCILLE: What zoo? We don't have a zoo.

DOT: That's not my point. Beware of elephants, Lucille. They can just reach over and, before you know it, you're a goner. If I were you, I'd steer clear of elephants.

LUCILLE: I've never seen an elephant in my life. Not in person.

DOT: Well, if you do, just ease on by him. Don't park. Don't even go near him. Elephants spell trouble. And that's my point. Now . . . isn't that a better story than anything you've read in that paper today? Isn't it?

LUCILLE: Are you sure that story is true? Why have I never heard it?

DOT: Sure it's true. And you've never heard it because you never listen. Open your ears, Lucy, you've got a lot to learn!

LUCILLE: That's why I'll just read my paper. (*She goes back to reading*)

DOT: I mean about life, Lucy, life! You can't always believe what you read, except in the Bible.

LUCILLE: Why's that the exception?

DOT: Because it's the truth. I never read anything but the Bible, that's why I speak nothing but the truth. "Ye shall know the truth," Lucy, "and the truth shall set ye free."

LUCILLE: Well, I think there's some truth to the news-paper.

DOT: Just some, Lucy, some! How are you going to separate the truth from the lies? You're not smart enough. You didn't do too well in school, did you? I would have felt just awful if I'd been the last in my class.

LUCILLE: Someone's got to be last.

DOT: Seems to me . . . if I knew I was going to be last, I would pull myself up by my bootstraps and try harder.

LUCILLE: I didn't know I was last. I knew I was near the end, but not last.

DOT: Did it just kill you when you found out? Did you just want to go jump in the lake? End it all?

LUCILLE: Like I said, someone's got to be last. Being the one hasn't ruined my life.

DOT: It hasn't helped it any. So get your head out of that paper, you might miss something.

LUCILLE: There's nothing to miss. What's there to miss?

DOT: Plenty. You'll miss something good and never know it. Why read that old paper?

LUCILLE: There are things I want to know.

DOT: Well, you won't find what you want in the paper. What do you want to know? Well . . . what? I'll answer all your questions. Ask me anything. I'm better than a newspaper. Ask me! (*Dot grabs the paper away from Lucille*)

LUCILLE: Do I have to?

DOT: Yes! Ask me a question and I'll tell you no lies.

LUCILLE: Oh, I don't know.

DOT: Where's your curiosity? Pop me a question.

LUCILLE: Oh, well . . . why is it so hot?

DOT: I know that! It is hot because it is summer. See?

(*Dot and Lucille probably play these kinds of question and answer games every day. Dot loves the game*)

LUCILLE: Well, why do you think you can answer my questions?

DOT: That's so simple. Because I wasn't the last in my class. Give me a hard one.

LUCILLE: Well, why live?

DOT: What?

(*Lucille usually doesn't ask such serious questions. She is out to stump Dot with this one*)

LUCILLE: Why live?

DOT: Ah, ha! That's a goodie. That's the sixty-four thousand dollar one. The best one yet. And the answer is, Lucy, because God put everyone on this earth for a purpose.

LUCILLE: What's yours?

DOT: Well . . . one doesn't always know.

LUCILLE: So you don't know what you're doing?

DOT: I know, I know . . . I haven't lived all these years in the dark. I know what I'm doing. I'm doing what God is doing with me. And I'll know what I've done when He decides to tell me.

LUCILLE: When will that be? What if some elephant picks you up and slams you against the sidewalk before He lets you know?

(*Lucille is winning at this point and Dot is not so quick with her answers*)

DOT: Well, you see . . . I am sure He told Mrs. Vickery her purpose the minute before that elephant threw her.

LUCILLE: And it was, "Mrs. Vickery, you have lived to be killed by an elephant?" Was that it?

DOT: How should I know? Don't be silly! Whatever He told her was between her and God. He didn't tell me . . . He told her. God just expects you to keep on doing whatever it is you do until He gives you the meaning of what you are doing.

LUCILLE: So you're just going to sit and wait here on the porch?

DOT: Sure I am. What else can I do? Besides . . . it's too hot to do anything else. I'd do something else if it was cool, but it's hot. I didn't make it hot. God did. He knows what I do when it's hot. I sit here. If He didn't like that He'd make it cool. Then I'd go inside and do what I do then.

LUCILLE: Which is?

DOT: Sit in the living room.

LUCILLE: I see.

DOT: Do you, Lucille? Sometimes I wonder. You're so slow to catch on.

LUCILLE: Well, if God made you to sit, maybe He made me slow.

(*Lucille goes and gets her paper from Dot*)

DOT: No. You did that, all by yourself . . . out of meanness. God does not set your pace. He puts us all at the starting gate and how fast you come out is your business.

LUCILLE: You really think it's the entire purpose of your life to sit on this porch?

DOT: Well, I hope that's it, because if it is then I've done it. Did my duty.

LUCILLE: Maybe I'm doing mine then. Maybe I'm doing exactly what God intends. (*She goes back to reading the news*)

DOT: Now, Lucy . . . I know God means for you to do more than just read the newspaper. I don't think God even likes the paper. I'm sure He'd rather have you read His book. The only one He ever wrote.

LUCILLE: The Bible?

DOT: Yes. (*Singing*)
      "Oh, the B.I.B.L.E.
      That's the book for me,"
How does that song go?

LUCILLE: I don't remember.

DOT: Oh, you sang it in Sunday School. Remember?

LUCILLE: I never sang it.

DOT: Oh, you did. I got the words but I can't remember the tune.
      "Oh, the B.I.B.L.E.
      That's the book for me,
      La, la, la, la, la, la, la . . ."
Help me! Help me with the tune! (*The buzzing sound of a fly*) Whew! Whew! Get away! Get! Silly fly! Get! I'm gonna get you, mister! Where'd he go? Oh . . . (*Swat, swat, swat—she hits the fly with her fan*) DIE! DIE! DIE! (*A short pause*) Lucille, I got him.

LUCILLE: Well, it can't be said about you, "She wouldn't kill a fly."

DOT: I don't know where that expression came from. I really don't. Why not kill a fly?

LUCILLE: Remember . . . "Thou Shalt not kill?" Your B.I.B.L.E. says that.

DOT: That doesn't apply to flies. That means men. "Thou shalt not kill thy fellow man."

LUCILLE: What about women?

DOT: It means women, too. Man means woman.

LUCILLE: Why didn't God say, "Thy fellow man and woman?" He said man. He said fellows.

DOT: He means both! Whatever His reason for writing man, He meant woman. God does not discriminate because of gender.

LUCILLE: What?

DOT: Gender!

LUCILLE: Then answer this . . . why are all the books of the Bible named after men? Why were all the Apostles men?

DOT: Well, I don't know, Lucille.

LUCILLE: Because God is partial to men.

DOT: There are many great women in the Bible, Lucille. There's, of course, Eve and Mary. Actually the two Marys. I always refer to them as Mary and Mary M. Now Mary M. wasn't as nice a girl as plain Mary. Then there was Ruth and sister, Naomi. And . . . and Sarah. Who could forget Sheba . . . the one who cut the hair.

LUCILLE: A beautician?

DOT: No! She cut Solomon's hair. Took away his strength. She didn't cut hair for a living. She was a queen! Now I forget, was Sheba the same as Bathsheba? Or was Sheba a country and Bathsheba the one who messed up Solomon? Or was it Samson and Delilah? Well, it's all confused, but it's all in the Bible. They were all women. They just didn't all know each other like the Apostles did. They sort of went their own ways doing deeds. But God, my dear, does not discriminate against women. After all, He gave us the power to have babies.

LUCILLE: The "power" to have babies?

DOT: That's why He made you the way you are. See how little you know? See what you learn from your newspaper and magazines? You ought to pick up the good book. That's where you get all the answers. It's not called good for nothing.

LUCILLE: What's it good for?

DOT: It's a total delight. Adventure, drama, pathos, a few laughs . . . not many, but a few. (*A short pause*) It's very well written. (*A short pause*) Better than a newspaper. (*She sings*)

"Oh, the B.I.B.L.E. . . . ."

LUCILLE: If you say so.

DOT: Boy, you can't beat the Bible.

LUCILLE: (*Suddenly putting down her paper*) Oh, look, Mr. Ferguson. (*Yelling*) Yoo hoo! Mr. Ferguson!

DOT: Lucille, what are you doing? Yelling at that old man? Have you lost your mind?

LUCILLE: (*Getting out of her chair*) Yoo hoo! Look it's me! Over here on the porch! (*She strikes a pose*) Do you like my swimsuit?

DOT: (*Screaming*) You have lost it, Lucy, gone berserk! Shut up talking to that old man!

LUCILLE: If you're going to the post office, I sure could use a magazine.

DOT: Oh, Lord, you don't need another thing to read!

LUCILLE: Get me a *Modern Screen* or a *Photoplay*. I'll give you some money when you get back.

DOT: You're not getting a nickel from me, Lucille.

LUCILLE: (*Waving*) Much obliged! Bye bye, Freddy!

DOT: Freddy! Lucille, are you crazy? Screaming at that old man? What will people think? Standing there exposing yourself! You're as naked as a jay bird! Hide, Lucy, hide!

LUCILLE: I'm not naked.

DOT: It's as close to naked as you can get in this world. That little swimsuit offers no surprises. Someone's liable to come up here, whisk you off and turn you into a white slave!

LUCILLE: People don't do that.

DOT: What do you know about people? I've been around and let me tell you it's bad out there. From what I've seen, I warn you, the only really safe place to wear that "bikini" is in the bathroom with the door locked. And if I'd known you could buy such things through the mail, I'd never gotten a 1956 Sears catalogue. What's happened to them? Who can you trust?

LUCILLE: I don't know.

DOT: No, you don't know. You'd never have ordered that if you knew. You threw away nine ninety-five on that swimsuit, as well as your reputation. Lucille, you don't even swim!

LUCILLE: But I'm awfully cool.

DOT: Yeah, well, I'm plain disgusted! Go on! Throw decency to the wind! I wish there was a little breeze . . . I'm about to die. (*A short pause*) I said, I'm about to die! Pass on!

LUCILLE: (*She screams*) So? What can I do about that? Don't scream at me. Yell at God. He controls the weather. Tell Him to turn the heat down.

DOT: You think you're very smart. Well, talking smart don't make you have more sense. Smart talk is senseless talk, Lucille, and you don't make no sense. Plum cuckoo, that's you.

LUCILLE: (*Angry, going to her newspaper*) I've got another question for you.

DOT: You do?

LUCILLE: Do you know Christine Clowe?

DOT: Oh . . . yes. Christine works down at the slack factory. She's a seat seamer. Is she in the paper? Is she dead?

LUCILLE: No. Arrested.

DOT: No?

LUCILLE: Passed some bad checks.

DOT: She, like you, never did have a lick of sense.

LUCILLE: And Beth Ellen Bonner?

DOT: Arrested?

LUCILLE: No. She called the police and said a prowler broke into her house and used bad language.

DOT: Called her filthy things?

LUCILLE: So it seems.

DOT: I'll bet she owns a bikini, too.

LUCILLE: And that woman who used to sell shoes, Miss Pugh?

DOT: Cussed out? Arrested? Robbed?

LUCILLE: Dead.

DOT: I thought you were reading the police news? Now you're back to the obits?

LUCILLE: I skip around. It makes it more fun.

DOT: Does it? Does it? Well, it just sounds silly, Lucille. Straighten up and fly right!

LUCILLE: What's a three-letter word meaning "Happiness?"

DOT: You're not now doing the crossword?

LUCILLE: Did you know rump roast is one fourteen a pound at the A&P? Or that Dear Abby says that you shouldn't feel obliged to write a thank you note to someone who's killed your mother, no matter how thankful you are that she's gone?

DOT: No! No! I didn't know any of that. I don't want to know any of that! Stupid. And you made that up about Abby . . . I just know you did.

LUCILLE: Do you?

(*Lucille is winning this game and is confusing Dot*)

DOT: Don't bother me with your silly news. What's the use of reading if you're going to make things up?

LUCILLE: Sex.

DOT: My God, what a word! Where did that come from?

LUCILLE: I think that's the three-letter word meaning "Happiness."

DOT: Sex? Sex? Happiness? How would you know? You've never had it! (*The bells of an ice cream truck are heard coming down the street. The bells play "Pop Goes the Weasel"*) Ooh, ooh . . . here comes the Good Humor! Good Humor! If you had on some clothes you could run out and get me a popsicle.

LUCILLE: I'll go anyway. (*She gets up and starts to go*)

DOT: Not in the street you don't. If you go out like that, you'll be gone with the wind.

(*Lucille is defiant. Dot is angry*)

LUCILLE: I'm just going to the curb.

DOT: No, you're not! Curb it, Lucille, no! No! No! (*Lucille stops . . . she has heard Dot*) There he goes. (*The sound of the ice cream bells fades*) My one chance to enjoy life. There goes the Good Humor. A cone would have cooled me off! If you had some morals, I would be cool!

LUCILLE: Do you want me to bring my buzz fan out here? Blow the hot around? Huh?

DOT: Well . . . it doesn't make up for me not getting an ice cream, but at least it shows you've got a heart. It's usually in the wrong place . . . like hanging out of your bathing suit.

LUCILLE: I'll go in the house and get the fan. (*She exits into the house*)

DOT: (*Yelling*) And get an extension cord. That way you can plug it in in the living room and pull the fan way out here on the porch. Hear?

LUCILLE: (*From inside*) I hear you.

DOT: I'm gonna be cool. I'm gonna be cool. Ha, ha!

LUCILLE: (*Coming out of the house with an electric fan*) Here we go.

DOT: Point it at me! Flip it on! Ha, ha!

(*The buzzing sound of the fan is heard when Lucille turns it on*)

LUCILLE: There we go.

(*They now have to talk over the sound of the buzz fan*)

DOT: Oh, oh . . . ha, ha! I'm cool! I'm cool! Ha, ha! Did I ever tell you that Poco has a buzz fan in all her bedrooms? Even in the winter?

LUCILLE: Yes. (*She picks up a magazine and reads*)

DOT: Yes. Once when I went to visit her, she showed me to my room and said, "Here's your buzz fan," and I said, "Poco, why do I need that?" And she said, "Turn it on for privacy. It drowns out the noise so everyone in the house won't hear what you're doing." Can you believe it? What did she think I would be doing? (*A short pause*) Oh, dear . . .

LUCILLE: Oh, dear, what?

DOT: That thing sure is loud.

LUCILLE: Yes.

DOT: I can hear it running at night. I can hear it running in your room.

LUCILLE: So?

DOT: You have this buzz fan for coolness, don't you?

LUCILLE: Sure.

DOT: I don't suppose you use it to drown out noise?

LUCILLE: What?

DOT: (*Yelling*) What do you do in your room?

LUCILLE: Nothing.

DOT: Good.

LUCILLE: Why good?

DOT: I'm glad to know nothing's going on that I shouldn't hear. I don't want you sneaking around on me. You don't do sneaky things do you, Lucy?

LUCILLE: No . . . well, no. Well, sometimes Helen comes over. It's not sneaky, she just comes in.

DOT: When? Helen? Helen who?

LUCILLE: Helen . . . from down the block. I went to school with her and sometimes she drops by when she gets off work at the movie.

DOT: At night?

LUCILLE: She works at night.

DOT: She comes over often? Comes in when I'm asleep?

LUCILLE: What difference does it make? It's my room. I can ask over whoever I like.

DOT: Can you? Can you? Well, I know what you like! I suppose you have men in?

LUCILLE: What?

DOT: Men! Men! For God's sake, get rid of this buzz fan! Turn it off! Get rid of it!

LUCILLE: Why?

DOT: I want to know what's going on! I won't have a Watergate under my own roof! Turn that evil fan off! Off!

(*Lucille turns the fan off*)

LUCILLE: Okay, it's off.

DOT: What have you done to me?

LUCILLE: Nothing. I had a friend over.

DOT: Keep that Helen out! And don't bring men in here. I don't want strangers in my house.

LUCILLE: It's mine, too.

DOT: Daddy left it to me.

LUCILLE: He was my daddy!

DOT: He was my husband! (*A pause*) I earned this house. I deserve it. It's mine. Children aren't supposed to own their own homes.

LUCILLE: I'm not a child. I wish I had my own home.

DOT: How would you get your own home? Huh? How'd you pay for it? What money you have belongs to me. I won't give you the money.

LUCILLE: You won't even give me enough to take a bus ride.

DOT: I've given you money. I gave you nine ninety-five and look what you bought.

LUCILLE: I get your point!

DOT: Do you? Do you, Lucille? Your own home? Are you crazy? How in the world would you get one?

LUCILLE: (*This is an outcry of white anger and force . . . she makes perfect sense*) I would walk across the street and marry old man Ferguson. I could do that. After all, that's what you did. Marry an old man, sit on his porch, have a kid, got your own home. What you did didn't take any brains or money. I could walk across the street, do what you did, sit on Freddy's porch and stare at you. I could do that! Unless it's God's will that I should stay here for forty-five more years letting you make me miserable!

DOT: You wouldn't marry that old man!

LUCILLE: Sit on your porch and watch.

DOT: You don't even know old man Ferguson that well.

LUCILLE: I do. I talk to him at night, when you're asleep. Other times I wander down the block and see Tommy Vickery's daddy. Another nice widower. Ferguson's old, Vickery's young . . . both are lonely. So am I.

DOT: Well, you have yourself quite a night life. I'll bet you even hang out with the beatniks at the Dairy Queen?

LUCILLE: Oh, Mama, I have the time of my life when it's past your bedtime.

DOT: What makes you think any man would want to marry you?

LUCILLE: Out of pity. Out of loneliness. I don't know.

DOT: No, you don't know. You see, the whole world's lonely, Lucille. That's the state of things. That's no reason to wander up and down the block talking to the menfolk. Shame on you! That's no reason to marry one.

LUCILLE: But you did! Marry one!

DOT: That don't make it right. It was the one mistake I ever made, but I recovered . . . got over it.

LUCILLE: And got a house.

DOT: Oh, for Pete's sake, Lucy . . . hold your horses! I'm an old woman, I'll be dead soon.

LUCILLE: How soon?

DOT: What?

LUCILLE: How soon? If you make it short, I might stay around to see the end.

DOT: That's silly, you make it sound like you want me dead?

LUCILLE: Right now I wish I knew an elephant.

DOT: You've certainly got a smart mouth. I didn't raise you to be a tart!

LUCILLE: No, well, what did you raise me for?

DOT: Because . . . because you were born, you came along, you were there.

LUCILLE: Well, that's why the chicken crosses the road, Mama. Because it's there. Like Freddy Ferguson's.

DOT: Well . . . well . . . I don't know what to say.

LUCILLE: Finally.

DOT: Well . . . this is a fine how-do-you-do. Well, I think it's time for you to go in. You've had too much exposure, Miss.

LUCILLE: I don't want to go in, thank you.

DOT: Well, I won't sit here and talk to a crazy. You ought to get inside, get on some clothes and get ahold of yourself.

LUCILLE: Freddy's bound to be back soon with my magazines.

DOT: You wouldn't do that, would you? Leave poor old me and marry that poor old man?

LUCILLE: I'm the one who's poor.

DOT: I'll be gone soon. Just wait. Then you can have this

house, run all over creation at night in your silly swimsuit, get yourself involved with a hot rodder . . . if you want. I won't know. Right now I need you.

LUCILLE: For years you've said, "Lucy, don't go, I need you." So I didn't go and all you've needed me for has added up to nothing. I need to go. I got a lot to do.

DOT: After the Lord takes me, you'll be on your own.

LUCILLE: Finally.

DOT: And I'll bet you find out there's nothing to do, Lucy. Nothing is what there is to do. There's no need to go looking for anything you can't have right here. This is the best of nothing. Oh, I know you have dreams. Wild ideas put there by your newspapers and magazines about what's going on in the world. But this is the best place to be, Lucy . . . out here on this porch. When I go to my eternal rest, you can rest right here. Swing on the swing. Rock in the rocker. Watch the world go by. The view is so much better here than it is from old man Ferguson's. But don't go outside . . . in the world, Baby. You're a little person and you might get lost. (*Dot reaches out and touches Lucille . . . as a mother would touch a child*)

LUCILLE: I'm just going to read, Mama. Read the news of people who got robbed, arrested or shot. People who got out and did something.

DOT: Good for you.

LUCILLE: Good for me?

DOT: After all, you wouldn't want to wander off. I might start to die and you wouldn't be here. I'm ready to go. Been just waiting for ages. I can't wait to get to heaven. Every night, before I go to sleep, I pray, "Dear God, take me." I've seen the world for seventy some odd years. Seen my neighbors come and go. Watched Tommy Vickery swipe my roses and old man Ferguson trot off to the post office. Seen Lucille grow from a little girl into a grown woman. I've had an eyeful. Seen it all. Everything there is to see from this porch. Yes, Lord, I'm ready to come to heaven and see what the angels are up to! (*A short pause*) Well . . . I've had it with the porch. I'm going inside, Lucille, and wait. (*Dot puts down her fan and rolls her wheelchair inside the house. We hear Dot yell from inside*) Don't run off!

(*Lucille picks up Dot's fan and begins to fan herself*)

LUCILLE: (*To herself*) Sit and rock. Sit and rot. (*A short pause*) God, it's hot. (*A short pause*) God, I got to be going.
(*Lucille puts down the fan, goes to the steps of the porch and begins to step off. She does not leave. The sound of ice cream truck is heard again playing "Pop Goes The Weasel"*)
DOT: (*Yelling from inside the house*) Lucy? Is that the ice cream man again? Lucille? (*A short pause*) Yoo hoo? Lucille? Come put me in the bed! (*Lucille stares out at the world beyond the steps . . . torn between leaving and the calls from Dot. A short pause*) Lucy? I need you. Are you there? (*A short pause. She sings*) "When I'm calling you . . . ooh . . . ooh . . . ooh . . . ooh . . . ooh." (*She yells*) Yoo-hoo?
(*Lucille turns and exits into the house. The sound of "Pop Goes The Weasel" gets louder and louder until the final "Pop"*)

Curtain

James McLure

PVT. WARS

James McLure

One of the more auspicious Broadway playwriting debuts of the past season occurred on June 7, 1979, when James McLure's two short comedies, *Lone Star* and *Pvt. Wars,* opened at the Century Theatre, New York.

Originally presented earlier in the year as part of a new play festival at the Actors Theatre of Louisville (where *Lone Star* was given a full mounting and *Pvt. Wars,* its companion piece, performed as a workshop presentation), the impact was such that producers Michael Harvey and Peter A. Bobley who saw them there immediately arranged for a New York production of the double bill.

Although *Pvt. Wars,* which appears in an anthology for the first time in *The Best Short Plays 1980,* has an underlying seriousness as a tale of three wounded Vietnam soldiers who are passing the long, corroding days in a veterans' hospital, the stress is on comedy.

As Mel Gussow reported in *The New York Times:* "*Pvt. Wars* is a marvelous compendium of episodes and blackouts about desperate, lingering lives. Mr. McLure has an original, death's head-humor, one not unlike that of such novelists as Joseph Heller and John Irving, but peppered with the playwright's own special brand of cascading, spontaneous wit. In his noteworthy New York debut as a playwright, Mr. McLure draws from a diverse comic arsenal. I would not be surprised to see these plays repeated and acclaimed at theatres in diverse areas for these are good ol' boy comedies that anyone can laugh at."

Others found the double bill "hilarious and touching" while T. E. Kalem of *Time* magazine summarized the occasion by declaring: "The best one can do is to spot a 'natural'. James McLure looks like one. His effervescent gift for black comedy makes both of these plays bubble with the champagne of laughter."

James McLure was born in Shreveport, Louisiana, and received his B.A. from Southern Methodist University. He taught and performed for two years with the Pacific Conservatory of the Performing Arts and appeared at the Oregon Shakespearean Festival, the University of Rochester Summer Theatre and the Center Repertory Theatre of Cleveland. Subsequently, he came to New York in further pursuit of his acting career.

Asked by an interviewer why he had turned to writing, he replied rather succinctly: "Unemployment! I always wanted to write. But it took me a year to get started as an actor after coming East. So I had time and concentrated on writing." Playwriting was no new notion for him, however, for he had taken courses and had written plays at Southern Methodist. "There are perhaps six or seven plays, though *Lone Star* and *Pvt. Wars* are the first to have been produced."

As an actor, meanwhile, Mr. McLure also was establishing himself on New York stages with his appearances with the Lion Theatre Company in *K: Impressions of Kafka's The Trial; The Death and Life of Jesse James; Music Hall Sidelights;* and, most recently, in the New York Shakespeare Festival's Public Theatre production of *New Jerusalem.*

The author presently has several new stage works in progress and has just completed an original movie script for Columbia Pictures.

Characters:

WOODRUFF GATELY

SILVIO

NATWICK

*The play takes place on an outdoor terrace of an army veterans'
hospital.*
The time: the present, during several days and one night.

Scene One

A sunny day. Gately at the table fixing a radio.
Pause.
Silvio enters hurriedly. Pause. He notices Gately.

SILVIO: What the hell you doing?
GATELY: Fixing a radio.
SILVIO: What the hell for?
GATELY: It's for Hinson.
SILVIO: What's Hinson need a radio for? I need a radio
more than Hinson.
GATELY: Why?
SILVIO: Hinson doesn't have any arms or legs.
GATELY: Yes, but you move around too much. This has to
be plugged in.
SILVIO: I'll get an extension cord. (*Pause*) One thing I've
noticed about you. You concentrate and you do things slowly.
How do you account for this?
GATELY: Hard drugs.
SILVIO: I see.
GATELY: It's for my nerves.
SILVIO: Do the drugs help?
GATELY: Oh, yes. I hardly have any nerves left at all.
(*Pause*) Could you hand me that piece of wire? I want to do a

good job of this. I figure if I do a good job of this radio, they may let me out of here.

SILVIO: You can get out any time you want.

GATELY: I know that.

SILVIO: But you figure, if you finish that radio, they'll let you out.

GATELY: Sure. It's all part of the Free Enterprise system.

SILVIO: I see. (*Silvio refers to a pocket notebook*) Okay, I gotta go.

GATELY: Okay.

SILVIO: Yeah, there's some orderly over in C Ward givin' those guys a lotta shit. Can you believe that? So—I gotta go.

GATELY: Okay.

SILVIO: So, uh, you here a lot? You hang out here?

GATELY: Yeah.

SILVIO: You're Gately, right?

GATELY: Yeah.

SILVIO: Tell you what. I'll see you later.

(*Silvio exits. Gately watches him go. Blackout*)

Transition one

Atkins and Johnson wanted in C ward immediately. Disturbance between patient and personnel. It's Silvio again. Jesus Christ!

Scene Two

Gately fixing radio. Natwick enters in robe and slippers, carrying a newspaper. He is visibly upset. He sits, opens paper, covering his face. He lowers paper.

NATWICK: I don't want to talk about it.

GATELY: What?

NATWICK: I don't want to talk about it.

GATELY: What don't you want to talk about?

NATWICK: Look, I said I didn't want to talk about it, okay?

GATELY: Okay. (*Pause, Gately begins to whistle*)

NATWICK: Do you mind? I'm trying to read.

GATELY: Natwick, if you won't tell me what not to talk about, how do you know I might not *accidentally* start talking about it?

NATWICK: (*Confidentially*) The odds are ten trillion to one against it.

GATELY: Oh.

NATWICK: (*Darkly*) But I don't even want to take *that* chance.

(*Pause*)

GATELY: I'll bet I could guess what it is.

NATWICK: (*Amused*) Don't even waste your time.

(*Slight pause*)

GATELY: Is it something that just happened to you?

NATWICK: (*Guardedly*) What?

GATELY: Did someone do something to you?

NATWICK: (*Sinking*) I don't want—

GATELY: Was it staff?

NATWICK: One down, two to go.

GATELY: Was it someone in the ward?

NATWICK: Two down, one to go.

GATELY: Was it Gleason?

NATWICK: (*Exulting*) Three down, none to—

GATELY: Was it Silvio?

NATWICK: What?

GATELY: Was it Silvio?

(*Silvio enters with a smile to suggest he has eaten Natwick's first-born*)

SILVIO: Hello, Gately.

GATELY: Hello, Silvio.

SILVIO: (*Pause*) Hello, Natwick.

(*Blackout*)

Transition two: Natwick Letter

Dear Mother: There is a guy here named Silvio. Mother, I think there is something very wrong with him. He's violent and terribly anti-social. I don't know why they let people like this in the Army. Your loving son . . .

Scene Three: Underwear

Gately fixing radio.
Silvio standing looking off, intently, into distance.

SILVIO: Would you look at that. Would you *look* at *that*. (*Pause*) Hey, beautiful! Hey, gorgeous! Turn around! Ta-dah! (*Silvio unties robe, flashes, reties robe. Smiles contentedly. Silvio slips underpants on underneath robe*) I don't know. I like the floppy kind of underwear. It gives you more of a sense of freedom, you know? You can flop around. One has mobility.
(*Pause*)
GATELY: That's very good. You could go on TV. Advertise floppy underwear.
SILVIO: Yeah, if I wanted to I could. I ain't got the time though. But I could if I wanted to, y'know, because I believe in floppy underwear. (*Pause*) Only one drawback to floppy underwear.
GATELY: What's that?
SILVIO: They make you feel like an old man. That's the trouble with life, Gately. You may find something you like, but if it makes you feel like an old man—what's the point? (*Pause*) You get my point? (*Pause*) You know another thing makes you feel like an old man?
GATELY: An old woman?
SILVIO: Garters.
GATELY: You're right.
SILVIO: You damn right I'm right! I had to wear garters to my brother's wedding.
GATELY: Did it make you feel like an old man?
SILVIO: You damn right! Besides the garters didn't work.
GATELY: Maybe you were wearing the wrong kinda socks.
SILVIO: Maybe you're right.
GATELY: What kind did you wear?
SILVIO: Athletic socks.
GATELY: You wore athletic socks to your brother's wedding?
SILVIO: You see, Gately, I'm Catholic.

GATELY: Did the Pope make you do it?

SILVIO: Don't get cute, Gately. It was his second marriage. Okay? First time around I wear black socks. Second time around I figured, fuck it! You see, Gately, I respect the state of Holy Matrimony.

GATELY: So do I.

SILVIO: And I respect the Holy Catholic Church.

GATELY: So do I.

SILVIO: I know you do. Let's shake on it. (*They stand and shake on it*) Now, I'd like to return for a minute, if I may, to the subject of underwear.

GATELY: All right.

SILVIO: Now then. Floppy versus tight. Me? I don't see any comparison. 'Cause, I mean, in terms of underwear, what is a man looking for?

GATELY: Fashion?

SILVIO: Certainly fashion. I mean, you're with a chick, right? You don't want to take off your pants, right, and have her laugh at your underwear?

GATELY: She might though, if you're wearing floppy underwear.

SILVIO: That's why you gotta get a good pattern. Take a look at these. (*He opens robe*) Are these smart or what?

GATELY: They're pretty smart.

SILVIO: My sister sent me these.

GATELY: Your sister's got good taste in men's underwear.

SILVIO: Of course.

GATELY: Kinda makes you wonder though.

SILVIO: What?

GATELY: How your sister got such good taste in men's underwear.

SILVIO: (*Pointing finger*) Hey! Watch it. (*Pause*) Okay. So the way I see it. A guy needs fashion. And a guy needs mobility. And outside of that there's nothing else a guy needs.

GATELY: Snugness.

SILVIO: (*Unsettled*) What?

GATELY: Snugness.

SILVIO: Uh–oh. I think I hear the voice of a tight underwear man here.

GATELY: Well, a guy doesn't always want floppy underwear.

SILVIO: Now wait a minute.

GATELY: Underwear are like socks.

SILVIO: Stop! I don't know if I can let that get by.

GATELY: You don't want your socks slipping down. A man wants snug socks.

SILVIO: (*Pondering*) Socks are like underwear. (*Pause*) What kind you wearing?

GATELY: Black ones.

SILVIO: (*Troubled*) Oh, yeah?

GATELY: Yeah.

SILVIO: Are they tight?

GATELY: (*Underneath table, wiggles his foot*) They're pretty tight.

SILVIO: They're not black silk are they?

GATELY: Black polyester, I think. But all mine got holes in them.

SILVIO: Of course they've got holes. It's a modern convenience.

GATELY: I've got holes on the balls.

SILVIO: Holes on the balls!

GATELY: I've gotta get some new ones.

SILVIO: I guess so.

GATELY: But I've got a problem. I got different sizes. My left is bigger than my right.

SILVIO: Well, how much difference can there be?

GATELY: About an inch. One's about nine inches long.

SILVIO: What!

GATELY: The other's about ten inches.

SILVIO: Nine and ten inches?

GATELY: Yeah. I was born that way.

SILVIO: Jesus Christ! What about . . . you know . . . Mr. In-Between.

GATELY: What?

SILVIO: Never mind.

(*Pause*)

GATELY: I find though, if I buy, oh, nine to, say eleven, that fits everything.

SILVIO: You're not talking about around are you?

GATELY: Hell, no! I'm talking about length. What's the matter, Silvio?

SILVIO: I don't want to talk about it.

(*Silvio sinks into darkest depression. Natwick enters. Sits*)

GATELY: Hello, Natwick.

NATWICK: I don't want to talk about it. (*Pause. Notices Silvio's depression*) What's the matter with Little Mary Sunshine?

GATELY: He doesn't want to talk about it.

NATWICK: Very intelligent of him.

GATELY: Pretty soon I'll be talking to myself around here. Say, Natwick. What size feet do you have?

NATWICK: About a nine. Ten.

GATELY: Can I borrow some socks? Mine are wearing out on the balls of my feet.

NATWICK: Do you still have athlete's foot?

SILVIO: What?

NATWICK: Does he still have athlete's foot?

SILVIO: You were talking about the balls of your feet.

GATELY: Of course.

SILVIO: Oh, you were talking about socks!

GATELY: Yes.

SILVIO: Oh. You hear that, Natwick? He was talking about socks.

NATWICK: Yes. I'm overwhelmed.

SILVIO: Oh. Wow! Great! That's great. That's terrific. Jesus, that's a relief. Fucking socks! (*Exits relieved*)

NATWICK: What did you say about socks?

GATELY: I don't know.

(*They look off to where Silvio has exited. Gately returns to radio. Natwick reads paper*)

NATWICK: Why are you still fixing that radio?

GATELY: For Hinson.

NATWICK: Hinson's dead.

GATELY: How can he be dead? I saw him just yesterday. He was perfectly all right. He didn't have any arms or legs, but he was all right.

NATWICK: He died last night.

GATELY: One day he's alive, the next he's dead.

NATWICK: That's life.

(*Pause*)

GATELY: But this is a hospital.

NATWICK: That's the way it is in a hospital. Either you get better or you die or you rot. (*Gately, stunned, gets up, walks away from table. Turns. Looks at radio*) Look at it this way. At least you don't have to waste your time on that stupid radio. Gately, we all die sooner or later. You know, Gately, in many ways we're alike.

GATELY: We're nothing alike.

NATWICK: Of course we are. We're both intelligent and sensitive.

GATELY: Am I?

NATWICK: Well, you're sensitive.

GATELY: Am I?

NATWICK: You'd have to be either sensitive or just plain stupid to fix a radio for Hinson.

GATELY: Why?

NATWICK: Everyone knew Hinson was going to die. (*Gately returns to radio. He begins work*) Gately, what are you doing?

GATELY: Fixing the radio.

NATWICK: Gately, Hinson's dead.

GATELY: I know that.

NATWICK: Gately, don't be a fool!

GATELY: Someone else can use it.

NATWICK: You're deluding yourself.

GATELY: No, I'm not. If I fix this radio, they'll let me out of here.

NATWICK: You can get out anytime you want to.

GATELY: You see, Natwick, every cloud has a silver lining.

NATWICK: Yes. But that's just what it is.

GATELY: What?

NATWICK: A lining. You takes out that lining, you know what you've got?

GATELY: What?

NATWICK: A cloud. A very dark, dangerous cloud.

SILVIO: (*Entering*) Hello, Gately.

GATELY: Hello, Silvio.

SILVIO: Natwick, go fuck yourself! (*Natwick gapes and exits*) One thing about Natwick—you tell him to go do something and by God, he goes and does it.

(*Gately returns to radio. Silvio is seated*)

SILVIO: Gately, I've been thinking of buying a kilt.

GATELY: A kilt?

SILVIO: Yeah, it's a kind of dress that guys in Scotland wear. (*Pause*) It's kinda like a cheerleader's skirt.

GATELY: If you want a cheerleader's skirt, why don't you just buy a cheerleader's skirt?

SILVIO: I don't want no cheerleader's skirt.

GATELY: Oh.

SILVIO: What would I do with a cheerleader's skirt?

GATELY: I have no idea.

SILVIO: Hey, wait a minute. You think I want to wear a girl's skirt. You think that? Is that what you think?

GATELY: Look, I don't care—

SILVIO: Look, I don't care that you don't care! Who cares!

GATELY: Not me.

SILVIO: Look, I don't want to wear a dress, okay?

GATELY: Okay.

SILVIO: I want to wear a kilt. (*Pause*) Look, I read somewhere that Scots have a very high potency rate. So I said to myself, what have they got that we haven't got?

GATELY: Kilts?

SILVIO: Right. Gately, did you know tight pants weaken the sperm count?

GATELY: They prove that?

SILVIO: They've practically proved that. Gately, picture if you will, an Oregon stream in the spring of the year, the icy waters teaming with salmon. Indians poised, ready to spear them as they spawn. Returning from the sea to a very old place. Now these salmon returning to spawn are called grilse. The grilse overcome incredible obstacles in order to spawn. They have to fight their way past dams and rocks and Indians.

GATELY: Are we still talking about the sperm count?

SILVIO: Gately, I want you to think of your sperm as salmon.

GATELY: Okay.

SILVIO: Think of your sperm as grilse.

GATELY: Grilse!

SILVIO: The sperm is fighting it's way up the vagina! Thrashing on to the spawning grounds! Over rocks and dams and Indians.

GATELY: In the vagina?

SILVIO: But the weak sperm can't make it!

GATELY: They give out?

SILVIO: They poop out. So the sperm pulls over to the side of the vagina. Worse thing they could possibly do!

GATELY: Poor little guys.

SILVIO: In the end all the salmon die. They spawn and they die. And except for the one sperm that fertilizes the egg, this is also the fate of the sperm.

(They both stare out at the world, impressed by the majesty of Silvio's speech)

GATELY: Have you ever read Hiawatha?

SILVIO: No.

GATELY: It's full of rocks and rivers and Indians. *(Pause)* Do you think the sperm know they're gonna die?

SILVIO: At present, Gately, science doesn't know how much the sperm knows. But we can say this about the sperm. *(Thinks)* It has a helluva sense of direction.

(They both look out. Blackout)

Transition three: Natwick Letter

Dear Mother: The days pass quickly and I make new friends. So far my favorite person here is a fellow named Gately. We have many pleasant conversations.

Scene Four: Superior

NATWICK: Checkmate.

GATELY: Natwick, why do you act so superior?

NATWICK: I don't act superior. I am superior.

GATELY: You're not necessarily superior. I'll tell you something. Silvio's been working on this theory. If you wear kilts your sperm will be more like a grilse's.

NATWICK: What?

GATELY: Grilse are the salmon that fight their way upstream.

NATWICK: No.

GATELY: What?

NATWICK: Grilse are the salmon that fight their way downstream. Grilse are the young salmon, not the mature salmon.

GATELY: What do you call mature salmon?

NATWICK: Salmon.

GATELY: What about kilts? Silvio says we should wear kilts to make us more potent.

NATWICK: Silvio wants to dress like a pervert.

GATELY: Why?

NATWICK: Because he is a pervert. And if we ran around in kilts, we'd be just as perverted as he is.

GATELY: What about the Scots? They run around in kilts. What about them?

NATWICK: They're perverted.

(*Pause*)

GATELY: Have you ever read Hiawatha?

(*Blackout*)

Transition four

PSYCHIATRIST: Silvio, I want you to relax.

SILVIO: Doc, I am relaxed.

PSYCHIATRIST: I'm here to help you. Now just relax.

SILVIO: I am relaxed.

PSYCHIATRIST: Silvio.

SILVIO: What?

PSYCHIATRIST: If you were *really* relaxed, you'd put down the lamp and get off my desk.

Scene Five: Silvio's Monologue

SILVIO: I don't know. I have these strange thoughts. They're not violent. (*Pause*) Some of them are violent. The other day I, uh, was talking to this old woman. And she was talking and I just wanted to do some outrageous thing to her. Like slap her. Or pull her false teeth out. Or play with the flab on her face. I mean, I wouldn't. But—it's something I think about. (*Pause*) When I was little I used to think I could talk to God. In fact, I thought I could talk to God better than anybody in the world and I didn't understand why world leaders didn't come to me to pray to God to solve the world's problems. I'd sit in church with my family. And my mother—my mother is a very beautiful woman. She looks like Italian women on jars of spaghetti sauce. And she's got big old bosoms. And I like 'em. And I don't care what that sounds like 'cause it's one of my favorite parts of my mother. (*Pause*) And I remember when my father died, it, uh, she showed great dignity. She took my hand and she said, "You go take care of your sister now." And I said, "Who's gonna take care of you." And she said, "I can take care of myself, you take care of your sister." And I said, "But I want to take care of you." And she said, "Look, you get in there and take care of your sister before I knock you into the middle of next week." And I did. And my sister was so pretty when she—was in her confirmation dress. (*Pause*) Somebody's been flashing the nurses? I don't know anything about that. It wasn't me. (*Pause*) It wasn't me.

(*Blackout*)

Transition five: Natwick Letter

Dear Mother: My friendship with Gately grows warmer and warmer. He is a very perceptive person for a semi-illiterate. Mother, he's never even read *The New Yorker.* I think he appreciates our little chats.

Scene Six: Hemingway—Peaches

Gately fixing radio.

NATWICK: (*Groaning*) Another book on Hemingway.

GATELY: Hmm.

NATWICK: And yet, did he have the right to take his own life?

GATELY: Hmm.

NATWICK: Don't forget, he was no longer the man he once was.

GATELY: Who is, for Christ's sake?

NATWICK: I tell you, Gately, if I had any kind of courage at all, I'd go straight to my room, take out a razor and slash my wrists. Oh God, I wish I could.

GATELY: What's preventing you?

NATWICK: I use an electric.

GATELY: I'll lend you one of mine.

NATWICK: What kind of thing is that to say to a person?

GATELY: Well, if you really wanted to.

NATWICK: But I don't *really* want to.

GATELY: You don't?

NATWICK: No. Suicide is a plea for help.

GATELY: Well, I'm trying to help. I'll lend you the razor blade.

NATWICK: That's just great. A man reaches out to his fellow man, a hand reaches out into the darkness for a little comfort, a little compassion, I reach out—and you hand me a razor blade.

GATELY: Okay. I won't lend you the razor blade.

NATWICK: What's the matter? Don't you trust me?

GATELY: Yes.

NATWICK: You'll get it back.

GATELY: How? You'll be dead. You'll be stretched out on the floor—

NATWICK: Actually, a bathtub.

GATELY: Bathtub?

NATWICK: Gately, for instance, suppose I can't cope with the world when they let me out of here.

GATELY: You can get out any time you want to.

NATWICK: I know that. I see my suicide, Gately, as a beautiful thing. There I am in my mother's home, my wrists slashed, my blood filling the bathtub.

GATELY: But why a bathtub?

NATWICK: I don't want to make a mess.

GATELY: Why?

NATWICK: My mother would kill me.

GATELY: You'll be dead. She can't do anything to you then.

NATWICK: You don't know my mother. (*Pause*) You know, you don't know what it's like growing up rich.

GATELY: You know—you're right.

NATWICK: When you're rich there's only one way to go—down.

GATELY: Same thing when you're poor. Only it's a different direction.

NATWICK: All my life, I've known I was going to fail. My mother had a brilliant career planned for me. Anything less than Secretary of State would have been considered a failure. I remember my childhood as a succession of summer homes moving farther and farther out on Long Island. My sense of failure grew in proportion to the size of the houses, each one larger than the last. When we got the place at Montauk, I joined the Army. Everyone was surprised that the Army took me. Including me.

GATELY: Isn't it funny how some days we can shoot the breeze like this and other days, we just can't talk at all.

NATWICK: There are good days and there are bad days. On good days, I can talk. On bad days—well, one dares not eat a peach as they say.

GATELY: Eat a peach? Why wouldn't a person dare to eat a peach?

NATWICK: It's something someone once said.

GATELY: Who said it?

NATWICK: T. S. Eliot.

GATELY: T. S. Eliot was afraid to eat a peach?

NATWICK: Gately!

GATELY: Was he allergic to them?

NATWICK: Prufrock didn't dare to eat a peach.

GATELY: Was Prufrock allergic to them?

NATWICK: Prufrock is not a person. He's a poem.

GATELY: I know that. (*Pause*) Why wouldn't he dare to eat a peach?

NATWICK: Because he was afraid.

GATELY: Was there something wrong with the peach? Had it gone bad?

NATWICK: There was nothing wrong with the peach.

GATELY: What was he afraid of then?

NATWICK: Life.

GATELY: Life?

NATWICK: Yes.

GATELY: He was so afraid of life that he couldn't eat a peach? That's disgraceful!

NATWICK: It was the small things of life that defeated him. The momentary terrors.

GATELY: Like what?

NATWICK: Old age. Old women. Tea parties.

GATELY: Tea parties! Old women! Hell, that's just minor league stuff! I hope this Prufrock never runs into any of the MAJOR PROBLEMS OF LIFE. Then he really wouldn't be able to eat the peach!

NATWICK: Why are you getting so upset?

GATELY: Where'd he eat this peach?

NATWICK: On a beach.

GATELY: Well, that's just dandy. The guy's so sensitive he can't even eat a goddamn peach on a goddamn beach.

NATWICK: It's just a metaphor, Gately, okay?

GATELY: I just hope this guy doesn't get drafted, that's all I hope.

NATWICK: The guy can't get drafted. The guy's in a poem, Gately, you know what poems are?

GATELY: I read poems.

NATWICK: When?

GATELY: All the time! I read 'em till I'm sick of 'em.

NATWICK: What poems? Give me one.

GATELY: Hiawatha. It's a great poem! Look it up!

NATWICK: Well, it's like that.

GATELY: What is?

NATWICK: You can't draft Hiawatha.

GATELY: Even if you did, what makes you think he'd serve? Hiawatha was one of the greatest Indians of all time. What makes you think he'd fight for this shitty Army? He'd go to Canada first!

NATWICK: Are you saying Hiawatha was a draft dodger?

GATELY: Not if it was an Indian war. If it was an Indian war, hell, he'd put on his war paint, get in his canoe and go whip ass!

NATWICK: (Weary) But only his own wars.

GATELY: That's right! And if everybody would fight their own private wars, things would be all right. But no, people have to keep sticking their noses into other people's wars! You see what I mean, Natwick? You see what I'm trying to say?

NATWICK: No.

GATELY: The thing about the world is. . . . The thing about the world is. . . . The world is. . . . You see what I'm trying to say?

NATWICK: And that's why I don't want to talk about it.

GATELY: (*Pause*) You just can't stand to lose an argument. Can you?

NATWICK: (*As he exits*) One, two, three—aaaah!

(*Gately fixing radio. Offstage we hear Silvio's voice*)

SILVIO: Hey, gorgeous. Turn around. Ta-dah! Woo! (*Entering*) Did you ever ask yourself the secret of my incredible sexual power over women?

GATELY: No.

SILVIO: Why the nurses can't resist me?

GATELY: The nurses hate you, Silvio.

SILVIO: Ah. That's what they would have you believe.

GATELY: They got *me* believin' it.

SILVIO: You wanna hear a great line for picking girls up?

GATELY: Sure.

SILVIO: Now this works best for Catholic girls.

GATELY: Okay.

SILVIO: You tell 'em you're a priest.

GATELY: A priest.

SILVIO: Okay. Look, we'll set the scene. This is what they call settin' the scene. Now, you're sitting there. At the table. What can this table be?

GATELY: A table.

SILVIO: Okay. We'll make it a table. We're in a night club.

GATELY: Can it be a singles joint?

SILVIO: Gately, you been to a singles joint?

GATELY: No.

SILVIO: Okay, I tell you what. In settin' the scene we'll make this a singles joint.

GATELY: (*Awed*) Where'd you learn all this?

SILVIO: Once I hung around a USO group that was rehearsing. A Bob Hope thing. I tell you somethin', Gately . . .

GATELY: Yeah?

SILVIO: Never be afraid to mingle in the arts.

GATELY: All right!

SILVIO: Okay, so we're in a singles joint. And you're a broad. Everybody's being hustled. It's a fucking meat market!

GATELY: What's a nice girl like me doing in a place like this?

SILVIO: That's it! That's it! That's what's called gettin' into character!

GATELY: Am I lonely?

SILVIO: Are you lonely? A face like that. What do you think?

GATELY: I'm lonely, huh?

SILVIO: That's right. You're like ugly Catholic girls all over the world. You're like a different breed. You sit there being ugly, ruining life for everybody else.

GATELY: Are you lonely?

SILVIO: Gately! I'm a priest! Of course I'm lonely. I'm one of the loneliest, horniest guys on the face of the earth. Okay, you're sitting there by yourself. So I come in. And I'm very depressed. So I come in and I look around. No, you don't see me yet, Gately. I see you. I come over and I say, "Pardon me, miss, is this seat taken?"

GATELY: Yes, it is.

SILVIO: What?

GATELY: Buzz off.

SILVIO: No. You don't say nothing.

GATELY: You want me to call the management?

SILVIO: That's not the way it goes.

GATELY: Male chauvinist pig!

SILVIO: Gately!

GATELY: What?

SILVIO: Don't give me such a hard time, okay?

GATELY: I just wanted to make it realistic.

SILVIO: Okay. But you're making it *too* realistic. We'll do it again. So I come in very depressed and—you don't see me yet, Gately—I see you and I come over and I say, "Pardon me, miss, but is this seat taken?"

GATELY: Well, why not.

SILVIO: Mind if I sit down?

GATELY: Well, why not.

SILVIO: May I order you another drink?

GATELY: Well, sure.

SILVIO: Bartender. Two more of the same. Do you mind if I smoke?

GATELY: Well, why not.

(*Silvio takes out two cigarettes, puts them in his mouth, lights them both. He offers "her" one*)

GATELY: I don't want it.

SILVIO: Why not?

GATELY: You've slobbered all over it.

SILVIO: No, I haven't.

GATELY: You've had it in your mouth.

SILVIO: Gately, take the fuckin' cigarette! (*Gately takes the cigarette*) I hope you won't think I'm being too personal but . . . what's your name?

GATELY: Woodruff Gately.

SILVIO: Woodruff?

GATELY: Woodruff.

SILVIO: I've never known a girl named Woodruff before.

GATELY: You've never known a girl like me.

SILVIO: If I seem a little nervous, it's because I don't usually come to this kind of place. Have you ever come to this kind of place?

GATELY: I'm a Baptist.

SILVIO: You must be very lonely.

GATELY: Why, because I'm a Baptist?

SILVIO: (*Putting his hand on Gately's leg*) Can I tell you something very personal?

GATELY: Okay. But don't get smutty.

SILVIO: I just wanted to tell you that I don't get a chance to meet beautiful women. You see, actually, I'm a priest.

GATELY: Well, I don't get a chance to meet men. You see, actually, I'm a lesbian.

SILVIO: (*Gets up angrily*) That's it! Forget it, Gately!

GATELY: I'm sorry!

SILVIO: No! No! Let's just forget it. I try to teach you something! Give you the benefit of my experience, my life! You know what you are? I'll tell you what you are. A fucking ingrate, that's what you are! Why'd you make her a lesbian?

GATELY: I don't know.

SILVIO: Not even a priest could pick up a lesbian. Nobody could pick up a lesbian.

GATELY: A lesbian could!

SILVIO: Who cares! That does me no good. I can't become a lesbian every time I wanna get laid!

GATELY: No.

SILVIO: You see my point?

GATELY: You could become a transvestite.

SILVIO: What?

GATELY: Wear women's clothes.

SILVIO: But I don't want to wear women's clothes!

GATELY: I know you don't.

SILVIO: I know I don't, too.

GATELY: You want to wear a kilt.
SILVIO: That's right.
GATELY: Which is nearly women's clothes.
SILVIO: (*Pause*) You know something, Gately? At the rate you're going, you may never get laid!
(*Blackout*)

Transition six

GATELY: Silvio.
SILVIO: What, Gately?
GATELY: What's a seven-letter word for hemorrhoidal tissue?
SILVIO: Nat-wick. N-A-T-W-I-C-K.

Scene Seven: The Cup

Gately fixing a radio. Natwick enters in near panic.

NATWICK: Gately, you've got to help me!
GATELY: I'm busy.
NATWICK: Gately, this is a matter of life and death!
GATELY: I'm busy.
NATWICK: Gately, would you look at me! (*Natwick lifts hand from pocket secretively. He holds a cup in his hand. He lowers hand back into his pocket*)
GATELY: Natwick, you've got a cup in your pocket.
NATWICK: Yes.
GATELY: Why do you have a cup in your pocket?
NATWICK: Actually, I've got a cup glued to my hand in my pocket.
GATELY: Why would you glue a cup to your hand?
NATWICK: You idiot! I didn't do it! Silvio did it! He handed me a cup of coffee and suddenly I was glued.
(*Gately tries, unsuccessfully, to disengage Natwick from the cup*)
GATELY: (*Fascinated*) Let's see. He must have used that super epoxy glue. You know it dries in five seconds?
NATWICK: Yes, I know.

GATELY: I always wondered if this stuff would work.

NATWICK: Yes, well, it works.

GATELY: You better take that over to the shop.

NATWICK: I'm going to find an orderly.

GATELY: Why? You'll get Silvio in trouble.

NATWICK: I *want* to get Silvio in trouble.

GATELY: Natwick! You've got to understand. Silvio's wound has left him emotionally scarred.

NATWICK: You want emotional scars? I have a urine bag strapped to my side. You think that's fun? Going through life as a portable toilet?

GATELY: Silvio's wound is different.

NATWICK: I don't want to hear about Silvio's wound.

GATELY: Natwick!

NATWICK: I don't want to hear about Silvio's wound! I'm going to find an orderly.

GATELY: You do and Silvio'll kill you.

NATWICK: What kind of wound was it?

GATELY: Shrapnel.

NATWICK: Well. Shrapnel. That's not so bad.

GATELY: It blew off his testicles and his penis.

NATWICK: Wow! That explains a lot. Sure. He flashes the nurses to assert his lack of manhood.

GATELY: Sure! That explains the flashing!

NATWICK: It explains his macho act.

GATELY: Sure. It explains the macho act.

NATWICK: It explains everything.

GATELY: It even explains the cup.

NATWICK: No, it doesn't explain the cup.

GATELY: No. I guess he just hates your guts.

NATWICK: Yeah. That explains the cup.

GATELY: (*Pause*) What're you gonna do?

NATWICK: I don't know. Things can't go on like this. First they hang a urine bag on me. Now a cup. It's like I'm a Christmas tree.

GATELY: Why don't you make friends with Silvio?

NATWICK: How disgusting! (*Pause*) What do I have to do?

GATELY: First of all, loosen up. You make people nervous.

NATWICK: Why?

GATELY: You're uptight.

NATWICK: I am not uptight!

GATELY: You stand like you got a rod up your ass!

NATWICK: I'm from Great Neck.

GATELY: Here. Look. Snap your fingers. Act like you're cool. (*Natwick does so, mechanically*) You look like someone put a quarter in you. Say, "Hey, man, what's happening?"

NATWICK: Hey, man, what's happening?

GATELY: (*Pause*) Okay. We'll come back to that. (*Pause*) I know. You've got to take an interest in Silvio's hobbies.

NATWICK: Like what? Child molesting?

GATELY: No. Mainly flashing nurses, kilts, men's underwear.

NATWICK: Men's underwear?

GATELY: Yes, that and—oh, here he comes.

NATWICK: I think I'm going to be sick.

(*Silvio enters in a hurry*)

GATELY: Hey, Silvio, what's happenin', man?

SILVIO: Gately . . .

NATWICK: Hey, Silvio, what's happenin', man?

SILVIO: Gately, I gotta talk to you!

GATELY: Sure, Silvio, but Natwick just said hello to you.

NATWICK: Hey, Silvio, what's happenin', man?

SILVIO: (*Pause*) Gately, it's Nurse O'Brian. She's been transferred. All week I been planning on flashing her. I got her on the list for Tuesday.

GATELY: So.

SILVIO: Today is Tuesday.

NATWICK: Oh, man, what a bummer.

SILVIO: What's a matter with him?"

NATWICK: Hey, Silvio: "What it *is* baby?"

SILVIO: Why's he talking like a spade?

NATWICK: I mean, what is this *jive* about O'Brian leaving?

SILVIO: Jesus! What is your problem, Natwick?

NATWICK: No problem, baby.

SILVIO: Don't call me baby.

NATWICK: I think it's great the way you flash nurses. You got it down to an art form.

SILVIO: Exposing yourself is not an art form. It's disgusting. You ever flashed anyone, Natwick?

NATWICK: No.

SILVIO: So what do you know about it?

NATWICK: Nothing.

SILVIO: That's right. Gately . . .

NATWICK: Hey, Silvio, you wanna know what kind of underwear I'm wearing?

SILVIO: Do I what?

NATWICK: Very tight jockey shorts.

SILVIO: (*Backing off*) Hey, has he gone queer or somethin'? Jesus! First O'Brian got transferred, now Natwick goes queer. Jesus!

NATWICK: Silvio—

SILVIO: Keep your hands to yourself, Natwick!

NATWICK: I just want to be your friend.

SILVIO: You remember the cup? I'll glue you, Natwick. I swear to God I'll glue you!

NATWICK: (*Terrified*) Don't glue me! Don't glue me! Don't glue me!

SILVIO: Hey. It's just a little glue. (*Exits*)

GATELY: Well. You blew it!

(*Blackout*)

Transition seven

GATELY: Silvio.

SILVIO: What?

GATELY: If you had one wish, what would it be?

SILVIO: I'd like to be on Johnny Carson.

GATELY: Why?

SILVIO: I might meet Charo.

Scene Eight: Radio Parts Are Disappearing

Gately fixing radio. Silvio with baseball glove.

SILVIO: Gately. How can you work for weeks on one radio?

GATELY: You've got to keep the incoming parts ahead of the outgoing parts.

SILVIO: What?

GATELY: (*Looking around*) Silvio. Radio parts are disappearing.

SILVIO: When?

GATELY: All the time.

SILVIO: You think someone's stealing them?

GATELY: Possibly.

SILVIO: You could be losing them.

GATELY: Possibly. Anyway I have to replace the missing parts.

SILVIO: Where do you get the missing parts?

GATELY: You can't just get parts. You have to steal the entire radio.

SILVIO: From where?

GATELY: Administration.

SILVIO: . . . How many radios have you stolen?

GATELY: To date, twenty-seven.

SILVIO: I see.

GATELY: I'm not discouraged. The main thing is to keep your incoming parts ahead of your outgoing parts. America was built on this theory, Silvio. The Free Enterprise System. And if one guy like me can make a radio work—then America works.

SILVIO: Interesting theory.

GATELY: It's simple really. It's just a question of incoming parts and outgoing parts.

SILVIO: Gately . . . I wish you luck.

GATELY: Silvio, thank you.

(*They shake hands. Gately goes back to radio. Silvio steals a part. Blackout*)

Transition eight: Natwick Letter

Dear Mother: Thank you for sending the guppies for my aquarium. However, please do not send anymore, because Silvio took them out last night and smashed all my guppies with a ball-peen hammer. Please send socks.

Scene Nine: Jack Palance

Natwick alone. Silvio enters, unseen, comes up behind Natwick. Silvio is acting very strange.

SILVIO: Hello, Natwick.

NATWICK: (*Startled*) I wish you wouldn't do that.

SILVIO: Where's Gately?

NATWICK: He's obviously not here.

SILVIO: Good. We can have a little chat.

NATWICK: (*Rising*) I really don't—

SILVIO: Sit down.

NATWICK: Thank you.

(*Pause*)

SILVIO: Well, it's been lovely getting to know you this spring, Natwick.

NATWICK: Yes, I haven't known fun like this since the Tet Offensive.

SILVIO: You weren't no grunt. (*Pause*) You were a clerk.

NATWICK: Correct. (*Pause*) Silvio, are you stoned? Are you stoned? That's good 'cause when you're stoned you mellow out? Right? Mellow?

SILVIO: You know who people tell me I look like?

NATWICK: No.

SILVIO: Jack Palance.

NATWICK: There is a certain resemblance.

SILVIO: Thing is, I had this dream the other night about Jack Palance. I dreamed Jack Palance was the leader of a girl scout troop. And he was dressed like a girl scout. And you and me and Gately were members of this girl scout troop. And we knew Jack Palance was going to do something horrible to us. . . . So we decided to sneak up on him. And it was dark, Natwick, very, very dark. And then we opened the door. And there in this room was Jack Palance in this huge green girl scout uniform. And all around were dead girl scouts. He had bitten off their heads and drained their blood. (*Pause*) Well, what do you think of this dream?

NATWICK: Fascinating.

SILVIO: Yeah, I know. But I mean in the Freudian sense.

NATWICK: Oh. In a Freudian sense, I'd say it was very common.

SILVIO: Common.

NATWICK: Oh, yes. I think everyone's had that dream. I know I have.

(*Pause*)

SILVIO: You're from Long Island.

NATWICK: That's right.

SILVIO: Great Neck.

NATWICK: That's right.

SILVIO: Bet you had the shirts with the little alligators on them.

NATWICK: Uh-huh.

SILVIO: Bet you had a summer home in the Hamptons.

NATWICK: Montauk, actually.

SILVIO: Montauk, actually. (*Pause*) I picture your home overlooking the ocean. The water coming in and out. In and out. In and out.

NATWICK: That's the way it is when everything's working right.

SILVIO: You pussy!

NATWICK: What.

SILVIO: I'll bet your mother played mah-jong by the sea.

NATWICK: What's my mother . . .

SILVIO: And you went to private schools where they all wore the alligator shirts.

NATWICK: Silvio. (*Silvio takes out a knife. Puts it under Natwick's neck, stands him up*) Silvio! Don't!

(*Silvio releases Natwick and walks off. Blackout*)

Transition nine

General announcement for all patients. Radios are being stolen from Administration. This is counterproductive to the effort. This can't go on! Repeat. This can't go on!

Scene Ten: I Can't Go On

Gately fixing radio. Silvio listening to radio.

GATELY: (*Rising*) I can't go on! I'll never fix this fucking radio!

SILVIO: (*Going to him*) What seems to be the trouble here, trooper?

GATELY: (*Near tears*) I try and I try and nothing ever gets done!

SILVIO: Calm down. Take two deep breaths. (*Gately takes them*) Now then, tell me what your problem is here.

GATELY: It's that damn radio! I'll never get it fixed. Parts keep disappearing! Silvio, there's something wrong with me. Here. In my head. I think I'm—

SILVIO: Hey, you're just having a bad day.

GATELY: I am?

SILVIO: Sure. Did I ever tell you the story of the first day when I realized there was something wrong with me? That I needed help?

GATELY: No.

SILVIO: Well, I woke up one morning in Cleveland. I was living with my sister at the time. It was a beautiful day. I looked out the window. And I remember thinking, Ohio is a party dip. Not long after I attacked my fellow workers with a tire tool.

GATELY: Did you do that?

SILVIO: Sure I did that.

GATELY: But you're psychotic.

SILVIO: Exactly my point. And see, I couldn't even repair a radio.

GATELY: Well, it's not easy.

SILVIO: Hell, no, it's not.

GATELY: Radios are complicated things.

SILVIO: Of course, they are.

GATELY: They're a product of human evolution.

SILVIO: Gately. If there's one thing that's clear to us at this point in time, it is that man is making progress. Now, are you going to let yourself be defeated by an inanimate object? You are not. You are going to go over there and fix that radio.

GATELY: Will you go with me?

SILVIO: Of course, I will. (*They go to table. Gately sits*) Are you ready to resume?

GATELY: I am.

SILVIO: As you do, remember: "The flesh of man can be torn, beaten and destroyed, but the human spirit abideth forever and shall not perish."

GATELY: Who said that?

SILVIO: Casey Stengel.

(*Gately works. Blackout*)

Transition ten

PSYCHIATRIST: Silvio, do you realize you're afraid of women?
SILVIO: Look, Doc, I'm not afraid of women.
PSYCHIATRIST: Silvio, you're afraid of women.
SILVIO: I'm not afraid of women.
PSYCHIATRIST: Silvio, are you nervous around women?
SILVIO: Oh, well, yeah, maybe I'm nervous around women. (*Pause*) You didn't say *nervous*.

Scene Eleven: Silvio's Leaving

Gately sitting. Natwick enters, depressed.

GATELY: Hello, Natwick.
NATWICK: Don't talk to me. I'm terribly depressed.
GATELY: (*Absently*) That's good.
NATWICK: What?
GATELY: Did you hear the news about Silvio? (*Pause*) Silvio's leaving soon.
NATWICK: (*Pause*) What?
GATELY: He's going to live in Cleveland with his sister.
NATWICK: Well. . . . That's great.
GATELY: Yeah. Isn't that great?
NATWICK: How's the radio coming?
GATELY: Won't be long now. (*Natwick steals another radio part*) You know the only thing Silvio says he's gonna miss?
NATWICK: Us?
GATELY: Nurse Krullick.
NATWICK: Not Neanderthal Krullick?
GATELY: Yeah. He thinks he loves her.
NATWICK: But she's the ugliest woman in the world.
GATELY: That's why he loves her.
NATWICK: What?
GATELY: He says ugly women need love more. So he's going over to tell her goodbye and to tell her he loves her.
NATWICK: But . . . Krullick.

GATELY: She's really ugly, isn't she?

NATWICK: She's uglier than the guy in *Ben Hur* that got dragged behind the chariot.

GATELY: Is it possible that Silvio really loves Krullick?

NATWICK: It's possible.

GATELY: And that she loves him?

NATWICK: Well . . . people can fall in love but it's really a question of being faithful.

GATELY: People can be faithful to one another. It's hard. But they can do it. *(Pause)* The coyote does it.

NATWICK: What?

GATELY: The coyote mates for life. He's entirely faithful. *He* doesn't fool around. And he's got plenty of chances, too. I mean he's out there in the middle of the desert, he gets lonely.

NATWICK: How do you know?

GATELY: He howls.

NATWICK: *(Pause)* Dolphins, too! They mate for life!

GATELY: Good for them.

NATWICK: It just goes to show you, Gately.

GATELY: What?

NATWICK: Love is a many splendored thing.

GATELY: Why . . . that's beautiful. Love is a many splendored thing. Did you make that up, Natwick?

NATWICK: Yes, I did, Gately.

GATELY: I'm impressed.

(Silvio enters quickly)

SILVIO: I can't fuckin' believe it!

GATELY: What?

SILVIO: I can't fuckin' believe it! I was standing there waiting for Krullick over by the cafeteria.

GATELY: Yeah.

SILVIO: And I saw her coming.

NATWICK: Yeah.

SILVIO: And I was about to say something to her, when suddenly out of nowhere comes Gleason. And what do you think the son of a bitch has the nerve to do?

GATELY: What?

SILVIO: He flashes Krullick!

NATWICK: Gleason flashes Krullick!

SILVIO: Can you believe that son of a bitch right in front of my very eyes! He flashes my Krullick!

GATELY: What? You give him a shot?

SILVIO: I was going to, but he turned around and hauled ass.

NATWICK: Gleason got away from you?

SILVIO: Gleason can move that wheelchair when he wants to.

NATWICK: Did you tell Krullick you loved her?

SILVIO: Natwick! Have a little sensitivity, would you? The woman had just been flashed by a horny paraplegic! Romance was the last thing she had on her mind.

NATWICK: I hear you're leaving soon.

SILVIO: Yeah, that's right. Tomorrow.

GATELY: (*Shocked*) Tomorrow?

SILVIO: Yeah. Uh. My schedule got pushed up.

NATWICK: Guess you'll be glad to get back?

SILVIO: Fuckin' A! Y'know. See the old neighborhood. Check it out.

GATELY: (*Trying to smile*) Well. We'll have a going away party.

SILVIO: Yeah. Sure. Well, look, I gotta go pack and everything. See you later.

(*Gately and Natwick watch him go out. Blackout*)

Transition eleven: Natwick Announcement

Hello, there. This is your entertainment director, Pfc. Natwick. Tonight's movie is *Bigger than Life* (1956) starring James Mason. The frightening story of a cortisone addict. (*Groans*) It's very well acted. (*Boos*) Barbara Rush is *very* good.

Scene Twelve: The Party

Gately and Silvio are very drunk. A bottle of Canadian Club and two glasses are out on the table.

SILVIO: I mean, am I right or am I right?

GATELY: You're right.

SILVIO: You're damn right I'm right! (*Pause*) What're we talking about?

GATELY: Cleveland.

SILVIO: Yeah. I just don't want it to be like last time.

GATELY: Last time you attacked your fellow workers with a tire tool.

SILVIO: I know. (*Pause*) Say, where's the asshole?

GATELY: Natwick's been in his room all day.

SILVIO: How come?

GATELY: (*Delicately*) I think he's depressed 'cause you're leaving. (*Pause*) You know Natwick.

SILVIO: Yeah.

GATELY: You worried about going to Cleveland tomorrow?

SILVIO: No . . . well . . . yeah . . . a little.

GATELY: What're you worried about?

SILVIO: I'm worried about that damn Protestant.

GATELY: What?

SILVIO: My sister married a Protestant. I mean, how do you talk to a Protestant?

GATELY: I'm a Protestant.

SILVIO: You're different.

(*Natwick enters. He has been drinking heavily*)

NATWICK: (*Despairing*) A party. Of course. I might have known. No one invites me anywhere.

GATELY: Natwick, you know perfectly well I invited you.

NATWICK: I couldn't hear you. The door was locked.

SILVIO: What were you doing in there, Natwick? Holding your breath?

NATWICK: That's right! Insult me! I just came out here to give you this. (*He hands Silvio a letter*)

SILVIO: It's from my sister. (*He begins to open it*) I'll read it later.

(*Pause*)

NATWICK: Well, don't anybody offer me a drink.

SILVIO: Okay, we won't.

NATWICK: Who needs your party!

GATELY: C'mon, sit down here, Natwick. I've got a surprise for you guys.

NATWICK: I've got martinis in my room. I have many martinis in my room.

GATELY: Sit over here, Natwick.

SILVIO: I think he's drunk.

NATWICK: I am not drunk.

SILVIO: Tell the truth, Natwick. You drunk?

NATWICK: Go fuck yourself!

SILVIO: Natwick is *very* drunk.

NATWICK: I am not. Gimme a drink.

GATELY: Okay. Wait. We don't have enough glasses.

NATWICK: That's all right. I brought my own. (*He lifts hand out of pocket. The cup is glued to it*)

GATELY: (*Reprovingly*) Silvio!

SILVIO: (*Good-naturedly*) Hey—a going away present.

(*Silvio and Natwick are seated on opposite sides of the table*)

GATELY: Now, put on your party hats. (*He gives them their party hats*)

NATWICK: Oh, boy, party hats!

SILVIO: Jesus Christ, do we have to?

GATELY: Yes.

NATWICK: (*Wrestling with his hat*) Jesus Christ!

GATELY: Here. I'll give you a hand.

NATWICK: It's all his fault! Can't even put a party hat on.

GATELY: (*Adjusting hat*) There. (*Becoming quite solemn*) I suppose you're wondering why we're gathered here this evening?

SILVIO: To wear these little hats?

GATELY: We're gathered here to say farewell and good fortune to our friend Silvio.

NATWICK: (*Giving a raspberry*) FFFTTT!

GATELY: And to celebrate the completion of the radio.

SILVIO: (*Sober*) What?

NATWICK: (*Sober*) What?

SILVIO: Have you tried it?

GATELY: Not yet.

SILVIO: How do you know it's gonna work?

GATELY: I've decided it will.

SILVIO: Radios are very complicated things. Remember we talked about this?

GATELY: I know, but I've worked long enough on this. I can't work on this thing the rest of my life. So today I screwed up the back and said to hell with it. It's now or never.

SILVIO: It's never.

GATELY: What?

SILVIO: There's no way that radio can work.

GATELY: Why not.

SILVIO: Because I've been stealing radio parts.

GATELY: You? I knew it! I knew something was happening. Do you know how many radios I've had to steal to replace those parts?

NATWICK: I took some, too.

GATELY: You what? Do you know what this means? Do you have any *idea?*

SILVIO: It means the radio won't work.

GATELY: It's true people are always stealing from me. It's horrible. I leave my room in the morning and when I return in the evening it's been stripped bare. Last week someone stole my dirty clothes. Stole my dirty underwear. (*Pause*) All my life people stole from me. Bicycles. Baseball cards. My shoes. Shit! (*Silence. Suddenly Gately gives out a loud . . .*) I'm through being stole from! That's it! No more stealing from old Gately! That's it! No more stealing. From now on I'm giving it away! Take my shoes! (*Takes off slippers*) Take my shirt! (*Takes off shirt*) Take my pants! (*Takes off pants*) Take it all! Damn vultures! (*Stands in rage and defiance in his socks and underwear*)

NATWICK: Can we have your socks?

GATELY: Take the damn things? (*Takes off socks. Stares at the radio*) And take the goddamn radio!

(*He goes to the radio with savage intensity. Grasps it, lifts it over his head. Is about to smash it into a million pieces when, miraculously, it comes on playing very loudly "The National Emblem March." The scene turns from one of pain to one of dazzled awe. Softly, Gately places the radio on the table. Turns off radio*)

SILVIO: Gately . . . you fixed the radio. You know what this means, don't you? (*Gately nods*) So. When you thinking of getting out of here?

GATELY: (*Quietly*) When they let me out.

SILVIO: You can get out anytime you want.

GATELY: I know.

(*Pause*)

SILVIO: Say, Gately, where you from?

GATELY: Georgia.

SILVIO: I know that, but where? What did you do there?

GATELY: Started out on a red dirt farm near Macon with my old man. He was a funny old guy. Big old hands. He couldn't seem to make nothing work. He fucked up everything he touched. He fucked up the farm, he fucked up runnin' a fruit stand. He fucked up workin' for the state. Finally we moved to Birmingham. He said that's where people like him moved to when they'd fucked up everything. He went to work in textiles. One day I come home and there he was in the middle of the afternoon leaned up against the house. Them big old hands. That's when I joined the Army. I couldn't stand to see him fuck up no more!

SILVIO: Say, Gately, when you were a kid, you ever do the Tarzan yell?

GATELY: Sure. Everyone did the Tarzan yell.

NATWICK: I never did.

GATELY: Why?

NATWICK: I had asthma.

SILVIO: Stand up here, Gately. I'm gonna show you how to do the Tarzan yell.

GATELY: Hell! I bet I do it better than you.

SILVIO: Are you fuckin' kiddin' me?

GATELY: I ain't kiddin' you.

SILVIO: I used to win prizes doing the yell.

GATELY: Big deal.

SILVIO: I did the Tarzan yell at a Bar Mitzvah once.

NATWICK: Hm. Must have been reform.

GATELY: Okay. Who goes first?

SILVIO: I go first. Give you something to shoot for. (*He does the yell*)

GATELY: I'm not impressed. (*He does the yell. Unexpectedly, Natwick does the call*)

SILVIO: (*Realization*) Natwick!

NATWICK: (*Pause*) I did the Tarzan yell. I did the Tarzan yell!

SILVIO: This calls for a drink.

(*They pour drinks, solemnly*)

SILVIO: A toast . . . to Tarzan.

ALL: To Tarzan. (*They drink*)

GATELY: To Cheetah.

ALL: To Cheetah. (*They drink and sit*)

GATELY: Sometimes I wished we were in a jungle somewhere.

NATWICK: (*Nodding*) You know, all over Africa apes and other wild things that climb are falling out of trees at an unprecedented rate.

SILVIO: Why?

NATWICK: Civilization. There's no place anymore for wild and wounded animals. There's just all sorts of ancient things that disappear. They get obsolete. Like the dodo bird. And elephants.

GATELY: And Indians.

NATWICK: And Indians.

GATELY: And salmon.

SILVIO: And grilse.

NATWICK: Did you know that the universe is collapsing? That's right. The universe is collapsing. The energy in stars eventually collapse in on themselves. Eventually the entire universe will collapse in on itself.

SILVIO: Where will it go?

NATWICK: Nowhere.

GATELY: What will be left?

NATWICK: Nothing.

SILVIO: No. There's gotta be something left..

NATWICK: Nope.

GATELY: A couple of little planets.

NATWICK: Not even a little card table and a little radio.

SILVIO: At least there'll be a lot of open space for development.

NATWICK: No. When stars collapse, they create a vacuum and suck space into it.

GATELY: There won't even be any space?

(*Natwick shakes his head*)

SILVIO: Jesus Christ, Natwick, no wonder you don't get invited to parties. You are the most depressive son of a bitch that ever lived!

GATELY: He's an asshole!

SILVIO: Gately! You've admitted it! You've finally admitted that Natwick is an asshole!

GATELY: Yes.

SILVIO: Now I can die happy.

NATWICK: Big deal. He admits I'm an asshole. I *am* an asshole. Even I'll admit that.

SILVIO: Natwick . . . even you will admit you're an asshole?

NATWICK: Of course.

SILVIO: That's wonderful! Let's all say it out loud. Natwick is an asshole!

ALL: Natwick is an asshole!

SILVIO: Louder!

ALL: Natwick is an asshole!

SILVIO: One more time!!

ALL: Natwick is an asshole! Gately is an asshole! Silvio . . . Silvio is an asshole!

(*A contented silence*)

SILVIO: Natwick. How long is it gonna take for everything to start collapsing in on itself?

NATWICK: Oh, trillions and trillions of years.

SILVIO: Natwick, then there's nothing to worry about.

NATWICK: There's not? Okay. Goodnight.

SILVIO: I'm gonna be in Cleveland tomorrow. (*Reads letter*) "My darling brother . . ."

GATELY: Look, Silvio, the sun's coming up!

"By the shores of Gitchiegoomie
By the shining big sea waters.
At the doorway of his wigwam
In the pleasant summer morning
Hiawatha stood and waited.
All the air was full of freshness.
All the earth was bright and joyous."
Natwick, you awake?

NATWICK: Hm. Aarg.

GATELY: Look at the dawn, Natwick. When was the last time you were up this early?

NATWICK: Last week.

GATELY: Yeah?

NATWICK: I had diarrhea.

(*Gately sees Silvio*)

GATELY: Good morning, Silvio. See how the world looks this early. All dewy. It's like Eden, Silvio. Listen. It's like Eden.

SILVIO: My sister don't want me. She's gonna have the Protestant's kid.

NATWICK: *(Pause)* I'm sorry, Silvio.

SILVIO: *(Miserably)* Yeah.

GATELY: Why are you so miserable, Silvio?

SILVIO: I'm a fucking psychotic with his pecker blown off!

GATELY: Things could be worse.

SILVIO: How? How could things possibly be worse?

NATWICK: It could rain.

SILVIO: Lemme tell you guys somethin'. Big news flash. Whether it rains or not really doesn't make that much difference. It wouldn't change anything.

GATELY: It would ruin a perfectly nice day. Look at it, Silvio! This day is special. It's like no other day that's ever been. It's like no other day that ever will be. This day will never come again.

SILVIO: Promise?

Slow Blackout

Ernest Thompson

A GOOD TIME

Ernest Thompson

Born on November 6, 1949, in Bellows Falls, Vermont, Ernest Thompson admits to having a lifelong fascination with writing. "When forced, I will confess to writing a high school church Christmas play, aptly titled *A Christmas Play*. Otherwise, such expression was carried out in total privacy and shyness."

Originally, he studied to be an actor at the University of Maryland, Colorado College, Catholic University, and American University, graduating in 1971. "Thereafter, I divided the seventies between acting, collecting unemployment insurance, and writing (privately and shyly)." His acting highlights during the period included starring on Broadway in the 1975 revival of William Inge's *Picnic* (rewritten as *Summer Brave*), a television adaptation of Lanford Wilson's *The Rimers of Eldritch,* and a television film called *F. Scott Fitzgerald and the Last of the Belles.*

After the second of two television series was canceled, there was, according to Mr. Thompson, "a reassessment of priorities and a more aggressive go at writing, resulting eventually in three short plays collectively titled *Answers,* of which *A Good Time* is a part." The plays were taken under option and served to give the author sufficient encouragement to continue. A full-length play, *Lessons,* followed, and then, in the spring of 1978, Mr. Thompson wrote *On Golden Pond.*

With Frances Sternhagen and Tom Aldredge in the leads, the play was produced at the Off-Off-Broadway Hudson Guild Theatre, became a sellout success, and was transferred to Broadway (after an engagement at the John F. Kennedy Center for the Performing Arts in Washington, D.C.) in February, 1979. Lauded in the press, the author was hailed as "a fresh voice in our theatre" with "an agreeable combination of wit and heart. Ernest Thompson makes an impressive professional playwriting debut with the enchanting *On Golden Pond.*"

After a season at the New Apollo Theatre, the play moved several blocks uptown to the Century Theatre where it continued to attract large audiences. A West Coast company, with Julie Harris and Charles Durning costarring, opened in February, 1980.

Chosen as one of the "ten best plays of the New York theatre season, 1978–1979" by Otis L. Guernsey, Jr., editor of the theatre yearbook, *On Golden Pond* subsequently earned many productions in countries around the world, and soon will be made into a movie. As a result of *On Golden Pond,* Mr. Thompson received the first George Seaton Award for play-wrights and was commissioned to write *The West Side Waltz,* which is scheduled to have its premiere at the Ahmanson Theatre in Los Angeles.

During 1980, the author also will be represented by a pro-duction of *Lessons* (at the Tennessee Williams Repertory Theatre, Key West, Florida) and a television movie, *Hospice.*

Mr. Thompson, who presently is "not married, but close to it," divides his time between New York and Los Angeles.

The play is dedicated to Patricia.

Characters:

MANDY MORGAN
RICK SELBY

Scene:

The living room of a New York apartment. It is straight from the pages of Vogue or the Sunday Times. There is a pillow couch, matched by two pillow chairs. There is a round antique oak table, and there are other "period pieces," old mirrors, a modern chrome and glass table, a director's chair, two cracker cans that serve as end tables, a fringed floor lamp, etc., all producing the desired mixture of moods and styles. In addition, the room is a veritable jungle: huge plants and small trees looming up everywhere, drooping vines and spider plants hanging from the ceiling. All very comfortable and tasteful, if a little self-conscious. A tall grandfather clock stands in a corner. It is three o'clock.

The entrance to the apartment is stage right, a heavy metal-looking door with an array of locks and peepholes. Through an open door down left can be seen a refrigerator or kitchen cabinets. In the center of the upstage wall there is a large picture window showing bits of other high-rise buildings and traces of blue sky. In the up left corner is the bedroom door, closed now.

The pillow couch is now pushed to one side of the room against a chair, and the two cracker cans are piled up beside it. Standing in the center of the room is Mandy Morgan. She is very pretty, in her early thirties, shortish, but she carries herself high. A lot of dance classes and all that. She is a smart-ass, cynical and quick, but soft and warm and lonely inside. She has seen more in life than she probably would have liked to, and she has come to this point slightly jaded and disillusioned. But she is still eager and still moves fast. She wears tights and is barefoot. She stands perfectly still for a moment and then, suddenly dances downstage. She doesn't dance badly, but would not be mistaken for a ballerina. She counts as she moves.

MANDY: 1-2-3-4-5-6-7-8 and h-o-l-d . . .(She balances one leg before her, her hands outstretched. She holds for several counts. She kicks and dances to the right) 1-2-3-4-5-6-7-8 and h-o-l-d . . .

(*She lands on one foot, one leg behind her, her hands overhead. Again she holds for several counts, and then springs to her left and dances across the room*) 1-2-3-4-5-6-7-8 and . . .

(*The phone rings. She holds her pose for the ring. Then dances to the right again*)

1-2-3-4-5-6-7-8 and . . . (*She gestures to the phone. It rings. She holds her position, then dances to the phone*) 1-2-3-4-5-6-7-8 and . . . (*She gestures. The phone rings. She picks it up*) Hello, Mother. (*She dances back across the room, carrying the phone, mouthing the counts. She stops*) Who is this? . . . Harold who? . . . Harold the account executive who? . . . Harold Bean the account executive. I don't know any Harold Bean the account executive . . . I did not meet you in Maxwell's Plum. I don't meet people in Maxwell's Plum . . . What other night? . . . Oh, Tuesday. Ohhhh. Oh-oh. Are you a sort of tall person with very sensitive, soft blue eyes and a tennis player's physique? . . . (*Standing in place, she begins a series of pliés and relevés while she talks*) Are you of medium height and dark complexion with a quick smile and warm, dark eyes? . . . It was very crowded in Maxwell's Plum on Tuesday night . . . Tall with brown hair and baby blue sunglasses . . . Why were you wearing baby blue sunglasses inside a restaurant at night? . . . Well, I don't think that's very good for your eyes . . . You don't smoke a little corncob pipe, do you? . . . You're kidding. Now, I remember you. You're Harold Bean the liar . . . Yes, you are. You said if I gave you my phone number you would leave me alone. But you're not leaving me alone, Harold, you're calling me up. In the middle of Jazz Two . . . Yes, Harold, I think I understand the discrepancy. You meant—leave me alone for dinner. I meant—leave me alone for life . . . Thank you, Harold. You're very sweet . . . Sure . . . Yes, I'm writing it down. (*She's not*) Harold Bean . . . LE-5-9913. Got it. Good. Bye, Harold.

(*She hangs up, goes to the center of the room and begins kicking her leg high into the air. She enjoys it. She stops, crosses to the bedroom door and pulls out a large, antique mirror, set in a wheeled frame. Now she resumes her kicks in front of the mirror. After a few her attention is drawn to her thigh muscle. She grabs it as she kicks. She lowers her leg, studies her thighs, not pleased at all. She walks back and forth in front of the mirror, eyes focused on her thighs. She tries different walks, doesn't like any of them. She stands and stares at the mirror. She grabs it and pulls it back to the bedroom. Now she goes back to her dance floor and resumes her kicks in peace. The phone rings. Mandy kicks over to it and picks it up)*

MANDY: Hello, Mother. . . . Oh, hello, Ren. . . . No, you don't sound like my mother. My mother doesn't have a French accent. . . . Because my mother usually calls when I don't feel like talking to her . . . I might feel like talking to you. Let me ask you a few questions. Do you think I'm attractive? . . . Thank you. Do you like my lifestyle? . . . Do you think I'm a considerate and giving person? . . . Then, I guess I feel like talking to you. . . . I sound out of breath because I'm out of breath. . . . Sure. Paul Newman is here. . . . Hold on, I'll ask him. *(She calls)* Paul, you want to talk to my silly French girlfriend, Ren? Sorry, Ren, he'd rather not. . . . I was dancing, dummy. . . . Yes, dancing the afternoon away. . . . No, I chanted this morning. Chant in the morning, dance in the afternoon, that's my program. . . . I dropped Yoga. I was flunking it. I can't do everything, Ren. *(She reaches into one of the end tables and pulls out a tobacco tin. From it she removes a rolled joint, which she proceeds to light and smoke)* . . . Lighting a joint. *(She coughs)* I always smoke a joint after I dance. . . . That's not true, Ren. It's supposed to be *very* good for you. It said that in *Rolling Stone.* . . . I don't know. . . . Oh, guess who just called me. . . . Wrong. Harold Bean, account executive, little corncob pipe smoker, Maxwell's Plum habitué, cruiser. . . . The very same. . . . No, I'm not going out with him. Do you want to go out with him? . . . I didn't think so. . . . I gave him my number because I panicked. Because I never know what to say when people ask me for my number. Usually I give them your number, but you were with me. . . . What are you talking about? I've sent some very interesting people your way. . . . That's not true, Ren. If they're really weird, I give them my shrink's number. I've sent some very interesting people his way. . . . It's all sex, Ren. . . . Eighty-five percent of the things we do we do for sexual reasons. It said that in *New Woman* magazine. A pleasant enough, attractive enough man comes up to me and says, "The Panama Canal is a technological political swamp." Do you know what he's really saying? . . . Well, that's a little graphic, but that's basically what he's saying. Why is that, Ren? Why is it all sex? . . . You're right. It is fun. I just wish everybody was a little more upfront about it. A little honesty, you know? I don't think it's very nice to *use* sex like that. Here, here . . . nothing . . . nowhere. It's Saturday night and I ain't got nobody. . . . I don't want nobody. I've quit. I'm turning in my diaphragm. . . . No, I don't want to go to a party, thank you. I've been invited to five parties and as a gesture of fairness, I'm not going to any of them. I'm tired of parties, Ren. I'm tired of account executives and boring politicians and bisexual actors and nasty writers. I'm tired of people with burnt nostrils. I'm tired of Sardi's. I'm tired of Regine's. I'm all boogied out. I'm staying in . . . I'm going to needlepoint a cover for my couch. It was in last month's *Vogue*. . . . No, I don't. . . . So far I have a needle and some yarn. . . . Thank you. (*The sound of a buzzer fills the room*) Hold on, babe, I'm hearing bells. (*She puts down the phone and walks to the front door. On the wall beside it there is a small intercom. She pushes a button and speaks into the box*) Yes?

DOORMAN: (*His voice is slightly garbled, but unmistakably Puerto Rican*) Uh. Missus Morgan?

MANDY: Yes, Francisco?

DOORMAN: Uh, this is not Francisco. This is Julio?

MANDY: Yes, Julio?

DOORMAN: Um, there's a cop, he coming up to see you.

MANDY: What?

DOORMAN: You know, a cop? A policeman?

MANDY: I know what a cop is, Julio. What's he coming here for?

DOORMAN: I don' know, Missus Morgan. Maybe you gonna get busted.

MANDY: What? (*She's getting nervous*) What? Are you sure it's a cop?

DOORMAN: Oh, yes. He got a badge and everything.

MANDY: (*She steps back from the intercom, stands frozen a minute. She drags on the joint. She remembers Ren and picks up the phone*) Ren! The cops are coming! . . . *A cop* is coming *here!* . . . To my apartment. What have I done, Ren? I haven't done anything . . . That's not illegal, Ren. None of those things are illegal. Ren! I have outstanding parking tickets! *Five* of them! (*She takes another drag on the joint*) Of course I'm still smoking. I always smoke when I'm nervous . . . It's illegal? You're kidding . . . God! What am I going to do? . . . Hide it? Where? . . . Good idea. (*She takes the tin box and dumps it into a plant pot*) Maybe it'll grow there . . . No, I'm all right . . . I'm fine. I just panic when I have to deal with the pigs . . . Yes, I know, Ren, I don't like authority. That's what my shrink said . . . I'm working on it. Another two hundred sessions and I'll be ready to talk to my father again . . . No, I'm just kidding. I'm fine, babe . . . I'll talk to you later. Really, I'm in total command. (*The doorbell rings*) My God, Ren! He's *here!* What have I done? I haven't done anything. I'll write him a check for the parking tickets. Will he take a check, Ren? Ren! (*In a loud whisper*) I still have this little *joint* in my *hand!* . . . No, it went out . . . Oh, yeah. Good idea, Ren. (*She pops the litle piece into her mouth. And swallows it*) Listen, call me back in twenty minutes to make sure I'm okay, okay? I might need a lawyer . . . Sure you do. I gave your number to some lawyer I met in Bloomingdale's . . . Well, he said he was a lawyer. Well, call me anyway. (*She hangs up the phone. The doorbell rings again. She freezes. She waves her hands in the air to clear the smoke. She steps toward the door. Stops, stands still, arms at her sides. Softly:*) Nam-myo-ho-rengay-kyo. (*Then, a little louder*) Nam-myo-ho-ren . . . Oh, fuck it! (*She opens the door slightly. It is chained*) Are you the cop?

RICK: (*Outside the door*) Yes, ma'am.

(*Mandy undoes the chain, and opens the door. Rick Selby enters. He is twenty-five, boyishly handsome, blond, not tall. He is straight-forward and sincere, says exactly what he means. He is enthusiastic and a little bit shy. He is dressed in neat blue jeans and shirt, with a windbreaker. The word* Dodgers *is written across the back. Rick stands in the middle of the room and smiles at Mandy*)

RICK: How ya doin?

MANDY: Fine. (*She suddenly realizes she is dressed in her tights. She turns*) Excuse me.

(*She exits into the bedroom. Rick waits in the middle of the room, looking around. Mandy returns wearing a rather dressy jogging suit. She has covered herself up adequately, but still looks smashing*)

RICK: That's really pretty.

MANDY: Thank you. Why aren't you in uniform?

RICK: Ha-? I hate that uniform. It's real tight around the crotch and it pulls when I walk around.

MANDY: Oh. Well, that's . . . a good reason.

RICK: This is a great place you've got here.

MANDY: Thank you. It's a dump.

RICK: It looks like something I saw in *Vogue* magazine.

MANDY: Oh, really? What month?

RICK: I don't know. (*He sniffs. And smiles*) It smells like dope in here.

MANDY: Oh, yeah? (*She sniffs. And sniffs again. A third time*) I don't smell anything. (*Rick steps toward her and sniffs. She steps back*) It could be my perfume.

RICK: Oh, yeah? Old Mary Jane perfume, huh? Promise her anything, but give her Mary Jane. That's good. (*Mandy smiles*) Got any more?

MANDY: (*Indignantly. And dramatically*) Oh, come on! Who do you think you're dealing with here, huh? I watch *Kojak*, too; I go to the movies. You're going to have to do better than that, buster! You've got to get up pretty early in the morning to try to pull that old crap on me. I've lived, buddy. And I *know* my rights, too. You understand me?

RICK: (*Amazed*) Uh. I guess so. (*Looking around*) You sure have a lot of plants.

MANDY: (*Jumping between Rick and the plant where she stashed the dope*) Stay away from my plants, buddy! (*Rick doesn't move*) You're going to have to get yourself a warrant before you can search my plants.

RICK: (*He smiles. Then laughs*) You don't know who I am, do you?

MANDY: You're a cop . . . aren't you?

RICK: You don't know me though, do you?

MANDY: No.

RICK: I didn't think so.

MANDY: Wait a minute. Let me see your ID.

RICK: Oh, sure. If I show you my ID then you'll know who I am. That's cheating.

MANDY: Whip it out, buster!

RICK: (*He reaches into his pocket and flashes his wallet at her. She can see the badge, but she's not close enough to read it. He flicks it closed and pockets it*) Now do you know?

MANDY: No.

RICK: (*Shaking his head, reaches in his pocket and brings out the ID again. He reads it*) Lt. Rick Selby, California Highway Patrol.

MANDY: You're kidding.

RICK: No.

MANDY: Then you're lost.

RICK: No.

MANDY: Um. This might sound like a real trivial question, but what's a California Highway Patrolman doing in New York City? Patrolling?

RICK: (*Laughing. He puts the ID back*) You mind if I sit down?

MANDY: No. Please, sit down.

RICK: (*Settling into the couch. Its pillows are very soft and he sinks into them*) Not a good couch if you're stoned.

MANDY: What do you want . . . Lieutenant?

RICK: (*He smiles*) You really don't remember me, do you?

MANDY: No.

RICK: (*He digs in another pocket and produces a folded-up traffic ticket which he unfolds*) Do you remember this?

MANDY: No. What is it?

RICK: It's a traffic citation.

MANDY: I don't remember traffic citations.

RICK: It's got your name on it. Right here. Mandy Morgan.

MANDY: Huh?

RICK: Great name.

MANDY: I really don't remember getting a traffic citation in California. Are you sure it's not a parking ticket?

RICK: Yup. Do you remember driving west on the Ventura Freeway, near Sherman Oaks, one day in August, 1975?

MANDY: Um . . . gee, I really don't.

RICK: August 14th, to be exact.

MANDY: August 14th I remember. That was my um . . . birthday.

RICK: Yeah. Your thirtieth birthday. I guess you would remember that.

MANDY: I don't believe it was my thirtieth birthday, exactly.

RICK: Well, it says here you were born August 14, 1945. Must have been your thirtieth birthday.

MANDY: (*She does a little quick figuring*) Huh? I guess so.

RICK: Don't you remember being pulled over for doing sixty-eight in a fifty-five?

MANDY: Huh? I . . . vaguely . . . remember something about that.

RICK: That was me. I was the arresting officer.

MANDY: Oh, is that right?

RICK: Yep. You probably just don't remember me without my helmet.

MANDY: Put it on.

RICK: Hey, I don't have her with me. (*He laughs*)

MANDY: Were you riding on a motorcycle? With little blue lights?

RICK: Yes.

MANDY: I think I remember your motorcycle. I thought you were taller though.

RICK: Oh, ha! That's because you were sitting down and I was standing up.

MANDY: Of course.

RICK: (*He stands and steps to her chair. He leans over her. She looks up at him*) Now do you remember me?

MANDY: Right.

RICK: (*Sitting back down. There is a pause*) It's great to see you again.

MANDY: Great to see you.

RICK: You look really foxy.

MANDY: Thank you. How did you find me?

RICK: (*Holding up the ticket*) Got your address right here.

MANDY: Oh, yeah. . . . Um, Lieutenant . . .

RICK: Rick.

MANDY: Rick. At the risk of sounding redundant, um . . . what do you want?

RICK: Hey . . . Mandy.

MANDY: No, really, what do you want?

RICK: Don't you remember what you said to me?

MANDY: No.

RICK: You told me you were real sorry for breaking the speed limit and you felt awful about it and you usually drive very carefully, except that you were really bummed out that day because it was your birthday and you didn't have any real friends in L.A., and you couldn't wait to get back to New York, and if you got one more speeding ticket you were going to have to go to driver's rehab school, and I said that was really shitty and that I was feeling very low and anxiety-ridden myself because the Cincinnati Reds had just beat the Dodgers three times in a row, which always brings me way down, and I said your name, Mandy Morgan, reminded me of Manny Mota of the Dodgers, and that I was a real Dodger fan, and I just wanted to be out at the beach and try to mellow out. And you said that if I'd just let you off you'd make it up to me somehow, and I said that was attempting to bribe an officer, and you said you wouldn't tell anybody, and we both laughed about that, and I went ahead and wrote up the ticket, and then you said, "Listen, officer, you throw away that ticket and if you ever come to New York City, I'll show you a real good time."

MANDY: (*Considering this*) I . . . vaguely . . . remember something about that.

RICK: Well, I didn't throw the ticket away. But I didn't send it in, either.

MANDY: Oh? Well. Wasn't that sweet of you?

RICK: Uh-huh.

MANDY: And now, here you are in New York, two and one-half years later.

RICK: That's right.

MANDY: You're kidding.

RICK: Oh, I don't kid around.

MANDY: I believe that about you. (*She pauses. It all sinks in*) Huh! Huh, huh, huh! So, now I guess I know what you want. (*Rick smiles at her*) You know—fifty-five is a rather abnormal speed to have to drive at.

RICK: Really. I don't make the laws, I just try to enforce them.

MANDY: Bully for you. Um . . . how much would that fine have been?

RICK: Sixty-eight in a fifty-five? Probably about forty-three dollars.

MANDY: God! What a rip-off! Would you like me to pay it? I could write you a check.

RICK: (*Smiling*) No. I don't want you to pay the fine, I want you to show me a good time, like you said you would.

MANDY: Huh? (*She's getting nervous. She looks from Rick to the phone, to the plant, to the window, back to Rick, back to the phone*) How long have you been here?

RICK: Three days.

MANDY: What? No, *here*. In this apartment. Since you rang the bell, how long has that been?

RICK: (*Checking his watch*) Twelve minutes. Why?

MANDY: No reason. I'm expecting a phone call, that's all. From my boyfriend, Boris.

RICK: Oh. Well, I've been here twelve minutes.

MANDY: Uh-huh. (*She stands*) Um. Stand up, Rick. (*He does*) Don't move. (*She crosses down behind the couch and begins to push it to the center of the room*) This couch belongs over here, not over there. (*Rick makes a move to help her*) Hold it. I'll move the couch. It's my couch. Thank you. It's part of my exercise program.

RICK: Oh?

MANDY: (*She gets it back in place. He stares at her*) Sit down. (*He does*) There you go. Very good. (*She stands away from him*) I'm going to be needlepointing a new cover for this couch. It's my project for today. I hope to have it finished in time for the 1988 Olympics.

RICK: Oh? I did a little needlepointing once.

MANDY: You did?

RICK: Yes. It takes a tremendous commitment, but it's super therapy.

MANDY: I'm glad to hear that. I need super therapy. (*She pauses*) Um. Rick. This is a little awkward, isn't it?

RICK: What do you mean?

MANDY: This . . . don't you feel a little awkward?

RICK: Nope.

MANDY: Lucky you. I feel very awkward.

RICK: Well, you should relax. You seem uncomfortable.

MANDY: That's because I'm uncomfortable.

RICK: Would you like some coffee, or maybe a little drink?

MANDY: Um, I live here. I'll handle this. Now, would *you* like some coffee, or maybe a little drink?

RICK: No, thanks. But you go ahead. Do whatever you want to do. I know I probably kind of surprised you dropping in like this.

MANDY: Yes. You kind of did.

RICK: Well, do whatever you feel like doing.

MANDY: Thank you. (*She turns toward the bedroom. She screams*) Acchhhhhhh! Excuse me.

(*She steps into the bedroom. Rick stands, looks around. He crosses to the two can/tables. He puts one at one end of the couch and brings the other to the other end. Mandy enters. Now she's wearing baggy jeans and a workshirt. Looks awful*)

RICK: You changed.

MANDY: Yes.

RICK: That looks good. You feel more relaxed now?

MANDY: No. You moved my cans.

RICK: Yeah. I figured they probably belong over here.

MANDY: Wrong-o. (*She picks up the can at the left end of the couch and carries it to the right end. Drops it. Picks up the right one and carries it left*) There.

RICK: Now I see the difference.

MANDY: You do?

RICK: You're a real independent woman, aren't you?

MANDY: Sort of.

RICK: That's great. I knew you were special when I first saw you.

MANDY: Is that why you arrested me?

RICK: No. I pulled you over because you were doing sixty-eight in a fifty-five. You're not a very good driver.

MANDY: Uh-huh.

RICK: But it didn't take me long to realize that you were a pretty neat person.

MANDY: Uh-huh. (*She stares at him a moment*) Excuse me. (*She steps to the kitchen and disappears inside. Rick watches her go. He's a little confused. There is the sound of the refrigerator door and a rattle of dishes. Then Mandy's voice can be heard, softly chanting*) Nam-myo-ho-rengay-kyo.

RICK: (*Standing. He calls to the kitchen*) Far-out! Are you chanting?

MANDY: (*Off*) Nam-myo-ho-rengay-kyo.

RICK: I thought so. Far-out!

MANDY: (*She steps into the doorway. A glass of Scotch in her hand*) Nam-myo-ho-rengay-kyo.

RICK: I chant, too.

MANDY: Nam-myo-ho-rengay-kyo.

(*Rick steps to her. He joins her chant*)

MANDY and RICK: Nam-myo-ho-rengay-kyo. Nam-myo-ho-rengay-kyo. (*The chant gets faster and more intense. It's almost sexual*) Nam-myo-ho-rengay-kyo . . .

MANDY: Stop!

RICK: What's the matter?

MANDY: I don't chant with strangers. Besides our chants are in conflict with each other.

RICK: Maybe not.

MANDY: Let's just sit down and compose ourselves, shall we?

RICK: You got it. (*He goes back to the couch. Mandy to her chair*) What's that?

MANDY: Johnny Walker Red. Want some?

RICK: No, thanks. Alcohol dulls my senses.

MANDY: Oh? Sure you don't want some?

RICK: Sure.

MANDY: How long have you been here?

RICK: Three days. Oh. Eighteen minutes. Listen, if you're worried about your boyfriend, go ahead and call him. I don't mind.

MANDY: What? No. I can't call him. He's busy. He's a karate instructor.

RICK: Oh, wow. I'm into karate.

MANDY: Oh? You're quite a well-rounded pig, aren't you? I'm *sorry!* That's left over from my revolutionary days. I took some night courses at Columbia a few years ago, and was a sort of commuter radical for about a month. I got very intense about upping the pigs.

RICK: That's okay. There's all sorts of weird stigmas attached to my job. That's part of the reason I do it. I'm trying to help change the image of the highway cop.

MANDY: Well, you've certainly gone out of your way to accomplish that.

RICK: Well . . . there's all sorts of ways to change images.

MANDY: Do you still wear those sunglasses that look like little mirrors?

RICK: Yes.

MANDY: Then you've got a ways to go.

RICK: Well, I only wear them in the daytime.

MANDY: Oh? There's a good sign.

RICK: I mean, you know, I wear those same glasses skiing, too.

MANDY: You ski?

RICK: Yes.

MANDY: Huh.

RICK: Do you?

MANDY: No. I'd like to, though.

RICK: I'll take you skiing. You come back to California and I'll take you skiing up at Mammoth Mountain.

MANDY: Sure.

RICK: Sure. I'll show you a real good time.

MANDY: Ha-ha-ha!

(*A moment passes. Mandy drinks her drink*)

RICK: Got any more weed?

MANDY: Huh? Um, maybe. You going to bust me?

RICK: Naw, of course not. At least not until I've been shown my good time.

(*Mandy looks at him whimsically. She steps to the plant pot and removes the tin box and a handful of joints. She sits on the couch, some distance from Rick*)

RICK: Those are very neatly rolled.

MANDY: They're from Zabar's. (*He looks at her blankly*) It's a little joke. It's a little deli on the West Side.

RICK: Well, they're certainly neatly rolled.

MANDY: Yes. (*She holds a joint in her mouth. He lights it*) Thank you. (*She passes it to him*) So.

RICK: So.

MANDY: So. God help me! I think my phone's on the blink. Um. How long have you been chanting?

RICK: Oh. About three years and two months. It's really helped my head through a lot of heavy weather.

MANDY: Uh-huh.

RICK: I'm really committed to it, too. I chanted that you'd still be living here when I got to New York City.

MANDY: Yeah?

RICK: Yep. It works. A couple of years ago I chanted for snow when I was going skiing in Colorado and, sure enough, it snowed.

MANDY: Was this in the wintertime?

RICK: Yep. February.

MANDY: You believe in chanting because it snowed in Colorado in February? Isn't that a little like doing a rain dance in Seattle?

RICK: It didn't work last year.

MANDY: But you still have faith in it?

RICK: Sure. You're still living here, aren't you?

MANDY: Yes. So, you're the reason why?

RICK: You got it. Now aren't you glad I chanted for you?

MANDY: Um. Maybe. (*There is a pause. They pass the joint*) How did you happen to remember me after all this time?

RICK: How could I forget you?

MANDY: You must get interesting little offers and bribes everyday.

RICK: Yours was one of the better ones.

MANDY: Huh. Then why'd it take you so long to get here?

RICK: Well, I had to wait for my head to tell me the time was right.

MANDY: And your head just now instructed you . . . to pick up and boogie on in to New York?

RICK: Yeah, sort of. I made my reservations a month in advance. Saved me one hundred and something dollars.

MANDY: No kidding. You're smart, aren't you? (*He smiles. She smiles*) So. How long have you been here?

RICK: Twenty-four minutes. You mean here? Or here? Three days.

MANDY: Why'd it take you so long to get *here*?

RICK: Well, I've been staying with my cousin-in-law in Stamford, Connecticut. You know where that is?

MANDY: Never heard of it.

RICK: It's kind of weird out there, but it's nice. Anyway, I wanted to get all that family crap out of the way. Because the real highlight of my trip, of course, would be coming into the city and seeing you.

MANDY: Oh . . . (*The phone rings. Mandy is staring at Rick. She fumbles for the phone behind her, finds it, lifts the receiver to her ear*) Give me ten more minutes, Ren. (*She hangs up the phone. She slides a little closer to Rick and hands him the joint*) That was Ren.

RICK: (*Smiling at her*) I thought your boyfriend's name was Boris.

MANDY: It is. Boris. And also Ren. He has two names, just like anyone else.

RICK: Oh? I don't think I've ever known anyone named Ren.

MANDY: It's short for Renegade. He's nine feet tall.

RICK: Uh-oh.

MANDY: So bear that in mind.

RICK: Okay. (*A moment passes. They finish the joint*) All gone.

MANDY: Yep.

RICK: How do you feel now?

MANDY: I have no idea. You know something? You're the nicest cop I've ever gotten stoned with.

RICK: Oh. Thank you.

MANDY: Wouldn't you like to take off your jacket?

RICK: (*He does*) Thank you.

MANDY: Don't you have a little Mrs. Cop back in Los Angeles?

RICK: No. I'm single.

MANDY: Me, too.

RICK: But you have a boyfriend.

MANDY: Do I?

RICK: Yes. Boris-Ren. Remember?

MANDY: Oh, yes.

RICK: Were you ever married?

MANDY: Oh, yes. I was married for seven years. To my husband.

RICK: What happened to him?

MANDY: I gave him back. He wore out.

RICK: I imagine it's not easy to have a good marriage.

MANDY: I'm sure you're right. Why aren't you married? You'd make a cute husband.

RICK: I thought I'd wait til I stopped being cute. I'm just starting to get my bearings, you know?

MANDY: Yeah.

RICK: Can I ask you something?

MANDY: Sure.

RICK: Are you happy?

MANDY: Sure. Except for the fact that I live in New York and hate the people I know, I'm perfectly happy.

RICK: Why don't you move?

MANDY: What? That would be too easy. I can't move. I'm stuck.

RICK: I don't like L.A. either.

MANDY: *You* could move. You could move to the mountains and ski in the snow with your mirror sunglasses.

RICK: I'd like to. But I'm stuck, too. Besides, I'm having too much fun arresting people.

MANDY: Right.

RICK: I'm just kidding. I hate arresting people. I just can't help myself.

MANDY: All in the line of duty.

RICK: Uh-huh.

MANDY: Sergeant Preston of the Yukon.

RICK: Right.

MANDY: Aren't you ever scared?

RICK: Sure. I'm scared a lot of the time. Aren't *you* ever scared?

MANDY: Well, sure, but I don't usually chase people on a motorcycle.

RICK: But you live in New York. That's scary.

MANDY: You're right. Now I'm scared.

RICK: Oh, you don't have to be scared. I'm just trying to answer your question. My job is scary, but so are a lot of things in life. So—might as well just get in there and do it. Besides the danger is part of the fun.

MANDY: Oh? How'd you happen to become a cop?

RICK: Well, I started out being a lifeguard and just sort of grew into it. Traded in my surfboard for a motorcycle.

MANDY: Oh? What's next for someone like you?

RICK: I don't know. Maybe acting.

MANDY: That sounds like a logical progression. That's the sort of logic I seem to follow in my life. That's why I'm taking up needlepoint. So I'll make a good granny. I should be working on being a mommy, but I'll get back to that later.

RICK: (*After a pause*) You know what I've noticed about you? You're a real smart-ass.

MANDY: Oh?

RICK: Yeah. But at least you find a little humor in a lot of things that aren't really very funny. You make me laugh.

MANDY: You're not laughing.

RICK: Inside I'm laughing.

MANDY: That's nice.

RICK: That's a pretty good trait to have, I think, finding humor in things. But you shouldn't laugh at yourself. I mean you can *laugh* at yourself, but you shouldn't *think* of yourself as a *joke*.

MANDY: I don't. I think of myself as a Snickers candy bar.

RICK: Huh?

MANDY: Yes. Little nutty, little tough, little sticky, artificial flavor and coloring, but very sweet inside.

RICK: Huh? Wow!

MANDY: I didn't make that up. A writer I know described me that way on the last night of our relationship. And he's right.

RICK: You're sure honest about yourself.

MANDY: Yes, I am. No, I'm lying. I'm mostly honest. I'd like to be. I like honesty.

RICK: So do I.

MANDY: I don't really have a boyfriend named Boris.

RICK: I didn't think so.

MANDY: I don't really have a boyfriend at all.

RICK: Why?

MANDY: Just don't.

RICK: I can't understand why you wouldn't have a boy-friend.

MANDY: I'm too nice. Men shy away from niceness. Tell me something. Honestly, Richard. Do you really think I meant it when I told you I'd show you a good time?

RICK: Sure. Didn't you?

MANDY: No.

RICK: You didn't?

MANDY: That's just the sort of thing people say, when they can't think of anything else. It's not supposed to mean anything. Don't you say things like that?

RICK: No. When I told you to come to California and I'd show you a good time, I meant it.

MANDY: I'll bet.

RICK: No, I did.

MANDY: You really think it's that easy? One person says, "Come to New York and I'll show you a good time," and then the other person boogies on in to New York and they have a good time? You think that's the way life works?

RICK: Yes.

MANDY: You're probably right.

RICK: That's the way it works for me. With other people I know.

MANDY: Well, I'm not other people, Officer. I am Mandy Morgan. A thirty . . . two-year-old woman of the world, a chanter, a dancer, an alimony collector, an involved, aware, total, liberated Snickers candy bar. And I play by my own rules.

RICK: What are they?

MANDY: I'm not sure. (*She stares at him. She stands*) Excuse me.

(*Mandy exits into the bedroom. Now Rick is even more confused. He stands. Puts on his jacket. Looks around. He reaches into his pocket, pulls out a pack of chewing gum. Opens a piece and puts it into his mouth. He chews thoughtfully for a minute. He studies the cracker cans. He steps to them and switches them back. Mandy reappears. Now she's wearing basically a flowing robe and nothing else. She looks quite lovely. Rick stares at her, amazed. He stops chewing*)

MANDY: Um. Leaving?

RICK: Well, I don't know.

MANDY: Leave now and you'll miss the good part.

RICK: You sure look pretty.

MANDY: Thank you. (*She sits on the couch*) Would you hand me my Scotch, please? (*He does*) Thank you. Sit down. (*He does. He sits awkwardly on the couch beside her*) Wouldn't you like to take off your jacket? (*He does*) Okay. Now. Um. Let's see. I've decided to follow through on this. I've decided to show you a good time, as the saying goes.

RICK: (*Skeptically*) Yeah?

MANDY: Yeah. So would you like to kiss me, or what? You want to chant a little bit?

RICK: I'd like to smoke another joint.

MANDY: No. Sorry. No more artificial sweeteners. This is the real thing, Lieutenant.

RICK: Well . . .

MANDY: Come here. (*She pulls him to her. She kisses him*)

RICK: Wait! (*He lifts his head. Takes his gum out of his mouth. He digs in his pocket for the wrapper*)

MANDY: What's that?

RICK: Chewing gum.

MANDY: You're kidding?

RICK: Uh-uh. (*He pockets the wrapped-up wad of gum. She kisses him again. After a moment, he lifts himself up again*) Um . . .

MANDY: What's the matter?

RICK: Nothing.

MANDY: But we've stopped kissing. It was fun.

RICK: Yeah. But, this isn't exactly what I had in mind.

MANDY: Oh?

RICK: Yeah. Um. You know, when you, like told me you'd show me a good time, this isn't really the way I pictured it.

MANDY: Oh? No? What do you want, violins? My doorman plays the bongos.

RICK: No. I mean, I might like to make love with you. Matter of fact, I'm pretty *sure* I'd like to make love with you. But I'd have to get to know you a little better.

MANDY: You're kidding?

RICK: No. You're sort of strange, you know.

MANDY: Oh, I know.

RICK: I don't mean that unkindly. I *like* you. A *lot*. You're a real foxy lady. But, you know, when I was thinking about you showing me a good time, I think I was thinking along different lines.

MANDY: What did you have in mind?

RICK: I wanted to have fun.

MANDY: Making love with a thirty-two-year-old foxy lady is not fun for you?

RICK: Oh, sure. It's just not what I was thinking of.

MANDY: (*Staring at him*) Pass me a joint, would you?

RICK: No. Listen. It's just that I've never been to New York before, and I sort of imagined we would, like, go around to the Statue of Liberty and the Empire State Building and the U.N., and stuff like that. And maybe we could see some shows and go to Radio City Music Hall, and have a drink in some famous bar. Things like that.

MANDY: You're kidding?

RICK: No.

MANDY: Do you mean that I have been coaxing myself through this major catharsis, and agonizing over my ever-so-slight lapses in honesty for nothing? Do you mean to tell me that I have *forced* myself to the point where I'm ready to share the wonders of my womanness with a *California Highway Patrolman,* and you want to go to Radio City Music Hall?

RICK: Well, I want to go to Radio City Music Hall *first,* let's put it that way.

MANDY: Ha! (*She laughs*) That's very funny. You should have told me that before I changed my clothes three times.

RICK: I think we had a little communication block. I wondered why you kept changing your clothes.

MANDY: I think you're right. I *like* to change my clothes.

RICK: That's why you have to be careful when you say things you don't mean. Sometime somebody's going to take you literally. I've enjoyed your various outfits, though.

MANDY: You never know, do you? Which was your favorite?

RICK: You never know. This is actually my favorite. But it's not real practical for sightseeing.

MANDY: Depends on who's sightseeing, I'd say. You um . . . you *are* interested in me, though, aren't you?

RICK: Yes.

MANDY: I'm comforted by that. I've got to tell you, in the nearly twenty years that boys and men have been looking to

me for that ever-elusive good time, you are the first who has
ever insisted on getting to know me better.

RICK: Well?

MANDY: Well, well, well! Sergeant Preston of the Yukon.
My hero. I don't believe this! Radio City, huh? (*Rick nods*) I
haven't been to Radio City since my class trip with the Stamford elementary school.

RICK: Yeah? You *do* know where Stamford is.

MANDY: I know where it *was*. I'm afraid I wouldn't be a
very good person to go sightseeing with. I'm afraid of heights.

RICK: So, don't look down. I'll hold your hand. You'll love
it.

MANDY: Hmm. You might be right. Oh, boy! Next time
I'm going to pay my traffic fine like a good American.

RICK: Hey, come on! We can have fun.

(*Mandy stares at him. The phone rings*)

MANDY: Excuse me. Hello? . . . Hello, Ren . . . What do
you mean, what's the matter? What's the matter with you?
. . . Oh . . . Nothing . . . Listen, Ren, I have to ask you a
very important question. How do you get to the Statue of
Liberty? . . . Oh? Good idea, Ren. (*She hangs up*) She said,
take a cab. (*She stares at Rick. He smiles at her. She smiles. Stands.
She walks toward the bedroom*) Excuse me.

(*Rick watches her go. He stands. He digs into his pocket, brings out
the gum wrapper. He carefully removes the wad of gum and pops it
into his mouth. Mandy calls from the bedroom*)

MANDY: (*Off*) So. You wanna have a good time, copper?

RICK: Um. Yes, I do.

MANDY: You *really* wanna have a good time?

RICK: Yes. Yes!

MANDY: Okay. I'm going to *show you a good time*. (*She storms
into the room. She wears jeans and a heavy sweater, a floppy hat. A
camera hangs around her neck, and she carries a bag*)

RICK: All *right!*

MANDY: Let's go, Lieutenant. (*She heads for the front door. He
pulls on his jacket and follows*) Wait! I've got to find my keys. It's
part of a ritual. (*She rummages in her bag. Rick opens the door. She
pulls out a small spray can*) I guess I won't be needing my mace.
I don't usually travel with a cop. (*She throws the can onto the
couch*) You didn't want that, did you? (*She smiles at him. He
shakes his head*) Ah, my keys. Let's go, kid. The tour bus is

leaving. (*The phone rings. She walks to it*) Excuse me. (*She answers it*) Hello? . . . Oh, hello, Mother . . . I can't talk right now. . . . No, I'm not just saying that. I'm going out. . . . I'm going to the Statue of Liberty with a very nice policeman . . . Thank you, Mother. I knew you'd be pleased. . . . Okay. Bye. (*She hangs up. She heads for the door, smiling at Rick. He grabs her arm*)

RICK: I just want to give you a little thank you in advance. (*He kisses her, quickly but warmly, on the mouth*)

MANDY: You're kidding!

(*He shakes his head. He smiles. She smiles. They exit*)

Curtain

Frank D. Gilroy

DREAMS OF GLORY

Frank D. Gilroy

With *Dreams of Glory,* Frank D. Gilroy makes his third appearance in *The Best Short Plays* series. As with its predecessors, *Present Tense* and *The Next Contestant,* the play initially was staged at the Ensemble Studio Theatre, a major innovative force in the realm of Off-Off-Broadway.

The author was born in New York City on October 13, 1925. He attended DeWitt Clinton High School in the Bronx and soon after graduating went into the U.S. Army. While in service he managed to do some writing and contributed two stories to the divisional paper. Coming out of the army with "a burning desire and determination to write," he enrolled in Dartmouth College. Although he had been writing poems and stories for some time, a playwriting course taken in his junior year made him realize that drama was his proper genre. During his tenure at Dartmouth, he wrote two full-length and six short plays that were produced at the college. He also served as editor of the college newspaper. Graduating from Dartmouth in 1950 *magna cum laude,* he won a year's postgraduate study at the Yale School of Drama.

After Yale, Mr. Gilroy held a succession of odd jobs, all the while continuing to write. Television drama was coming into its own at the time, and he decided to make "an all-out total assault" on the medium. The breakthrough came in 1952 when he sold a sketch for Kate Smith. This soon was followed by other scripts performed on almost all of the major dramatic shows during television's Golden Age. He also started to write for films, notably the screenplays for *The Fastest Gun Alive* with Glenn Ford, and *The Gallant Hours* with James Cagney.

He next invaded the theatre with *Who'll Save the Plowboy?*, presented Off-Broadway at the Phoenix Theatre in 1962. The play and author were hailed by most reviewers and it brought him his first theatre award, an Obie for the best new American play of the year.

The Subject Was Roses, his second produced play in New York, opened at the Royale Theatre on May 25, 1964, and it was greeted with critical acclaim. Richard Watts, Jr. declared in the *New York Post* that Gilroy had written "a powerful drama" and "established himself as one of the high hopes of the American theatre." The play ran for 832 performances and won drama's triple crown: the Pulitzer Prize, the New

York Drama Critics' Circle Award, and the Antoinette Perry "Tony" Award.

In 1967, Mr. Gilroy was represented again on Broadway with *That Summer-That Fall,* with Jon Voight and Irene Pappas. This was followed in 1968 by *The Only Game in Town,* a three-character vehicle that costarred Tammy Grimes, Barry Nelson, and Leo Genn. It later was filmed with Elizabeth Taylor.

Mr. Gilroy also has served as author and director of several films including *Desperate Characters* starring Shirley MacLaine, *From Noon Till Three* with Charles Bronson and Jill Ireland and, most recently, *Once in Paris,* which he also produced.

After a hiatus of eleven years, Mr. Gilroy returned to Broadway in 1979 with a new drama, *Last Licks,* which was directed by Tom Conti, who earlier in the year won a Tony Award for his performance as the paralyzed hero of *Whose Life Is It Anyway?*

The author, a former president of The Dramatists Guild, lives with his wife and three sons in their upstate New York home.

Characters:

GEORGE BREWSTER
ADA BREWSTER
BILL FARLEY
GINGER FARLEY

Scene:

A country club terrace.
A summer evening—the present.
Two couples—George and Ada Brewster, Bill and Ginger Farley—late forties, evening clothes, share a table. The sound of an orchestra, in the Glenn Miller mode, from off.
Bill pops the cork of a champagne bottle into a napkin.

BILL: Barely a whisper.
ADA: Bravo!
BILL: (*Filling Ada's glass*) *Voilá.*
ADA: *Merci.*
BILL: (*Filling Ginger's glass*) *Voilá.*
GINGER: *Merci.*
BILL: (*Filling George's glass*) *Voilá* . . . Well?
GEORGE: What?
BILL: You missed your cue.
(*George just looks at him*)
ADA: Bill filled your glass.
GEORGE: *Merci.*
BILL: *De nada.* (*Raising his glass as do the women*) To the two nicest couples at the twenty-seventh annual summer dance all of which we've attended together except for the year we went to Europe and the time I had the mumps.
GINGER: Long may we wave.
ADA: Cheers! (*They look to George*) Well?
(*George offers no reaction*)
BILL: You're on.
GEORGE: To the two nicest couples at the dance.
ADA: Bill said that.
GEORGE: Long may we wave.
GINGER: That's my line.

GEORGE: (*To Ada*) Let me guess—you said "cheers."

GINGER: The fizz will be gone soon.

GEORGE: Bottoms up.

(*They touch glasses and drink. We hear the orchestra conclude a number to applause. And then the Leader's Voice:*)

LEADER: After a brief intermission we shall return. Don't go away.

BILL: Excellent band.

ADA: As always.

GEORGE: Isn't it amazing that in the twenty-seven years we've been attending these affairs, less the summer in Europe and the time Bill had the mumps, we've never had a band that was less than excellent.

GINGER: It's a tribute to the dance committee.

GEORGE: Or shabby standards.

BILL: Are you saying the band's no good? And if so by what authority?

GINGER: Bill has one of the best record collections in town.

ADA: And George got up on the wrong side of the bed. Ignore him.

GEORGE: The brass is weak, the reeds need tuning, and the drummer lags.

BILL: Thus spake Benny Goodman.

GEORGE: *The brass is weak, the reeds need tuning, the drummer lags.*

BILL: You win—they stink. Agreed?

GINGER: Agreed.

ADA: Agreed.

GEORGE: I didn't say "stink."

BILL: Raise your hand for a refill.

GEORGE: Last year's band stank. And the one the year before was even worse. These fellows are passable.

BILL: How would *you* know?

GEORGE: When I was sixteen I played with Tommy Dorsey.

(*The incongruity of the statement and the matter-of-fact way it's made arrests reaction for a moment. Then they laugh*)

BILL: Is that Tommy Dorsey the shoemaker on Elm Street?

GEORGE: Tommy Dorsey, "the sentimental gentleman of swing."

(*Again the sincerity of the pronouncement prompts laughter*)

BILL: What did you play with him—handball?

GEORGE: Piano.

(*Laughter*)

BILL: No more booze for this lad.

GEORGE: Tommy Dorsey performed at our prom. His piano player was late so I played the first set.

ADA: Dreams of glory.

GINGER: If I were you, I'd get the car keys.

GEORGE: At the end of the set, Tommy Dorsey said, "Kid, if you ever decide to give the music business a whirl—look me up."

BILL: *Golden Boy* with William Holden!

ADA: His father wanted him to be a violinist but he became a boxer.

GEORGE: He gave me his card with a private number written in.

GINGER: They laughed when I sat down to play. (*Raising her glass*) Refill.

GEORGE: *Tommy Dorsey gave me a card with his private number.*

ADA: What's the punch line?

BILL: When he dialed the number he got *Jimmy* Dorsey who Tommy disliked and was always playing dirty tricks on.

(*Laughter*)

GEORGE: I never called him.

GINGER: I'll bite: Why?

ADA: This better be good.

GEORGE: I knew my family, my father, would never approve.

BILL: That's not funny.

ADA: His father wanted him to be a boxer.

GEORGE: *That's* funny.

GINGER: How come we never heard you play?

ADA: Having achieved the pinnacle with Tommy Dorsey, he vowed never to play again.

GEORGE: Bull's-eye!

GINGER: *Boo—hiss.*

BILL: Ginger likes happy endings.

GEORGE: I married Ada—have four great kids.

BILL: And any day now will become the new president of Ridgeway Products.

ADA: We agreed not to talk about that till it happens.

BILL: Only kidding, God.

GEORGE: Murray Hill seven-four-six-five-three. (*They regard him*) Tommy Dorsey's number.

BILL: Don't look now but I think we've exhausted that gag.

ADA: Seconded.

BILL: In favor?

BILL, ADA and GINGER: *Aye.*

GEORGE: It's not a gag.

BILL: Ginger and I are thinking of Bermuda for Easter. You guys want to come?

GEORGE: *It's not a gag.*

BILL: Prove it. Go inside and tickle the ivories like you did with Tommy Dorsey.

GEORGE: It's been thirty years.

GINGER: Put up or shut up!

GEORGE: What would you like to hear?

ADA: Ignore him.

GEORGE: *What would you like me to play?*

BILL: How about one of the songs you performed with Tommy Dorsey?

GEORGE: All right. (*He rises*)

ADA: And just where do you think you're going?

GEORGE: To tickle the ivories.

ADA: Down boy!

GEORGE: How about "I'll Never Smile Again"?

BILL: Fine.

(*George starts away*)

ADA: George. (*He stops*) I don't know what you're up to or why, but Mr. Ridgeway is in there and he isn't going to like it if you make a fool of yourself. It could affect his decision.

GEORGE: No.

ADA: What do you mean "no"?

GEORGE: There's nothing I can do now that would influence Mr. Ridgeway's decision.

ADA: *He's decided who's going to succeed him. He told you.*

GEORGE: Yes.

ADA: You didn't get it. I knew something was wrong.

GINGER: I told Bill when we got out of the car, "George isn't himself tonight."

BILL: After twenty-five years and all you've done for that company. It's a damn shame!

ADA: *It's an outrage.*

GINGER: I could cry.

GEORGE: So could I. As a matter of fact, I did.

ADA: We shouldn't have come tonight. Why didn't you say something?

BILL: At times like this, a person should be with those closest to them.

GINGER: What are friends for?

ADA: So Paul Stockwell, yea-sayer and ass-kisser par excellence, is the new president of Ridgeway Products.

GEORGE: No.

ADA: Paul Stockwell didn't get it?

GEORGE: No.

ADA: Who then?

BILL: Don't tell me old man Ridgeway turned the company over to his nephew? Don't tell me it's Bertram?

ADA: Of course it's Bertram.

BILL: Bertram is barely literate.

GINGER: Bertram was chased from the playground for staring up little girls' dresses.

ADA: Once again blood proves thicker than gray matter. Bertram—*my God!*

GEORGE: Bertram is not the new President.

BILL: Who else is there besides Paul Stockwell, Bertram and you?

ADA: An outsider! The old bastard brought in an outsider!

BILL: Some hotshot from a totally unrelated field, hardly dry behind the ears, who dazzled him at a cocktail party.

GEORGE: Cold—very cold.

GINGER: Mr. Ridgeway changed his mind—decided not to retire after all.

GEORGE: Getting colder all the time.

BILL: He's liquidating. Selling the company lock, stock and barrel.

GEORGE: Frigid.

BILL: I give up.

ADA: So do I

GINGER: Ditto.

GEORGE: Mr. Ridgeway summoned me to his office at two-thirteen this afternoon. I noted the time because I sensed he'd made his decision—the occasion would be historic.

ADA: Just say who it is.

BILL: The man's had a traumatic experience—don't rush him.

GEORGE: Knocking at his door, the usual two raps neither timid nor bold, I wondered if I would ever knock at that door again.

ADA: Why?

GEORGE: Crossing to his desk, steps rendered soundless by the deep carpet whose colors and design registered with unprecedented clarity, I sensed how familiar things appeared to those en route to the guillotine.

ADA: *You made up your mind that if you didn't get the presidency you were going to quit.*

GEORGE: Yes.

ADA: How could you without consulting me?

GEORGE: Arriving at his desk, I waited for Mr. Ridgeway to look up.

ADA: Kids in college, savings zero. You had no right.

GEORGE: *I waited for Mr. Ridgeway to acknowledge me!*

GINGER: *(To Bill)* I think we'd better go.

GEORGE: And miss the denouement?

ADA: *The denouement is we're broke and you're out of work.*

GEORGE: I am not out of work.

BILL: You said you'd quit if you didn't get the presidency.

GEORGE: Correct.

GINGER: You realized that would be a foolish thing to do—changed you mind.

GEORGE: No.

BILL: I don't get it.

ADA: I think I do: George is the new president of Ridgeway Products. *(To George)* Well?

GEORGE: I cannot tell a lie.

BILL: *You got it?*

GEORGE: I got it!

BILL: *He got it! Eee-Yow! You dog—putting us on like that!*

GEORGE: I never said I didn't get it.

GINGER: You said you cried.

GEORGE: I did cry.

ADA: *(Tearful)* Because he was so happy like I am now.

GEORGE: I did not cry because I was happy.

BILL: Relieved. Weeks of uncertainty and tension and suddenly it was over.

GEORGE: Strike two.

ADA: How did Mr. Ridgeway, who hates any sort of emotional display, react to your tears?

GEORGE: It happened later—after he left for the day. I slipped into his office, the room I'd coveted for twenty-five years, leaped on the desk and proclaimed it mine—all mine.

BILL: At which point, overwhelmed, you commenced to weep.

GEORGE: Not yet.

BILL: (*To Ada and Ginger*) Not yet.

GEORGE: Contemplating the changes and alterations I would make, I felt euphoria give way to the most exquisite melancholy I've ever known.

BILL: Prepare for tears.

GEORGE: I had striven for the prize too long and too hard. It would never justify the expenditure.

BILL: (*To Ada and Ginger*) I think we're almost there.

GEORGE: Looking out the window, at the view that would have to sustain me for the rest of my working life, I remembered the night I played with Tommy Dorsey, and the card he gave me.

BILL: Once again from the Hotel Astor it's that sentimental gentleman of swing!

GEORGE: With moistened eye . . .

BILL: *At last.*

GEORGE: . . . I extracted the card from the corner of my wallet where, worn and folded, it had resided these many years. Decided to avail myself of Tommy Dorsey's offer.

ADA: I think this is where I came in.

GEORGE: Using Mr. Ridgeway's private line I dialed Murray Hill seven-four-six-five-three.

BILL: It's best to humor them.

GEORGE: After several rings someone picked up and a voice said "Lombardo's Music School—Professor Lombardo speaking." I said my name was George Brewster—that Tommy Dorsey had invited me to call this number. Professor Lombardo reminded me that Tommy Dorsey died in nineteen fifty-six—asked what kind of a sick joke I was up to. I assured him it wasn't a joke—that I was just trying to verify that the number I called had once belonged to Tommy Dorsey. "No," he said, "it's my number, the number of the Lombardo Music School and has been for forty years." I wondered aloud why Tommy Dorsey would give me the number of a music school. "Dorsey was a good friend of mine," Professor Lombardo

said. "He used to steer pupils to me whenever he could."
"Tommy Dorsey told me this was his private number," I insisted. Professor Lombardo chuckled. "I remember now," he
said. "That's what he used to tell them so they'd be sure and
get in touch with me. What's your instrument?" I said I played
the piano. "Piano's my specialty," he said. "I can give you an
hour on Tuesday at six. Usual rate twenty dollars but since
Tommy sent you it'll only be fifteen." "I'm fifty years old," I
said. "Better late than never," he said. "I haven't played in
thirty years," I said. "It's like swimming," he assured me. "You
never forget." He was telling me how to get to the school when
I hung up.

GINGER: That's the saddest story I ever heard.

GEORGE: Quite the contrary. For thirty years I'd been carrying that card wondering how much more exciting and satisfying my life might have been if I'd called that number. As of
this afternoon and my chat with Professor Lombardo I am rid
of such doubts. Tommy Dorsey conned me. My life is exactly
what it should have been. I am a happy man.

BILL: I don't suppose I could see that card.

GEORGE: Having no further need, I tore it up—scattered
the pieces from my office window.

BILL: Why did I know he was going to say that?

GINGER: Because you're cynical—have no soul.

ADA: (*To George*) I believe you.

GINGER: So do I.

GEORGE: Thank you.

GINGER: (*To Bill*) Make it unanimous.

BILL: Why?

ADA: That's what friends are for.

BILL: Okay, it's unanimous. Now what about Bermuda at
Easter?

GEORGE: You're on.

BILL: (*Raising his glass*) To the two nicest couples in Bermuda at Easter.

GINGER: Long may we wave.

ADA: Cheers . . . George?

GEORGE: Bottoms up.

(*As they touch glasses they freeze*)

Curtain

Richard Wesley

GETTIN' IT
TOGETHER

Richard Wesley

Richard Wesley, one of the leading playwrights of the Black Theatre Movement, was introduced to readers of *The Best Short Plays* in 1975 with his poignant drama of a father and son relationship, *The Past Is the Past.*

His second work to appear in these annuals, *Gettin' It Together,* is described by the author as "a steady rap" and is "dedicated to the Sisters, who gotta take so much jive from alla us Brothers." Initially presented by Joseph Papp at the New York Shakespeare Festival's Public Theatre, the play appears in an anthology for the first time in *The Best Short Plays 1980.*

Mr. Wesley was born in Newark, New Jersey, in 1945, and attended Howard University in Washington, D.C., where he studied under the noted black writers Owen Dodson and Ted Shine. He received a Bachelor of Fine Arts Degree in 1967. In 1965, while a sophomore at Howard, he received an "Outstanding Playwright Award" from Samuel French, Inc. for his play, *Put My Dignity on 307.* This same play was later mounted as an experimental production at Howard in 1967, and subsequently was seen on a local television show.

In September, 1969, Mr. Wesley joined the New Lafayette Theatre of Harlem as the managing editor of *Black Theatre Magazine* which the theatre published at that time. He remained with the New Lafayette in this capacity through 1973 and during this period he also served as a playwright-in-residence.

Mr. Wesley has written over a dozen plays, both short and full-length, and has seen them all produced, either in New York or in theatres and colleges throughout the country. His most prominent works include *The Black Terror,* for which he won a Drama Desk "Outstanding Playwright Award." Produced by the New York Shakespeare Festival, it opened on November 10, 1971, and ran for 180 performances. In 1973, The New Phoenix Repertory Company performed his *Strike Heaven on the Face* as a workshop production. It was this play that first brought him to the attention of Sidney Poitier, who was then preparing *Uptown Saturday Night.* He was engaged as a screenwriter for the film that was to co-star Poitier, Harry Belafonte and Bill Cosby and which became one of 1974's most successful motion pictures. (This was followed by another popular screen comedy, *Let's Do It Again.*)

In that same year, the author's *The Sirens* was presented at the Manhattan Theatre Club and prompted Mel Gussow to report in *The New York Times:* "As in all his plays that I have seen, the author elevates the seemingly commonplace into remarkably human drama."

The Mighty Gents, for which he received much praise, was a Broadway entry in 1978 and was revived by the New York Shakespeare Festival during the summer of 1979.

A recipient of a Rockefeller Fellowship, Mr. Wesley also has taught courses in Black Theatre at Manhattanville College in Purchase, New York, and has participated in a number of major symposiums on theatre and film.

Characters:

NATE, *twenty-five, an auto mechanic, but dreams of a better life for himself and the woman he loves. Hard because he feels he has to be; tender when it suits him. Wishes he could relax sometimes. A Brother on the go.*

CORETTA, *twenty-three, a woman in many respects, a child in others. Mother of Nate's baby. Wants his love, wants him to love her.*

Scene One

Evening. Weequahic Park in Newark, New Jersey.
The remnants of a picnic can be seen strewn about. We see Nate and Coretta lying on a blanket.

NATE: C'mon, baby, it's time for us to go. It's getting late.
CORETTA: Late? It's only eight-thirty. We ain't been here but two hours.
NATE: Well, I wanna split before it gets dark.
CORETTA: We just got out here.
NATE: I don't wanna be here after it gets dark.
CORETTA: It ain't my fault we late. You coulda got to my place sooner. You ain't never been on time to take me anywhere.
NATE: I told you I had some business with Marvin to take care of.
CORETTA: Yeah, I'll bet.
NATE: Now, what's that supposed to mean?
CORETTA: It means I don't believe you.
NATE: (*Sucks teeth in disgust*) C'mon, let's go. (*Coretta picks up newspaper and begins reading it*) Now look, Coretta, I ain't playin' with you. I said let's go. (*Coretta ignores him*) You hear what I said?
CORETTA: Yeah, I heard you.
NATE: Then why don't you act like it?
CORETTA: You know why. I ain't gonna go in early, so you can go on back out to see your other woman.

NATE: Now look, don't bring that up again, 'cause I don't want to hear it.

CORETTA: You just go on back to the house without me, hear?

NATE: Now, don't be gettin' me mad. Shit! (*Coretta ignores him. Knocking the newspaper from Coretta's hands*) Move.

CORETTA: If you think I'm gonna just let you use me like a fool, you got another think comin'. Spend all your time with that other woman, ain't hardly got time for me or your son.

NATE: I was with the boy all afternoon.

CORETTA: I thought most of your time was spent with Marvin.

NATE: I took the boy over to Marvin's with me. You can ask him.

CORETTA: You probably got him to lie for you.

NATE: Coretta, let's go before I get mad.

CORETTA: I saw you talking to her over by the baseball stands just after we got in here. You was supposed to be in the men's room.

NATE: I told you once before I never saw that woman before in my life. She mistook me for someone else.

CORETTA: You lyin' to me. You goddamn well know who that musty heffer is!

NATE: Now, why I gotta be all these liars to get along with you?

CORETTA: If the shoe fits, nigger . . .

NATE: I may do a lotta things, baby, but I don't lie. Now get up off your behind and let's go. It's gettin' dark an' I don't want these mosquitoes feastin' offa me.

CORETTA: (*Picking up fallen newspaper*) I told you I ain't goin'. I'll get home by myself. Besides, you can go meet your other woman.

NATE: Hey, baby, you gonna make me do somethin' I don't wanna in a minute.

CORETTA: Whatchu gonna do, kick me in my ass?

NATE: Maybe.

CORETTA: You can kiss my ass, nigger. You don't care enough for me to do nothin' like that.

NATE: Stop talkin' stupid. I ain't gonna hit you. Just get up and let's go.

CORETTA: I told you once I ain't leavin' here. I paid that babysitter for the whole night and I ain't hardly goin' in this early.

NATE: Look, don't try my patience, Coretta.

CORETTA: Try *your* patience?! You got a lotta nerve! You think you can make a fool outa me like you did by the grandstand and then act like ain't nothin' ever happened? You plannin' to get rid of me, man. You gonna get rid of me, and as soon as you done cut me loose you gonna go to that other woman of yours, naturally. Soon as you and Marvin go into business for yourselves and start makin' it, she'll be on your arm all over town, and I won't even be a memory.

NATE: There ain't no other woman. How many times do I gotta tell you.

CORETTA: You gonna drop me for that other woman!

NATE: You crazy. Let's go.

CORETTA: I ain't crazy. It's the truth. You lyin'!

NATE: I told you once it ain't true, and don't call me no liar.

CORETTA: Liar! Liar! Liar!

NATE: Shut up and let's go. (*He starts to pull her up but she slaps him. They stand looking at each other for a long time. She stares at him defiantly, hands on hips. Nate is still for a long time. Then suddenly he smacks the hell out of her. She falls to the ground screaming. Nate kicks her*) Get up! Get up, I said!

CORETTA: (*On the ground, screaming*) Nate, leave me alone, goddamnit!!!

(*Nate bends over and beats her some more*)

NATE: So, you was gonna play man, huh? Gonna sell me some woof tickets, huh? (*Smacks Coretta*) Gonna be so bad, huh? (*Kicks at her, but misses as she scrambles away from him*) You still wanna play man, Miss Lady? You still wanna sell some woof tickets? (*He grabs her and pulls her to her feet*) Now, that's what you gonna get every time you try to act like a man with me. Don't ever slap me, woman. Not long as you live. 'Cause every time you raise your hand to me and swing on me I'm gonna beat your ass just like I would a man. Every time you jump in my face, I'm gonna jump twice as heavy on your ass. You remember who you are and what you are, woman, you hear me? You are my woman, understand? In a fight, I will kick you in your ass every time, an' when I get tired of hittin' on you, I know some butches who'll be glad to take you off themselves. They don't like your ass, anyway. Always tellin' me how stuck up you are. You better start gettin' it together, baby, you better start gettin' it together. You a woman, and I shouldn't have to kick you in your ass to get you to behave like one. Now, go on down by the lake, wash your face, so we can get ready to go.

CORETTA: Nate—

NATE: I didn't ask to hear no words, woman. Walk. (*Coretta exits. Nate lights a cigarette, then moves about straightening up the picnic area. Presently, Coretta returns and stands by silently as he finishes. Nate hardly glances at her. After a while everything is packed away. Coretta starts off. Nate stares at her a moment*) Coretta.

CORETTA: Leave me alone, Nate.

NATE: Wait, hold it, baby. I wanna talk to you.

CORETTA: I don't wanna talk to you.

NATE: Please, baby, please. I'm sorry. (*He moves to her*) See now, baby, why you wanna make me treat you so hard? You know I don't like to. You *know* that. (*Coretta turns her back to him. Nate is about to blow up again, but thinks better of it*) Aw, Coretta, come on, now. You know how I feel about you.

CORETTA: Yeah man, you love me so much 'til you can't keep your hands off me.

NATE: Aw, bay-bee, c'mon. Now, you know I ain't hurt you all that much. I mean, hey look, whatchu expect. You made me lose my temper an' you know how I am when that happens, but baby, I promise I won't lose my temper with you knowing how I am. I'll walk away before I touch you again. But, Coretta, me an' Marvin been plannin' this deal out a long time. Now everything is just about cooled out and I can't be worryin' about that deal on the one hand and you actin' up on the other. Any man would break under pressures like that. Know what I mean? Huh?

CORETTA: What about the other woman?

NATE: Hell, no, there's only you, baby. Only you.

CORETTA: An' you ain't gonna get rid of me? Not ever?

NATE: Naw, baby. Ain't never gonna be no days like that.

CORETTA: Then stay with me tonight.

NATE: Baby, that was my intention all along. (*Kisses her on the cheek*) C'mon, let's go.

The Lights Dim

Scene Two

Later that same evening.
Coretta's apartment in Newark's South Ward. When we first see it it
will be very neatly furnished and we'll be in the bedroom. In fact,
quiet as it's kept, that's the only place we'll be, so the set ought to be
together enough to imply that the entire apartment is as together as
the bedroom.
Open in total darkness. Silence. We hear sounds of lovemaking. A
few grunts, soft moans, here and there.

CORETTA: Aw, man, you come already?

NATE: Yeah, baby, sorry.

CORETTA: (*Sucks teeth in disgust*) Shit!

NATE: Sorry, baby, my mind just ain't on what I'm doin'.
(*Sound of stirring*)

CORETTA: No, don't get up. Lay on me awhile.

NATE: Yeah, okay.

(*Silence*)

CORETTA: Nate?

NATE: What?

CORETTA: You feel alright?

NATE: Do I feel alright?

CORETTA: You ain't never stopped before; not this early.

NATE: I just got something on my mind, that's all.

CORETTA: Well, it ain't your mind I'm concerned with
right now. C'mon, Nate, honey, c'mon. Ba-a-a-y-b-e-e-e. Uh!
(*Movement as though someone is getting up*) Where you goin'?

NATE: I just wanna get up, Coretta, you mind?

CORETTA: Well, damn, you don't have to bite my head off.

NATE: I ain't bitin' your head off. I just wanna do some
thinkin' an' I can't do nothin' with your grindin' on me alla
time.

CORETTA: Well, go on and think then; don't let me stop
you. (*Stirring sound in bed*) Get off me, get off me, shit! (*We hear
a body hit the floor*) You can think all night and day, for all I
care.

NATE: See, now why you wanna do that, Coretta? You still
mad 'cause I hit you in the park (*Suddenly we hear a loud thud as*

though something were knocked over) Owww! Godamnitmother-
fuckershit!!

CORETTA: Why don't you turn on the light if you gonna
stumble around in the dark?

NATE: Don't worry about it. (*Bumps into something else*)
Damnit!!

(*Coretta turns on a lamp near her bed. We see her lying half under
the covers wearing a slip, and Nate, wearing only his shorts, is
sitting in a lounge chair frowning and holding his foot*)

CORETTA: See. You so hard-headed.

NATE: Later for you.

CORETTA: Nate?

NATE: What?

CORETTA: How come you don't feel like makin' love to me?

NATE: I told you, baby, I got things on my mind. I had a
busy day.

CORETTA: (*Ruefully*) Yeah, I know.

NATE: Huh?

CORETTA: Nothing.

NATE: You tryin' to be smart or something? You tryin' to
start up again?

CORETTA: No. (*Pause*) Nate?

NATE: What?

CORETTA: There ain't nothin' special you wanna tell me, is
there?

NATE: No, not really. Why?

CORETTA: No special reason. I just thought that maybe
what was on your mind so much might concern me.

NATE: It don't.

CORETTA: You sure?

NATE: Yeah, I'm sure.

CORETTA: Okay, if you say so.

NATE: Yeah, I say so. (*Peeved*) Hey look, what's botherin'
you, anyway?

CORETTA: Whatchu startin' to get mad for? I just asked a
simple question.

NATE: More like the third degree, if you ask me.

CORETTA: Be quiet. You'll wake up your son.

NATE: He sleeps like a log, can't nothin' wake him.

CORETTA: Where'd you and him go this morning?

NATE: To the airport. I used to work out there, just before

I met you. I showed him the airplanes and the hangars and things. He asked questions from the minute he got there until the minute he left. Then we went over to Marvin's for awhile. Yes, sir, that boy liked to drove me outa my mind.

CORETTA: Yeah, he was talkin' about his trip when me an' the babysitter put him to bed. Did you go in and say good night to him before we left? You know you're so forgetful about little things like that.

NATE: Yeah, I said good night. He made me tell him a story, but I didn't know too many.

CORETTA: You coulda told him the ones about the three bears. He's only five. He woulda liked that one.

NATE: I ain't tellin' him none of that corny stuff. I made up one about Shine and Stago-Lee. He really dug that one and went right to sleep.

CORETTA: He really loves you. Asks about you all the time. He always wonderin' when he gonna see you again. So is his mother. Today was the first time I had seen you in a week.

NATE: Yeah, baby, I know.

CORETTA: Nate?

NATE: I'm sorry I got mad at you.

CORETTA: I'm sorry I got mad at you, too.

NATE: Damn, I'm so tired. Wow.

CORETTA: Come here and lie next to me. I'll massage your back. It'll help you relax.

NATE: Yeah, I need to do that. I need to relax. I get so tired, and that little boy in the next room like to walk me to death out at the airport. Those planes really took him out.

CORETTA: C'mon, honey, c'mere.

(*Nate moves to her and plops down across the bed beside her. Coretta kisses his back*)

NATE: (*Smiling*) Hey, I thought you was gonna massage my back.

CORETTA: I am, but I had to get you to relax first.

(*They laugh*)

NATE: (*As Coretta massages him*) Mmmm. Yeah, baby, that feels so good. Lord have mercy.

CORETTA: Nate?

NATE: Yeah, baby?

CORETTA: Do I really get on your back a lot?

NATE: (*Smiling*) No, but you do a nice job massagin' it.

CORETTA: That's not what I meant, nigger. See that, you always ready to make fun of me.

NATE: I'm sorry, baby, you know I was only foolin' with you.

CORETTA: Well, I wanna be serious.

NATE: Okay.

CORETTA: You still ain't answered my question.

NATE: No, baby, you don't get on my back a lot. I was mad at you when I said that. You know how I am when I get mad. I didn't really mean it.

CORETTA: Well . . . if I don't get on your back a lot and you really like me and everything, why don't you stay with me?

NATE: Coretta, we talked about that a million times already.

CORETTA: Nate, I ain't askin' you to marry me. But I need you and so does your son. I want you here. Nate, you know I love you.

NATE: Coretta, I told you a million times, baby, I can't make that trip. I'll take care of you and my son for life. I'll be at your side whenever you need me . . . but stayin' here and marriage and alla that. Wow, baby.

CORETTA: Then what's supposed to happen?

NATE: Whatchu mean?

CORETTA: Am I supposed to sit around here and wait until you decide to come around? I ain't got no other man except you. I don't want none.

NATE: Coretta, I can't stay with you.

CORETTA: No, you never can do nothin' except knock me up and hurt me like you do.

NATE: Hey look, Coretta, I told you that you was free to see any man you liked. It ain't my fault that you haven't.

CORETTA: Nate, I love you. Don't that mean nothin'?

NATE: Yeah, Coretta, it means a lot. It really does. You know that.

CORETTA: Then why you treat me like you do?

NATE: Love and marriage is not where I'm at. Can't you understand that? You know I've told you so many times my feelings on the subject, but you just refuse to listen.

CORETTA: You could stay with me if you really wanted to, you could do that.

NATE: Well, I don't want to, okay?

(*Coretta turns from him*)

CORETTA: Then why don't you just get outa my life? Why don't you?

NATE: Don't push it, baby.

CORETTA: Don't push what? Maybe you just better not come around here anymore. Maybe I should just forget you ever existed.

NATE: (*Trying to hug her*) Hey, sweetheart, c'mon, c'mon, now.

(*Coretta frees herself from him, gets up and sits in a far side of the room*)

CORETTA: Stay away from me, Nate. Just stay away.

NATE: Hey, baby, c'mon. You know we ain't never been able to stay apart for very long. (*Smiling*) C'mon, now, c'mon. (*He laughs quietly*)

CORETTA: What's so funny? You think hurting my feelings is funny?

NATE: For a woman of twenty-three, you can sure act like a kid a whole lot.

CORETTA: Well, you just stay away from this kid. Besides, you ain't so grown yourself.

NATE: Aw, c'mon, woman, you know you ain't mad. Hey, baby, please? C'mon and finish doin' my back.

CORETTA: No. Leave me alone.

NATE: Okay, then later for you.

(*Coretta is sitting in a chair with her arms folded, legs crossed and is pouting. Nate lies flat on the bed saying nothing. They try not to look at each other, but invariably steal glances at each other, trying to detect if any effect is being had on the other*)

CORETTA: Nate?

NATE: What?

CORETTA: You don't love me, do you?

NATE: I love you, Coretta. I always have.

CORETTA: But not enough to marry me.

NATE: It has been said among men way smarter than me, that some men make good husbands and lousy fathers while other men make lousy husbands and good fathers. I guess I fit in the second group.

CORETTA: I don't need a part-time lover, Nate.

NATE: No, baby, I guess you don't. You want me to go? (*Coretta does not answer*) Do you? (*Coretta shakes her head*) Look, baby, I know what I am, and how I am. For me, marriage would not be too cool.

CORETTA: If you won't marry me, then why won't you at least stay with me?

NATE: If I stayed with you, it would be the same as marriage. I like to be on the go too much.

CORETTA: That's a flimsy excuse, nigger. I ain't never stopped you from bein' on the go before. You just don't wanna give up your other woman, that's all.

NATE: My other what? Woman, are you still on that kick? Am I gonna have to go upside your head one more time or what?

CORETTA: Don't be threatenin' me. Beatin' my ass ain't gonna change the truth.

NATE: So that's why you so concerned about whether or not I love you.

CORETTA: You spend a lotta time with her today? That why you too tired for me tonight?

NATE: Woman, I been with you and the boy all day. Use your head instead of your heart alla time. Now, how many times I gotta tell you, there ain't no other woman.

CORETTA: I'll betcha I could prove it if I wanted to.

NATE: Coretta, there ain't no other woman in this world who interests me more than you do. If there was another woman, why would I be here?

CORETTA: I don't know. Why are you here?

NATE: Because . . . hey, what kinda question is that? You know why I'm here. 'Cause of you, and how I feel about you.

CORETTA: You don't feel nothin' for me, Nate. Nothin' at all. You only come around here to see your son. You dress him up, take him out, show him off. The only reason you pay any attention to me is because I'm here so you just may as well take me to bed while you're at it.

NATE: You sure got a low opinion of yourself.

CORETTA: I'm like a lotta women I know. I'm like my mother and her mother before her. I ain't never had a man who made me feel like I was worth somethin'. Always makin' me feel so cheap. So unwanted. Nate, why you do me like this?

NATE: Hey, baby, look—

CORETTA: (*Cutting him off*) Just stay over there where you were. Don't come over here botherin' me.

NATE: Now, who's treating who bad?

CORETTA: I'm treating you like you deserve to be treated. But not nearly as bad as you treat me.

NATE: Coretta, you beginnin' to get on my nerves.

CORETTA: You gettin' on mine, too. Why don't you get dressed and go on back to your other woman?

NATE: You just ain't gonna give up that fantasy, are you?

CORETTA: It ain't a fantasy. It's fact.

NATE: I told you once, you were mistaken.

CORETTA: Oh, don't worry, I ain't mistaken. I ain't mistaken at all. I know what I'm talkin' about, you can believe that.

NATE: Woman, you don't know a goddamn thing. Don't be handin' me no okey-doke like that. You pissed off 'cause I ain't makin' love to you. Well, I told you I wasn't feelin' well . . .

CORETTA: You told me you had your mind on something else.

NATE: (*Angry*) Well, shit, same difference!!

CORETTA: Stop yellin' at me. I ain't deaf.

NATE: (*Loudly*) Who the hell's yellin'!!

CORETTA: All that loud talkin' just goes to show how guilty you are.

NATE: (*Softly*) I ain't guilty 'cause I ain't did nothin' to be guilty of.

CORETTA: Just gonna sit there and lie. Nate, you ain't shit, you know that? I don't know what I ever saw in you.

NATE: A bad motherfucker.

CORETTA: Man, if your honesty was as great as your ego you'd be into something.

NATE: Don't be funny, 'cause you ain't.

CORETTA: Neither are you. Neither is the kind of life we leadin'. It can't go on like this much longer, Nate. I ain't gonna have you walkin' all over me like you do. I waited all week just to see you. I cooked that picnic dinner we had especially for you. I been preparing that recipe all week. I wanted everything to be just right for you. I ain't never been on your back about nothin' and you know it. Ever since I first met you all I ever wanted was for us to be happy and honest with each other. There is nothing else I could have wished for, Nate. I loved you more than anything in the world. There was nothing I wouldn't have done for you, even after what I saw this afternoon.

NATE: This afternoon?

CORETTA: Ain't there something you gotta tell me, man?

NATE: I don't know what you're talking about.

CORETTA: You jiveass nigger, don't come talkin' that trash to me. Guess who I bumped into downtown today? My second cousin, Alicia. The name sound familiar?

NATE: Alicia?

CORETTA: Alicia Howard. I ain't seen Alicia in years. I used to go down to Baltimore with my mother to visit her and her family. I didn't know she was livin' up here. We stayed downtown talkin', eatin' at the Nedicks, shoppin' at Ohrbachs, everything. I was really glad to see that bitch. You can imagine my surprise when she started to mention her boyfriend's name. Your name.

(Nate groans)

NATE: Now look, baby . . .

CORETTA: No, you look! There ain't nothin' you can do or say that would change things for me. I feel like you cut my heart out. I even made myself feel that if you could just tell me the truth, not apologize, just tell me the truth . . . maybe I could forgive you. I know I ain't all that good-lookin', so I ain't gonna blame you if you go tippin' every now and then; mama told me to expect that, anyway. All men gonna tip sooner or later, but don't lie to me. Don't use me like that.

NATE: Baby, believe me. Me and Alicia . . . there wasn't nothin' between me and Alicia, honest. That's just a dream she cooked up in her own head. I can't help if the woman got a crush on me.

CORETTA: There go that ego again.

NATE: That ain't my ego. That's the truth. I mean it. Alicia Howard dig the hell outa me. I try to discourage her but it ain't no use. You know.

CORETTA: Aw, man, quit your lyin'.

NATE: Damnit, woman, I ain't lyin'!

CORETTA: You been with her today. That was her you was talkin' to in front of the grandstand at the park.

NATE: You knew all the time.

CORETTA: Some truth, that's all I wanted. Just a little truth for a change.

NATE: Boy, you really feelin' your Cheerios today.

CORETTA: No, I'm just tired of you bullshitting me, that's all.

NATE: Yeah, well okay, baby, then I think it's time we got something straight. I ain't answerable to no woman livin' for nothin' I do. Not a damn thing. If I wanna walk outa that door *tonight* and take off fifty women, I will do it and you ain't gonna do nothin' or say nothin' about it. You better get to that, baby. I put this roof over your head, I pay the rent here, I put clothes on my son's back, every stitch of cloth sittin' in your closet was bought with my money. I'm fuckin' you and you likin', so shut up! You ain't got nothin' to say. You women complainin' we men don't take care of our responsibility and we don't do enough for you. Well, I'm an example of that not bein' all together true. You better open up your eyes—all you women—'cause lookit me. I'm bustin' my ass for you and you still complainin', still runnin' your mouth. What the hell more you want?

CORETTA: Your love, your respect. That's what I want. That's all I ever wanted.

NATE: You had that.

CORETTA: No, not really. All I ever been to you is an easy mark. Just one more pussy. You brag to all your friends how I cling to you and moan your name when you do it to me? Oh, don't answer. I know you do. I got a brother. He brags like that a lot. I've heard him talking to his friends about all the women he gets. I've heard a lotta men talk that way. It shows how much respect they have for they women. How many times you brag about me? You just like 'em. Find 'em, fuck 'em, forget 'em. That's you. Only you can't forget me 'cause I got your baby. So, you give me a whole lotta material things and figure I should be happy and shouldn't want nothin' more from you. You say you love me, but do you really? You don't even respect me very much. I would have given anything if you told me the truth about Alicia. That's all I wanted to hear tonight, really. Even if you had said that you felt guilty about Alicia an' that's why you couldn't make love to me, I woulda dug that.

NATE: That's a lotta shit, too! You screamed and hollered and tried to kick me in my ass. Who you tryin' to kid?

CORETTA: I woulda been mad, but I woulda had to respect you for at least tellin' me the truth when it woulda been so easy to lie. A woman can take just about anything except bein' lied to by the man she loves.

NATE: I don't jive half as much as a lotta dudes I know. I don't see why you gotta be so hard on me. You women wouldn't be so jammed up all the time if you would stop actin' so damn babyish and start actin' like women.

CORETTA: Maybe we women won't start actin' like women until you men start actin' like men. Nate, I don't wanna be without a man. I don't like bein' hard an' strong all the time. I'm tired of bein' evil and always in a hassle over tryin' to keep my mind together. You hear?

NATE: Yeah, baby.

CORETTA: The doctor says I gotta start relaxin' more. Maybe I can't relax 'cause I ain't got a real man to help me, take care of me. I wanna have a man, Nate, to stand beside— or behind.

NATE: Yeah, baby.

CORETTA: I wanna have someone there when I'm lonely or when I'm frightened. Your son needs you to teach him how to be a man. I can't teach him that. He gotta see you more than just on weekends, man.

NATE: Yeah, baby.

CORETTA: Nate, honey, I love you; even when you hurt me like you do. Like tonight. Maybe I'm crazy, but you my man. I'd do anything to keep you, but I got pride, too. I can't go through too much more with you. You gotta start gettin' it together, man.

NATE: Yeah, baby.

CORETTA: Nate, you twenty-five years old. You a grown man, and just like my mama said to me, you the one who gonna determine the future lives of three people: Me, your son, and you. It can't be no off-the-wall jive between us, man. It's gotta be straight and true. If we ain't gonna be honest with each other, then our lives are just gonna be miserable. Nate, don't let us be unhappy like so many of our friends, like my parents. A day don't go by without my mama cursin' my father's name. I don't want that for me. I don't want our child to see me like that. You the only one who can change that. You my man, the father of my son. You everything, Nate.

NATE: Yeah, baby.

CORETTA: You hear me talkin', Nate. Ain't you got nothin' to say besides, "Yeah, baby?"

NATE: Yeah, baby, I gotta go. It's gettin' late.

CORETTA: (*Disappointed*) Oh . . . well . . . will you be comin' back?

NATE: If you want me to.

CORETTA: If you want to come back, you come back. You pay the rent here.

NATE: But do you want me to come back?

CORETTA: (*Quietly*) Yes.

NATE: Okay, then I'll be back. (*Pause*) Hey, come here. (*Coretta shakes her head*) Come here, baby, please.

(*Coretta is still kind of angry, but moves over to Nate. He takes her in his arms and kisses her, but she does not respond. He tries to kiss her again, but she turns her head from him. Finally, he lets her go. He moves across the room and begins to dress*)

CORETTA: When you comin' back?

NATE: Soon. Probably the day after tomorrow. I gotta work all day tomorrow, and I'll be too tired most likely.

CORETTA: I'll fix something special for you when you come . . . if you come.

(*The atmosphere is subdued. Nate continues dressing. Coretta watches him. She is still angry, but is now ready to forgive all. Nate is sorry, but doesn't want to show it. Once again, the game of stealing glances is played. Nate has finished dressing. He and Coretta look at each other for a moment, then he starts for the door. Coretta moves toward him. Melodramatically, they stare at each other a moment, then Nate kisses her long and hard. He moves toward the door as Coretta watches him. Nate stops at the door, ponders a moment, then turns toward Coretta*)

NATE: Uh, er, hey, baby, looka here: I think I'll stay here tonight.

CORETTA: (*Smiling, pleased, but speaking very softly*) If you want to.

(*They embrace and kiss. Nate picks her up and carries her back toward the bed as the lights go down to:*)

Blackness

Anna Marie Barlow

THE BICYCLE RIDERS

Anna Marie Barlow

Anne Marie Barlow was born in Albuquerque, New Mexico, but grew up in California and Louisiana. As the author recalls: "I wrote my first play—a terrible whodunit!—in high school when I was fourteen. I directed it, gave myself the leading part, did the scenery, props, program copy . . . all those things you do when you're already stage struck."

After receiving her B.A. from Louisiana State University, she came to New York to study acting and simultaneously did odd jobs writing for trade magazines and publicity offices. As an actress she appeared in summer stock, then made her Broadway debut in Sam and Bella Spewack's comedy, *Festival.*

"I wrote my first short play in order to have a piece of 'fresh' audition material. It came to the attention of Rodgers and Hammerstein who said of the piece, 'it shows one of the most promising writing talents in recent years.' They encouraged me to pursue playwriting and submitted me for membership in the New Dramatists. The play, *Ferryboat,* was entered in a short play contest, won first prize, and I was hooked!" Three other short plays followed, *Mr. Biggs, The Frizzly Hen* and *The Blue Tango,* all fragments of life in New Orleans. The triple bill was presented in summer stock under the overall title *On Cobweb Twine* and received considerable praise.

Further encouraged, Miss Barlow embarked on her first full-length stage work, *Cold Christmas,* which was seen at the New Dramatists and, later, in Dallas, Texas, and at the University of Delaware where it took first prize in a new play competition.

Miss Barlow was then given a John Golden Playwriting Award to complete her second full-length play, *Taffy.* According to the author: *"Taffy* went into rehearsal for a Broadway opening with a stellar cast including Kim Stanley, James Earl Jones, Lou Gosset, Michael Tolan and Cicely Tyson. But due to such catastrophic mismanagement of financing, the play, after four weeks of rehearsals, was never allowed to open anywhere and government regulations regarding financing of all future Broadway shows were permanently changed. And for a considerable time thereafter the play was tied up in the bankruptcy proceedings that followed. After that experience, I retreated from the theatre for a time to start a family and to write a novel with a Civil War background, but by page thirty I knew it had to be another play."

Meanwhile, Miss Barlow wrote the book for a musical, *Half-Past Wednesday*, which was presented in 1962 at the Off-Broadway Orpheum Theatre. Though it ran for less than a month, it served to launch the career of comedian Dom De-Luise.

The author then returned to the short play form and wrote *Limb of Snow* and *The Meeting*. Performed at the White Barn Theatre in Westport, Connecticut, and subsequently at the Off-Broadway Theatre De Lys, the pair of plays prompted Jerry Tallmer to write in the *New York Post:* "Hope springs eternal in the drama critic's breast, and sometimes, just sometimes, hope is rewarded as it was last night when we were introduced to some beautiful work by a new playwright, Anna Marie Barlow. . . . She knows people; she knows character; she knows how people think and talk; how they reveal, conceal; in short she knows how to write."

Next came a Ford Foundation Grant to complete work on her Civil War play *Glory! Hallelujah!* which was given its premiere by the American Conservatory Theatre in San Francisco under the direction of Edwin Sherin. Later, it was seen on National Educational Television.

In 1972, Miss Barlow returned to Broadway as co-author (with Don Ettlinger) of the book for the musical, *Ambassador.* Based on the Henry James novel, *The Ambassadors,* the musical starred Howard Keel and Danielle Darrieux. More recently, Miss Barlow's dramatization of Truman Capote's *Other Voices, Other Rooms* opened at the Studio Arena Theatre in Buffalo, and plans now are being formulated to bring the play to New York.

The author also has written for all of the television networks and presently is working on a new full-length play for which she received a National Endowment for the Arts Award.

The Bicycle Riders was initially performed in workshop productions at both the Actors Studio and the New Dramatists and appears in print for the first time in *The Best Short Plays 1980.*

Characters:

EDDY
PATSY

As house lights go out, there is the sound of razzmatazz music and applause. As sound builds, spotlight picks up Eddy and Patsy before the curtain, taking bows beside their bicycles. They clown with each other and with the audience.

Patsy wears clown make-up, her hair tied into several small tufts with colored ribbons. She wears bright colored knickers and wildly striped socks. Eddy is dressed in baggy pants and jacket. His make-up is exaggerated, but not as clownish as hers. Her clown effect is to be that of a sprite, his to be oafish. They are in their forties.

A loaf of French bread is tossed up onto the stage from the audience. Eddy picks it up, pretends to bop Patsy over the head with it. Getting their last drop of applause, they exit off opposite sides of the stage, rolling their bicycles with them.

Music and applause fade as lights dim and curtain rises, revealing the dressing room in a theatre that has seen better days.

The scenery is fragmentary, walls and doors are indicated, but not fully there. The effect is colorless, dingy, airless. There is a door upstage center. The dressing table is downstage center, facing audience. Two battered chairs are behind it. The table is littered with the usual clutter of jars of cold cream, Kleenex, make-up, tin make-up box, etc. The mirror that would be over the table will be indicated by the actors. A wardrobe trunk stands stage right. It is open, spilling out a few drab contents. Down right is a wash bowl. Down left is a battered chaise lounge; once grand with ornate carving, its springs are falling out and the damask is shredded.

Upstage a clothes stand holds a few articles of clothing. Running from the clothes stand to a hook on a wall behind the chaise lounge is a clothes line, which holds tights, socks and a shirt. A folding screen is up left. Up right is a large carton for packing the bicycles. A life-sized plush bear, battered, wearing a Tyrolean hat, rests against the trunk.

Patsy opens the door. She stands on the threshold a moment, almost unwilling to enter. The exuberance is gone. She looks tired, beat. She slowly moves into the room, mechanically moves down right with her bike and props it up. Leans on it, drained. Eddy enters, catches a glimpse of Patsy and wheels his bike down left. She keeps her face turned away from him. Eddy props up his bike, moves to the dressing table. He takes off his jacket, hangs it on back of chair on left side of make-up table, then sits in the chair.

EDDY: Oh, boy . . . oh, boy . . . oh, boy . . . oh, boy . . . oh, boy . . . oh, boy . . . *(He halfway sees her out of the corner of his eye; she hasn't moved. He settles back in the chair, waits a beat and then says again)* Oh, boy . . . oh, boy . . . oh, boy . . . *(There is still no answer, so he lets it wind down with a "hummmmmm" sigh and starts to take off his shoes and socks. He contemplates his foot, props the naked white foot up on the dressing table)* Look at that! God, is there anything uglier than a foot?

PATSY: Feet! *(She moves to the clothes tree, takes down an old chenille robe and crosses to behind the trunk to take off her costume and put on the robe)*

EDDY: Sometimes I say to myself, "Where are you riding to on that bicycle? Where in the hell are you riding to on that bicycle?"

PATSY: And what do you answer?

EDDY: Well . . . *(He realizes he never has an answer)* Well . . . *(He unwraps half of a sandwich left on dressing table)* Want a bite of sandwich? *(She shakes her head "no")* No? No. They put too much mayonnaise on them. Makes them soggy. Which is correct? *May*onnaise or *My*onnaise?

PATSY: The fanciest people seem to say *My*onnaise.

EDDY: Then it's probably wrong. *They're* the ones that break the rules. Too much *may*onnaise. Lousy mayonnaise at that. The oil separates. Lousy ham for that matter. God-damned lousy sandwich! *(He puts it down and gets up and starts pulling off his pants. He wears long underwear)* Isn't any better now than it was at supper.

PATSY: The pickles were good.

EDDY: Yeah, I should've gone into the pickle factory with my Uncle Charlie.

PATSY: What Uncle Charlie?

EDDY: *(He has put his pants over back of chair and sits to take off make-up)* The one I just made up, then.

PATSY: *(Tying her robe around her she moves downstage, takes his coat and pants and crosses to trunk with them, folding them neatly)*

Yeah . . . we should've gone into a lot of things I could make up. (*There is a sound of hammering offstage. Patsy stops and listens*) Are they really gonna tear this old building down? (*Sound of offstage hammering again*)

EDDY: Tomorrow. Sounds like they're starting tonight though, don't it?

(*Sound stops*)

PATSY: What do they do with all the old stuff in these buildings? (*She returns to make-up table and starts taking out the ribbons from her hair, which she rolls and puts neatly into a box*)

EDDY: Like what?

PATSY: The lights, chandeliers, carpets . . . the exit signs?

EDDY: (*Busy removing make-up*) Sell 'em to antique dealers . . . and collectors, kooks, that collect all that sort of stuff.

PATSY: I'd like one of those red exit lights.

EDDY: Why?

PATSY: Just would. (*Illustrates it with her hand*) "This way out." (*Pause*) I'd like one so I could always find the way out.

EDDY: The way outta what?

PATSY: Whatever it was I wanted to get out of, I suppose.

EDDY: (*Finished removing make-up, he takes off tie and shirt*) Oh? Well, you can probably buy one.

PATSY: From who?

EDDY: I dunno . . . whoever's tearing down the building.

PATSY: (*She takes the box of ribbons to trunk*) I really would like to know. I really do want to buy one.

EDDY: What do you want with one?

PATSY: I *told* you. (*She goes back to get his shoes, shirt, tie, etc., and takes them to trunk, packing them*) I *want* it. I think I'll come back over here in the morning and see whoever's in charge of the job and buy it then. What do you think they'd sell it for?

EDDY: Are you serious?

PATSY: Sure.

EDDY: Really?

PATSY: Yeah.

EDDY: Aw . . . you're putting me on.

PATSY: No. Cross my heart. I really want one. You can give it to me for Christmas.

EDDY: An exit sign?

PATSY: Yeah.

EDDY: Where we going to put it?

PATSY: (*Returns to dressing table and starts removing make-up*) With the other stuff that's in storage till I get a place for it.

EDDY: Why don't you wait and buy one when you get the place for it?

PATSY: Nope. I want to get it now. I bet they'd be what? Five dollars? Seven-fifty?

EDDY: Ought to give 'em away. They're worthless. (*He goes to his bike, rolls it to the carton and starts collapsing it for packing*)

PATSY: No, they're not . . . you can always . . . you always need an exit sign.

EDDY: I don't.

PATSY: I do.

EDDY: Where in the hell are you going to put it?

PATSY: I told you . . . in storage.

EDDY: Then don't buy it.

PATSY: I want it . . . and I want it *now!*

EDDY: Why?!

PATSY: I *told* you!!

EDDY: (*Very soft voice, but concentrated*) But why?

PATSY: (*She very softly now, too*) Because . . . I want to put it up to show me where to exit . . . when I don't know how to get out of someplace . . . see? (*She looks squarely into the mirror*) And more and more my life seems to be filled with moments of not knowing which way to go . . . so an exit sign on the wall leading to some avenue of escape would be very comforting in bad moments . . . see?

EDDY: (*Concerned, but puzzled*) You have a lot of bad moments?

PATSY: Enough.

EDDY: (*Still packing his bike*) Enough for what?

PATSY: To make use of an exit sign.

EDDY: (*Surprised; a little hurt*) I didn't think you had so many bad moments.

PATSY: (*Finishes removing make-up and starts packing everything into make-up box*) I don't have so many. Just enough.

EDDY: Enough for what?

PATSY: To make use of an exit sign.

EDDY: (*He has finished packing his bike and crosses down to get hers*) All right . . . you win!

PATSY: What?

EDDY: Whatever it was you were trying to win!

PATSY: I wasn't trying to win anything.

EDDY: Yes, you were and you won it. Let it go at that.

PATSY: Let it go where?

EDDY: Out the goddamned exit sign! . . . for all I care!

PATSY: See . . . that's another use you can put it to.

EDDY: What?

PATSY: Letting irritations out . . . open the door! . . . whee! . . . irritation out! . . . smoking pleasure's in . . . some such crap! You think we're going to get that dog food commercial? (*She is taking off her tights*)

EDDY: I don't know.

PATSY: How many bicycle riders do they have to audition? All you got to do is ride along and let all those dogs bark at you . . . what's that?

EDDY: (*Finishes putting up her bike*) He said he wanted the right kind of faces for the product image and they had to debate ours.

PATSY: My face isn't in line with dog food? He's right! I don't want the job.

EDDY: No. . . they didn't say that . . . they just said . . . that's why they'd let us know this week.

PATSY: They probably think we look too Semitic. We ought to wear a big sign saying we're Greek . . . that does not necessarily mean we're Semitic.

EDDY: I don't think I look Semitic. I think I look Norwegian.

PATSY: Norwegian? How many Norwegians do you know that *own* dogs?

EDDY: We aren't the dog *owners* on the bicycles. We are just the people the *dogs* of the dog owners follow. The dog *owners* are all at home in the houses we are bicycling by.

PATSY: Then why couldn't we be anything? Semitic? Norwegian? Greek? What the hell, is there some special kind of people dogs bark at?

EDDY: No, but there's some special kind of neighborhood they're trying to sell dog food to.

PATSY: Hmmmmmmm . . . that's what's wrong with show business.

EDDY: (*Takes more articles off table and up to trunk*) What?

PATSY: Too specialized.

EDDY: Oh, well . . . we can just bicycle right out of it.

PATSY: Yeah. (*Picks up partially eaten sandwich*) You're really not going to eat that sandwich?

EDDY: No.

PATSY: The ham's not so bad. What's wrong with it? It's liverwurst! That's not ham at all. It's liverwurst. Didn't you know it was liverwurst?

EDDY: No. I knew it tasted funny for ham.

PATSY: (*Pushes it away*) Liverwurst . . . and I hate liverwurst!

EDDY: Give it back to me then. I like liverwurst better'n ham anyway. (*Takes it and eats*)

PATSY: You don't still have your pickle, do you?

EDDY: Yeah, it should be around here somewhere.

PATSY: You know what I wish we could do? (*She gets her panty hose off the clothesline*)

EDDY: What?

PATSY: I wish we could get a booking on one of those cruise ships down to the Carribbean this winter.

EDDY: They don't have room for a bicycle act. You'd have to keep going round and round the deck.

PATSY: (*Laughing at the idea*) Yeah! (*She yells out*) Clear the decks. . . Fore! (*She laughs, looking up at her own hand in the air*) Yeah! (*She brings her hand down contemplating it. She puts her hand down on the oil cloth top of the dressing table and just looks at it*) Look at that hand . . . just look at it! Huh?

EDDY: I'm looking.

PATSY: And what do you see?

EDDY: Me?

PATSY: Yeah. You looking at my hand?

EDDY: Yeah.

PATSY: So what do you see?

EDDY: Your *hand.*

PATSY: No . . . I mean . . . really.

EDDY: I don't know. Nothing. Your hand.

PATSY: Yeah. Just a big, limp, lifeless, outstretched hand. It's nothing. Nothing motionless like that . . . isn't that something? Look at how nothing it is . . . stretched out like that in repose . . . but move it . . . just move it a little and see what a song it sings . . . huh? It's a whole poem to the human race.

EDDY: (*Goes to wash basin and starts washing his face*) What are those books you been reading at night?

PATSY: Translations from the Chinese.

EDDY: Yeah . . . well, China's changed a lot.

PATSY: It shouldn't have. Everything's changed. Even Yosemite Valley. Where it used to smell like the wilderness . . . now it only smells like Charcolite. God, I can't tell you how disappointed I was showing it to you last year. Here I've thought about it and remembered it since I was a little kid . . . I could always remember the smell of it . . . especially in the early mornings . . . and the way the sun slants down through those tall, tall, tall trees . . . and Goddamned! It was like a bloody trailer court! It's not fair . . . it's not fair the way things keep changing. There's nothing you can leave someplace anymore and go back and find it . . . (*He is drying off his face and she joins him to wash hers*) But what kills me the most is the way all the clean natural smells are all going. What are we going to do . . . hang toilet deodorizers from the sky? Oh God, that reminds me . . . speaking of crud . . . the john doesn't work . . . you gotta go downstairs.

EDDY: Did you tell 'em? (*He moves to chaise where he picks up his pants to put them on*)

PATSY: Are they going to fix it the last day?

EDDY: No.

PATSY: What I really want to do is get on that cruise ship . . . with my exit light . . . what else could we do? We could just go as the social directors. (*Hopefully*) I bet we could! We play cards. Dance. Tell funny stories. Smile a lot and have good breath . . . why not?

EDDY: No, I got a plan for us.

PATSY: (*Takes soap and towels to make-up table to pack them*) What?

EDDY: Not yet.

PATSY: We're going back to the bears?

EDDY: No . . . not that. I don't have it worked out yet.

PATSY: The one thing I'm not gonna do . . . is go back with any of those traveling circuses . . . no matter how much I may want to see California or Utah or any of those places I used to live . . . *no siree!* You know there are nights still I wake up and dream about that lion?

EDDY: What do you do that for?

PATSY: Because he damned near *ate* me! And that's a terrible feeling. You talk about dog food? Lions! Ought to tell them that! My face even appeals to lions!

EDDY: No, don't tell them that. It'd scare 'em.

PATSY: Why?

EDDY: They like milder dogs.

PATSY: No guts.

EDDY: (*Crosses to make-up table to look for* Variety) You know they went bust . . . ?

PATSY: The Great Western Shows?

EDDY: Yeah. I read it in *Variety* yesterday. I meant to keep it for you. I must've thrown it away.

PATSY: Jesus, no kidding?

EDDY: Well, what can you do? They lost all three of those lions, the trailer, and then the elephant died. Hard stuff to replace.

PATSY: You can't . . . you just can't beat a loss like that. Didn't they have any insurance? (*She crosses to screen up left and takes skirt from off top and steps into it*)

EDDY: There's never enough. And there was a ten-month maternity clause on the elephant and she was pregnant when she died so they lost all of that.

PATSY: We ought to get some insurance.

EDDY: For who?

PATSY: Oh, each other. If I died first you could get it . . .

EDDY: And if I died . . . you could get it.

PATSY: How much does insurance cost?

EDDY: Couple of hundred a year.

PATSY: I'd rather have a fur coat.

(*She starts taking down one end of the clothesline and he removes the other and they each start rolling up the line*)

EDDY: So had I.

PATSY: You want a fur coat?

EDDY: Yes. I've always wanted one. Just for awhile . . . anyway.

PATSY: You never told me that.

EDDY: I see myself getting off the Berlin express with it on . . . traveling the Trans-Siberian railroad.

PATSY: What about the Port Authority Bus Terminal?

EDDY: No. Kennedy International?

PATSY: Hmmmmmm. (*She thinks it over*) Maybe . . . they'd sort of *clear* the way for you! (*She parts the throngs with her arms*)

EDDY: Exactly!

PATSY: (*Eddy gives her the rope and she takes it to the trunk*) Hmm . . . I saw one in a thrift shop the other day.

EDDY: In good condition?

PATSY: I think so. I thought about buying it for myself
. . . cutting it down.

EDDY: You get the exit sign and I'll get the coat.

PATSY: When?

EDDY: Tomorrow. How much was the coat?

PATSY: Fifty dollars.

EDDY: That much? They might trade something for it.

PATSY: What?

EDDY: I don't know . . . something. Then no matter what,
we'd have the coat. What do you think they'd trade? (*He sits on
the chaise*)

PATSY: (*Coming to him*) A chandelier.

EDDY: We don't have a chandelier.

PATSY: We could unscrew one out in the lobby . . . a little
one. They're just going to give them to a wrecking crew anyway.

EDDY: Take it? Not pay for it?

PATSY: Right. I think I'm sort of entitled to it anyway.

EDDY: Why?

PATSY: Because . . . *we* were the lights when it was off
. . . and *it* was the light when we were off. It's sort of recip-
rocal . . . we belong to it.

EDDY: I don't know.

PATSY: That's the way it has to be. It's all a question of
illumination anyway. If you can't cast a little illumination in
this old world, what is there? (*The lights all go off. She gives a
little sort of a half-stifled cry*) Oh!

EDDY: What did you do?

PATSY: I didn't do anything! I was only talking about illumination.

(*The lights come back on again*)

EDDY: That's funny. Say it again.

PATSY: No.

EDDY: Why not?

PATSY: (*Moves a little distance away from him*) I'm scared!

EDDY: Aw . . . don't be.

PATSY: What could that be?

EDDY: (*Follows her*) Come on . . . say it again.

PATSY: (*Very tentatively*) Il-lum-i-na-tion . . .

(*Nothing happens*)

EDDY: (*Looks around the room like something ought to happen*)
No . . . say the whole sentence you said.

PATSY: I don't remember!

EDDY: Remember!

(*They are both whispering*)

PATSY: What are we . . . if we aren't a little . . . illumination . . . (*She hears herself and waits. Nothing happens. Relieved, she gestures "I told you so"*) See . . . (*And the lights go off again*)
Oh! I'm not doing anything, are you?

EDDY: No.

PATSY: (*Almost whimpering as a child*) I'm scared, Eddy!

EDDY: Shhh . . . say it again.

PATSY: I can't!

EDDY: Say it! Come on . . . (*He starts to spell it slowly*)
I-L-L-U-M-

PATSY: *I-N-A-T-I-O-N.* (*And the lights come back on*) Oh! (*She clutches at Eddy*)

VOICE: (*Offstage*) Hey . . . anybody left in here?

EDDY: (*Calling back*) Oh . . . yes . . . yes . . . we are . . .
we're here.

(*Patsy sinks down in chair at table. She has been really frightened*)

VOICE OF DOORMAN: Oh . . . okay . . . tell me when you
go . . .

EDDY: Righto! (*Laughing*) Oh . . . it was just him . . . it
was just the doorman fooling with the light switch . . . it was
just him . . . (*He looks at her. She slowly shakes her head*) You
don't think so? (*She shakes her head again*) What do you think it
was? (*She shrugs*) Or it's them taking down the fire curtain . . .
they've hit a cable and it keeps shorting it . . . you can hear
them down there still working on it. Oh God, but that was
funny . . . Oh God, that was funny it coming just when it did!
Ought to have an act like that . . . something magical . . .
something magical.

PATSY: (*Suddenly, with a shiver of premonition*) Let's get out
of here! It's so cold in here.

EDDY: Put your coat on instead of that flimsy thing. (*He
takes an old, beat-up coat off the clothes tree and crosses back to her*)

PATSY: It's not going to help . . . 'cause they don't have
the heat on . . . they turned it off early tonight.

(*Eddy stands her up, she is almost immobile with the cold as he puts
coat over her shoulders*)

EDDY: It's the last night. The *long* cold is setting in.

PATSY: Don't say that!

EDDY: But it won't be cold forever. The last thing they do with these old buildings is pile all the stuff that's left into a big heap and make a bonfire. A great, big bonfire. (*He goes back to screen to get her sweater*)

PATSY: (*She continues to shiver*) I don't want to talk about that either. The only thing I don't feel bad about are all the cockroaches.

(*During the following, Eddy comes back with the sweater and helps her take off coat and robe, she slips sweater on and puts coat back on over it*)

EDDY: Aw, they been moving out for weeks. There's a whole wagon train of them going up Main Street every night when I come in.

PATSY: Maybe insects are really going to take over the earth . . . become the superior intelligence.

EDDY: You don't have to become the superior intelligence . . . you just have to *survive*! Look at the Great Western Shows. Fourteen dollars is all they took in the last day in Mariposa. Poor bastards! But who wants to come to see somebody shot out of a cannon? . . . We're going to the moon! . . . (*He sits in chair to put on clean socks*)

PATSY: (*An idea suddenly dawning*) Eddy . . .

EDDY: (*Continuing*) . . . Who cares about the high wire acts? . . . What else is life every day but a high wire act?

PATSY: (*Now more insistent*) Eddy! You said they couldn't collect their insurance because the elephant was *pregnant*?

EDDY: Right! Bad luck!

PATSY: How could that elephant be pregnant? They only had the *one* elephant?

EDDY: Huh?

PATSY: How could she be pregnant? They only had *one* elephant. They only had the *one* elephant for three years.

EDDY: (*He thinks a second then dismisses it*) Well . . . I dunno . . . but she was . . . and that's why they didn't get the insurance.

PATSY: (*Afire with the idea*) Eddy! Jesus! They had the biggest attraction since Jesus Christ and they didn't promote it!

EDDY: What?

PATSY: An immaculate conception in an elephant!

EDDY: (*Like she is putting him on*) Oh, come on.

PATSY: (*Dead serious*) I mean it! How else?

EDDY: (*Shrugs*) They met another circus on the road.

PATSY: *Impossible!* Elephants are very slow to socialize.

EDDY: They don't necessarily have to socialize.

PATSY: Yes, they do. It's part of the same thing.

EDDY: No. If it was, socialism would be a more popular form of government.

PATSY: (*With the fervor of a Crusader*) Listen, Eddy, I'm telling you . . . this is *something!*

EDDY: Aw . . . (*He turns away from her*)

PATSY: (*Insistent*) Then how else?

EDDY: Well . . . I dunno . . . that whole bunch was pretty weird.

PATSY: Not *that* weird!

EDDY: What do you mean?

PATSY: What do *you* mean?

EDDY: Well . . . that trainer was a weirdo.

PATSY: Yeah . . . but I've heard of a lot of strange things . . . but never with an elephant! And anyway . . . she wouldn't have gotten pregnant . . . unless . . . (*She grabs hold of a new idea*) . . . unless it's a whole changing of the species.

EDDY: (*Rejects that*) No.

PATSY: (*Considering it, she agrees*) No . . . No . . . Then this is *really* . . . *really* something!

EDDY: (*Tries to brush it away, busies himself putting on a shirt he takes from the chaise*) Oh, Patsy.

PATSY: (*Follows him*) You stop and think about it. Wouldn't it be just . . . fantastic if the second coming of Christ would be in the form of an elephant . . . and we all just missed it . . . we all just blew it? The Hindus believe in a sacred elephant . . . a sacred white elephant.

EDDY: This one was grey.

PATSY: Colors change.

EDDY: *Everything* has an explanation.

PATSY: Christ was an immaculate conception! *No* explanation! None! Look at how many years that's lasted?

EDDY: But he wasn't an elephant.

PATSY: Well, all right . . . so it's different. That's the trouble with you and me . . . we always expect things to be the same . . . and they aren't. This old building won't even be here two months from now . . . the lights won't work and the faucets won't turn on water tomorrow . . . it's gone. And that surprises you and me . . . 'cause we can't get used to change . . . and yet change is all there is you *can* get used to.

EDDY: (*Crosses, get jacket from clothes tree*) But not elephants.

PATSY: Why not?

EDDY: (*He shrugs*) Because . . . I just can't.

PATSY: (*She thinks for a minute, then counts it off on the fingers of her hand*) Hmmm . . . first . . . I said, "What else are we here for . . . if not for . . ."

EDDY: Don't!

PATSY: (*Looks at him, and quietly, softly, determinedly goes on*) ". . . if not for . . . the purpose of illumination . . . illumination." And the lights went funny. Then, then, second, we make this discovery about the elephant!

EDDY: (*Rejecting her theorizing firmly*) No!

PATSY: You can't just say "no." You don't really believe in your heart of hearts that those lights were only the stage doorman . . . or them working on the stage . . . do you? Why is it you can't believe we are on the brink of a great *illumination?* (*The lights go out again*) Oh, God!!

EDDY: (*Loudly*) Now stop that! Stop it! Stop that!

(*A faint, faint blue light begins to seep into the dark*)

PATSY: (*This time not frightened. She stands with a sense of having been affirmed in her belief*) I'm not doing anything.

EDDY: Well, whatever it is you're doing . . . stop it! (*He starts feeling his way downstage in the dark*)

PATSY: (*Softly*) Eddy . . . stop being so scared. (*She begins to grope her way to the make-up table*)

EDDY: I'm not scared. Where are you? I can't feel you. Is that you? (*He touches her*)

PATSY: (*Her arm around him*) Yes. Listen to me. If we are big enough to be given a relevation, we must be big enough to receive it. Stop being scared.

EDDY: (*Trying to convince himself*) I'm not scared! My God! I did the cannon act, I did the high wire act.

PATSY: Yeah, but you're scared of what you don't know. I don't care . . . this is *something*.

EDDY: (*Feels around dressing table top, sits in his chair*) Where's the candle? I have a candle here in my make-up box.

PATSY: Don't light it! Let's wait. Let's wait a minute and feel what it is we are feeling in the dark.

EDDY: Cold. I'm cold.

PATSY: (*As one would evoke spirits*) No. More . . . more . . .

EDDY: More cold.

PATSY: (*Angry, but not breaking her mood*) Stop it! Stop trying to ridicule what you don't understand.

EDDY: I'm not.

PATSY: (*Coaxing him and whatever is there*) Listen and feel.

EDDY: I found the pickle.

PATSY: (*Sits in her chair*) Eddy.

EDDY: Yes?

PATSY: Do you feel a draft suddenly coming in through the door?

EDDY: No, it's been there for years.

PATSY: Listen and feel. (*Looking into mirror*) What do you begin to see?

EDDY: You . . . a little bit . . . in the dark.

(*As blue light, picking up a little luminous green, grows slightly brighter, she stares into the mirror*)

PATSY: And what else?

EDDY: (*He looks into the mirror*) Me . . . in the mirror.

PATSY: (*Hushed voice*) Yes . . . and what? . . .

EDDY: . . . and you . . . you and me in the mirror, growing brighter.

PATSY: (*Excited, urging him to keep going*) Yes?

EDDY: (*Turns away from mirror, but unable to really break out of her mood*) It's the blue light from the Canco sign . . . it comes through the window.

PATSY: (*Still hushed, but challenging him; focused on the mirror*) Is it?

EDDY: (*More hopeful than sure*) Yes, of course it is.

PATSY: (*Not breaking the mood*) It's getting brighter and brighter.

EDDY: You've been playing with that Ouija board too much.

PATSY: Eddy . . . when you move . . . the one in the mirror doesn't.

(*Eddy moves his hand, tentatively, watching the mirror, then gasps, seeing she is right*)

EDDY: Oh, God!

PATSY: (*Still not breaking the spell, almost hypnotized by the mirror*) Shhh . . . and me there. That's not me! I'm nothing but empty sockets where my eyes used to be! God, it's nothing. It doesn't move its mouth. It doesn't ask the questions. (*She puts her hand out to cover up the mirror*)

EDDY: (*Now transfixed by his own mirror*) I see me riding . . . riding endlessly, endlessly . . .

PATSY: Where?

EDDY: Up a hill, up a high hill . . . all the way . . .

(*Patsy takes down her hand to look again into the mirror*)

PATSY: Am I there?

EDDY: (*Still staring*) I don't know where I'm going. Where the hell am I going?

PATSY: (*Looking again into her mirror*) I wanted to be a revivalist at thirteen . . . there . . . right there.

EDDY: (*Still staring into his mirror*) Why didn't you?

PATSY: Because I joined the magic act instead. It seemed the same thing . . . almost . . . with that man in the tall hat. I've always been after something . . . something.

EDDY: . . . up hill . . . always up hill . . . all the way . . .

PATSY: But it always stays ahead of me . . . out of reach . . . over the cliff . . . I'm reaching . . . what does it all mean? . . . all the dead children? . . . all the hopes? . . . dead flowers? . . . but to keep going . . . to always keep going . . . keep going is the thing . . .

EDDY: . . . up hill . . . all the way. The wind at my back.

PATSY: And I'm getting closer to it . . . closer . . . it's almost mine. I can see it there . . . like a balloon in the sky . . .

EDDY: A gold balloon!

(*They both reach out for it*)

PATSY: It's lifting us . . . lifting us . . . (*They are both standing holding on to the imaginary gold balloon before them*) . . . over the cliff . . .

EDDY: . . . higher . . . higher . . .

PATSY: But what if there's *nothing* on the other side? . . . (*Then with sudden terror*) Nothing on the other side? (*There is a sound of a balloon bursting. They both see their balloon disappear. Anguished*) Oh!

(*The lights come on. For a moment, Eddy stands there beside the dressing table. He looks at Patsy, then quickly moves away from the table*)

EDDY: Come on . . . let's get going . . . (*She is motionless, transfixed*) Let's get out of here!

PATSY: (*Still breathless from what she has seen*) We are on the verge of some great revelation. Don't you see it, Eddy?

EDDY: No! My God, you just talk me into things. Why, you know what all this is? It's that doorman down there. That damn doorman down there is dead drunk! Dead drunk. That's all it is . . . (*He starts to laugh*) Oh, God, how many years has he been there? Thirty-five? And now they're putting him out to pasture. Even the cockroaches are going to another theatre. But he's going to his grandchildren who won't want him. So, why shouldn't he find what he wants it to be—in the bottom of a glass? Doorman through the whiskey glass! He is *drunk!* And he is deciding when there shall be light and when there shall be dark. It is his only time to play God, huh? . . . Before he steps out of here and slips off the curb into his grave. Maybe a slow descent of a month . . . a year . . . but he's slipping off the curb and he knows it. He sees that. So tonight is his night to write the book, see! 'Cause sometime a man has got to be in control. Maybe sometime he's got to play God, huh? Oh, my God, Patsy, he is down there laughing . . . laughing . . . at how he is scaring the hell out of us! The old drunk doorman is in charge . . . clocking in our entrances and exits . . . controlling our illumination.

PATSY: Don't use the word like that! (*She still sits transfixed*) I don't believe it is the doorman for one minute. It is not the doorman! (*She sits silent for a moment. The lights slightly dim*)

EDDY: Well, it's like I said . . . they hit a cable . . .

PATSY: No, we have been chosen. (*She hunches over her dressing table*) Oh, God, I feel so little . . . so infinitesimally little.

EDDY: (*Puts his arms around her*) Don't . . .

PATSY: I feel so little.

EDDY: We'll make out.

PATSY: That's not it. I just feel something so big is descending on me. I just feel we're on the verge of knowing what it's all gone for . . . what it's all about . . . (*She clutches at his hand*) I mean it, Eddy . . . Oh, God, I *feel* it . . . in these lights . . . in the curtain coming down . . . the shadows . . . dark corners of the room . . . everything . . . it's going to hit me like a knife in the back in a moment . . . here beneath the shoulder blades . . . it is going to come . . . the whole knowing of what the hell it is all about . . . I know it . . . (*Very breathless*) . . . don't you? . . . why else all this?

EDDY: (*Believing more than he would like to admit*) Maybe . . .

PATSY: You and me . . . we've been chosen . . . (*There is a crash offstage*) Oh, my God, what was that?

EDDY: I guess they . . . maybe they got the asbestos curtain down already.

PATSY: Now there's no separation between the imaginary world and the real . . . if a holocaust starts in one it will spread to the other. I've always taken such comfort knowing that curtain stood between. How funny . . . that's the first thing they take down before total destruction. Look at us, Eddy, which side are we really on?

EDDY: Here or in the mirror?

PATSY: In the mirror . . . it doesn't matter. It's all one now. Oh, Eddy, today's anchors must go deeper than today . . . they have to reach down to the bottomless *unknown* recesses of the sea! Let's get our exit sign now.

EDDY: Now?

PATSY: Yes. There's a screwdriver here. You can push the old candy vendor's case over in front of the door and stand up on that and get it. (*She hands him the screwdriver and pushes him out the door*) Go on. Now! Quick! I'll finish up. (*She turns back into the room to see what is left to put in the trunk. Sees the bear, holds it in her lap and begins to rock the bear like a baby*)

EDDY: (*Coming back in room with exit light*) You know, there's nobody out there at all . . . no stagehands . . . not even the doorman . . . what are you doing?

PATSY: Remembering. (*She gets up quickly. Refers to exit sign*) Oh, I love it! I love it . . . and I'm going to write them tomorrow and find out all about that elephant.

EDDY: She's probably burned or buried.

PATSY: I don't care . . . even Christ had to be dead to make it!

EDDY: (*Referring to the bear*) Are we taking this?

PATSY: (*Hands it to him*) Yes. To think we've been chosen to see—when the great disease is disbelief. Disbelief in the unknown . . . and what's so worth holding on to in the known? (*The lights go down and the exit sign begins to glow*) You see . . . (*She speaks in a hushed voice*) I am positive I am right.

EDDY: Patsy . . .

PATSY: Here . . . take my hand. Look, we can follow the exit sign. Look how it leads the way.

(*The lights are almost out, except for the red exit sign*)

EDDY: To where?

PATSY: Wherever we are going . . . our light is our exit . . . how strange . . .

(*They move out the door*)

Curtain

Robert E. Lee

SOUNDING BRASS

Robert E. Lee

Sounding Brass represents one of Robert E. Lee's few stage works written without his collaborator, Jerome Lawrence, and it is published in an anthology for the first time in *The Best Short Plays 1980.* Regarded as "a definitive dramatic study of St. Paul," the play was written to commemorate the 125th anniversary of the founding of the Reformed Church of Bronxville, New York. Its world premiere was held there on November 13, 1975, under the direction of Hugh McPhillips.

Mr. Lee was born in Elyria, Ohio, in 1918, and was educated at Northwestern University and Ohio Wesleyan University. He met Mr. Lawrence in 1942 at a New York restaurant that catered to radio talent and personnel and ever since that eventful meeting they have been one of the most productive and successful writing teams in the country. During their reign in radio, they turned out almost two thousand scripts for major network shows, won two Peabody Awards, and were co-founders of the Armed Forces Radio Service during World War II. (They also wrote and directed the history-making broadcasts for D-Day, V-E Day, and V-J Day.)

In 1948, the team journeyed from radio to the Broadway stage with their first musical venture, *Look, Ma, I'm Dancin'!* Produced and directed by George Abbott, with music and lyrics by Hugh Martin, choreography by Jerome Robbins, and with Nancy Walker starring as a bumbling ballerina, the show ran for 188 performances. Seven years later, they returned to the Broadway stage with a powerful drama, *Inherit the Wind,* based on the famous Scopes trial of 1925, with Paul Muni as the prototype of Clarence Darrow. A modern theatre classic, the play was performed 806 times in New York and subsequently was translated and presented in more than thirty languages.

After *Inherit the Wind,* the team's versatility again took successful hold with their adaptation of Patrick Dennis' novel, *Auntie Mame.* Rosalind Russell created the title role and the presentation delighted New York audiences for 639 performances. In 1966, the authors (with the invaluable assistance of Jerry Herman as lyricist and composer) turned out a musical version, *Mame,* and with Angela Lansbury as the irrepressible heroine it sang and danced its way through 1,508 performances.

Another of the collaborators' notable works for the stage,

The Night Thoreau Spent in Jail, was the most widely produced play of the 1970's. Performed in regional, community, and university theatres throughout the United States, it was presented under the auspices of the American Playwrights Theatre, an organization founded in 1963 to encourage dramatists to write for audiences beyond Broadway. Other plays by Lawrence and Lee include: *Shangri-La* (a musical based on James Hilton's *Lost Horizon*); *The Gang's All Here; Only in America; A Call on Kuprin; The Crocodile Smile; Sparks Fly Upward; Dear World* (a musical adaptation of Jean Giraudoux's *The Madwoman of Chaillot,* with score and lyrics once again by Jerry Herman); *The Incomparable Max; Jabberwock* (drawn from the boyhood of James Thurber); and, most recently, *First Monday in October,* a 1978 Broadway success that costarred Henry Fonda and Jane Alexander.

Recipients of innumerable honors and prizes, the team of Lawrence and Lee received an award for "distinguished service to the theatre" from the American Theatre Association in August, 1979.

Mr. Lee is married to actress Janet Waldo and has two children, both active in New York theatre. He holds Doctorates in Literature from Ohio Wesleyan University and in Humanities from Ohio State University. He is presently Professor of Playwriting at U.C.L.A.

Author's Note

SOUNDING BRASS *can be performed anywhere. Frankly, I wrote it for the chancel—because there seems to be a dearth of vigorous drama for the sanctuary.*

But pulpit and proscenium share the same historical roots. Religion should be dramatic; and many of our best modern plays of substance have been inspired by religious themes.

Paul fascinates me because of his imperfection, his admitted frailty, his inclination to err—which makes him one with us all.

SOUNDING BRASS *is a play about a man, not a saint. And the conflict in Corinth belongs to the secular stage no less than to the worship service.*

Characters:

XENOPHILUS, *a young Greek convert*
BOY-WITH-A-CRUTCH, *eight years old*
MONICA MAGA, *a Gnostic, a charlatan*
DEMETRIUS, *an Agnostic, a sailor*
PRISCA, *a Jewish exile from Rome, wife of Aquila*
TITIUS JUSTUS, *a well-to-do Jewish business man*
APOLLOS, *a scholar from Alexandria*
PLOUSIO, *a Hedonist, a fat Dionysian convert*
IONE, *a girl with a braised arm, an ex-virgin*
STULTISSIMUS, *a Jewish convert, devout but dull-witted*
PAUL, *the 13th Apostle*
CANTOR, *unseen*
ROMAN SOLDIERS, *unseen*
CITIZENS OF CORINTH, *Singers*

Time:

Autumn of 55 A.D.

Place:

Corinth, in the Roman Province of Achaia.

The play is performed without intermission, without scenery. It is designed for the sanctuary; the chancel is the house of Titius Justus, transept and nave are intersecting streets, at right is a raised level, the pulpit. A hinged wooden bar left marks the entrance to Titius' house.

Characterizations

(*Seven people represent the core of the corinthian church:*)

APOLLOS *has been left in charge of the church by Paul. He is charismatic, scholarly, a little vain. Though Jewish, his thinking is predominantly Greek—more logical than mystical.*

XENOPHILUS *is in his very early twenties, a Greek convert. He has a "Billy Budd" quality about him. The idea of a loving Christ infuses his whole existence. Xenophilus is not profound; he latches onto the easy catharsis of Glossalalia. He is friendly, open, vulnerable. He carries a guilt which, exposed, leads to tragedy.*

PRISCA *is in her middle years. She is a Jewish emigré from Rome. A longtime Christian, she carries a mixture of devoutness and bitterness. Prisca has deep admiration for Paul, but she resents his attitudes toward women and marriage, and she has the guts to tell him so!*

PLOUSIO *is a sensualist. A Corinthian pagan, he turned to Christianity because he could worship by eating and drinking. Plousio is bright but shallow, selfish and boisterous.*

STULTISSIMUS *runs errands, does menial work and complains about it with a stuttering stubbornness. He's young, quick, clumsy. An ardent "Judaizer," he wants the church to remain an exclusive Jewish "club," to enhance the value of his own membership in it.*

TITIUS JUSTUS *is in his sixties, the only well-to-do member of the church. His house, next door to the synagogue, is the place of worship. His late wife, whom he loved deeply, was an ardent Christian; chiefly because of her, Titius left the Synagogue to follow Paul. He is an uncertain and lonely figure of wavering faith.*

PAUL *is poorest of the lot. He is stooped, weary, unimposing. But the Holy Spirit can crackle through him like a forest fire. Paul has really only one gift—the greatest gift—a genius for being possessed. More Jewish than Greek, emotion takes precedence over logic. An exalted prophet who looks like a skid-row bum, he is in his mid-fifties but seems older. He is unshaven, greying, subject to epileptic seizures. The power of Paul comes from outside his own person; and when he is assailed on personal grounds, he reacts with a vehemence which borders on paranoia. The prophet is a mixture of man's pettiness and God's infinitude.*

(*Four people are not associated with the Corinthian Church:*)

MONICA MAGA *is a self-styled seer. She is a highly dramatic "operator" who feeds on fear and superstition. Utterly unprincipled, Monica is a flurry of veils and incantations.*

THE BOY *has the gamin freedom of an eight-year-old. He lives, like Oliver Twist, in the service of Monica's Fagin.*

IONE *is a lovely girl in her late 'teens. She has an almost barbaric fierceness. Ione has no self-pity—only outrage, pain—and wonder that people can be as decent and helpful as the Christians are.*

DEMETRIUS *is the compass needle of the play. He is a good-natured sailor from the Greek Isles. He lacks education, but he has a jester's keenness and wit. He's middle-aged—without illusions, but without bitterness. The world amuses him. Demetrius has infinite curiosity but faith in nothing—until he passes close to the magnetic field of Paul.*

Black—Distant, the melancholy chant of a Cantor.
Closer—The voice of Xenophilus, singing gibberish.
The two voices rise and fall in the darkness, a kind of musical "challenge."
The bang and clatter of brass, from another direction.
The Cantor subsides as lights rise on Xenophilus in the pulpit. Barely twenty, he has a free and open face, tousled hair. Like everyone else in the play, he wears "rehearsal clothes"—modern and causal.
His eyes are closed; he seems to be in a rapture of prophecy.

XENOPHILUS: De eenescopholis? Egalopolis? Oone-scalaba-labalis . . . ?
(*A Boy-with-a-Crutch scampers into the light*)
BOY: (*Shouting*) Get the Roman! Get the Roman!
(*The Boy is seven or eight. His crutch is only a forked tree-branch with which he knocks a battered blob of brass along the street—much as kids play street-hockey or kick-the-can. The Boy runs about easily, doesn't need the crutch. Xenophilus' concentration is easily broken*)
XENOPHILUS: What're you playing?
BOY: What do you care? Get the Roman! (*He gives the piece of metal another noisy whack with his crutch. Xenophilus leans over the pulpit, amused*)
XENOPHILUS: What's that thing you're hitting?
BOY: You can't have it—it's mine! (*The Boy holds up a*

battle-bruised helmet, puts it on his head; it's much too big for him.)
I'm a Centurion, see?

XENOPHILUS: A what?

BOY: Don't you know what a Centurion is?

XENOPHILUS: You're a Roman, and you're chasing a Roman. . . .

BOY: I'm both sides. That way I can't lose!

XENOPHILUS: (*Grins*) You can't win, either—!

BOY: (*He points his crutch accusingly at the young man in the pulpit*) You better watch what you say, or I'll have you crucified!

(*Monica's voice shrieks from off*)

MONICA'S VOICE: Brat! Little pig! Where'd you run off to?
(*The Boy reacts to the voice, scampers off in another direction. Xenophilus takes a deep breath, grips the pulpit, closes his eyes, erupts in a great cadenza of gibberish. The same syllables he uttered before. Demetrius, sitting in the audience, raises his voice*)

DEMETRIUS: Hey! Mate! You with the big words—!
(*Xenophilus keeps on going, an ecstasy of prophecy.*) Hey, crazy-mouth!

(*Demetrius whistles shrilly between his teeth. Xenophilus breaks off. Demetrius stands. He's a sailor, a rope for a belt, a stocking cap cocked on his head. He saunters into the light*)

XENOPHILUS: (*Hopeful*) Do you understand me?

DEMETRIUS: I've sailed from the Indies to Tarshish, and I know some words of almost every way men can talk . . . But *that's* a language I never heard in all my life!

XENOPHILUS: (*Sighs*) I guess that's why you can't understand me.

DEMETRIUS: What were you saying?

XENOPHILUS: (*A little wistfully*) I was hoping maybe you'd know . . . !

DEMETRIUS: (*Turning away*) You're looney. Or you're crocked—!

XENOPHILUS: (*Coming down from the pulpit*) I'm fishing. I'm a fisherman.

DEMETRIUS: Dry land is a poor place to catch fish.

XENOPHILUS: I'm fishing for men. That's what my Master did.

DEMETRIUS: Oh, you're a slave?

XENOPHILUS: (*Scornfully*) I'm not a slave, I'm— (*Breaks off, thoughtfully*) Well, maybe I *am* a slave, in a way . . .

DEMETRIUS: You don't know *what* you are, do you? Where do you come from?

XENOPHILUS: I don't come from anywhere.

DEMETRIUS: Everybody has to come from *some* place.

XENOPHILUS: If I went away from Corinth, I could tell you I came from Corinth. But since I haven't left Corinth, how can I say that I come from a place where I already am?

DEMETRIUS: Are you a drinking man?

XENOPHILUS: I'm intoxicated with the Holy Spirit!

DEMETRIUS: I don't know what kind of a grape *that* comes from, but it's done the job for you. (*Sits on the steps of the chancel*) In Rome, when you go to the theatre and some clown comes bobbling out on the stage up to his hair-line in wine, you know what they say? "Ahhh, here comes the Man from Corinth!" (*Both laugh*) It's got a wicked reputation, Corinth has. The crossroads between perdition and damnation. Any town with so many temples has got to be rotten with sin.

XENOPHILUS: You haven't heard the good news—!

DEMETRIUS: Is there any *left* in the world?

XENOPHILUS: (*He looks up, seized with another burst of ecstasy*) De eenescopholis? Egalopolis? Oonascalabalis—!

DEMETRIUS: (*Covering his ears*) Oh, let's not go into that again!

XENOPHILUS: I'm telling you the good news!

DEMETRIUS: Look, mate, all the good news I need is a place to sleep until my ship sails again.

XENOPHILUS: (*With a smile*) Someone in our church will find you a place to stay. (*Extending his hand*) My name is Xenophilus.

DEMETRIUS: Zen—?

XENOPHILUS: Xenophilus.

DEMETRIUS: (*Askance*) Is that one of those words you just made up?

XENOPHILUS: For twenty-two years it's been my name. You know what it means?

DEMETRIUS: (*Skeptically*) Do you?

XENOPHILUS: It means "Friend to Strangers" . . .

DEMETRIUS: (*He smiles, takes the young man's hand*) I'll make no quarrel with that. Xenophilus, hm? Well, you may be a little bit crazy. But who isn't? Madness is like salt: no good for a steady diet—but a dash of it seasons the meat of the mind— and keeps it from spoiling on a long voyage.

(*They laugh. Monica Maga storms on. Merely breathing is high drama for her. She wears something gauzy and flowing which she flails about theatrically*)

MONICA: (*Angry*) Boy? When I find you, I'll beat you until your backside is blue— (*Breaks off, sweetly*) I'm looking for a precious little boy; have you seen him?

XENOPHILUS: What does he look like?

MONICA: A mean little monkey—and about high enough to walk under a donkey's tail without stooping.

DEMETRIUS: Are you his mother?

MONICA: Mother! He never had one. He was *whelped!* And he'd be dead by now if it weren't for me. Oh, when I get my hands on that little brat-of-a-bitch! You see the kind of treatment people get today in return for sweetness and generosity . . . ?

XENOPHILUS: A boy came by with a crutch—

MONICA: You've seen him! Which way did he go?

XENOPHILUS: I don't think I'll tell you.

MONICA: Why not?

XENOPHILUS: I didn't see anything bad about him. Nothing evil.

MONICA: (*Disparagingly*) What do you know about evil?

XENOPHILUS: I know a lot of things. I'm a prophet.

MONICA: A prophet!? (*She laughs*)

XENOPHILUS: I'm trying to be a prophet.

DEMETRIUS: Oh, he's a prophet all right, I'll swear to it, I've heard him prophesy! And it's an awesome experience for the human ear . . .

MONICA: (*Skeptically*) I don't believe it.

DEMETRIUS: Now I wouldn't stand for that, Xenophilus! (*Pushing him toward the pulpit*) Get up there and give her a sample of how a good, first-rate prophet can rattle the air. I've sailed from the Golden Horn to the Gates of Hercules and never heard anything like it.

XENOPHILUS: (*In the pulpit*) I have to wait until the Holy Spirit moves me . . .

DEMETRIUS: (*To Monica*) It's worth the wait. (*Xenophilus lifts his arms slowly, his eyes toward heaven*) And he may go off sooner than you expect—!

XENOPHILUS: (*Chanting, loudly*) De eenescopholis? Egalopolis? Oonescalabalabalis . . . ?

MONICA: What's that supposed to be?

XENOPHILUS: I'm speaking in tongues . . . !

MONICA: (*With contempt*) That's no tongue and you're no prophet.

DEMETRIUS: How do you know?

MONICA: Because I'm Monica Maga, the magician. I can see past and future, I understand all languages and all mysteries—

DEMETRIUS: Except where a small boy has run off to.

MONICA: I'll find him! (*She starts off*)

XENOPHILUS: Oon—esca—laba—labalis!

MONICA: (*Calling back*) That's gibberish!

XENOPHILUS: (*Passionately*) It's truth! The wind of the Holy Spirit blows through me. I prophesy in the name of Christ Jesus, and if you really understood all—

MONICA: (*She stops short*) You're a Christian—? (*Xenophilus is wary, doesn't answer. Demetrius is intrigued. Cat-like, Monica begins to stalk back toward the pulpit*) Ahhh, the veil is lifting . . . ! But how foolish you are—to use the sacred language of the Christians on a public street—

XENOPHILUS: It isn't secret. The teachings of Jesus are for everybody . . .

MONICA: (*Scoffing*) How little you know . . . ! There's great magic in the art of Saint Jesus. But magic is fire: you have to be careful!—it warms, but it can also burn, like hot coals! Many times I've done miracles just by whispering the name of the mighty magician Jesus—along with certain words and wizardry known only to a few . . .

XENOPHILUS: If you're a Christian, why haven't I seen you worshiping at the house of Titius Justus?

MONICA: (*Soaking up the information*) The house of Titius Justus. . . ? Prove to me you're a prophet! I don't think you know where Titius Justus lives.

XENOPHILUS: (*Pointing toward the chancel*) There's his house—right beside the synagogue.

MONICA: That's very good! You may be a prophet, at that! —a minor one, when I teach you more of the mysteries . . . !

DEMETRIUS: Now hold on, hold on—just a minute. Both of you pray at the same faith, bend a knee at the same altar and all that . . . how is it you've never seen each other . . . ?

MONICA: (*She glares at the sailor*) My presence is not always known. Sometimes the human eye can't see me.

DEMETRIUS: You're invisible. Like that small boy you're yelling your lungs out to find . . .

MONICA: Doubter! Friend of fiends! (*Furtively, to Xenophilus*) He wouldn't trust a sign—even if the rivers ran blood and the clouds rained salt water!

DEMETRIUS: (*To Xenophilus*) She's a fake!

MONICA: He's got the key to hell in his pocket. Don't waste the breath of the Holy Ghost on him.

DEMETRIUS: If she's a Christian, I'm Alexander the Great. (*Poor Xenophilus is caught in the cross-fire. Monica has the last word*)

MONICA: Don't believe him, believe *me!* (*She starts off, turns, eyes narrowing*) Because I know who you are! (*She points a finger at Xenophilus*) Your father was killed in the Lydian Wars . . . ! (*She sweeps off*)

XENOPHILUS: (*Stunned*) How did she know that?

DEMETRIUS: The woman's a witch. Give her a wide berth, that's a sailor's advice. Keep her well to windward. (*The sailor sits on the chancel steps, toys with his stocking cap*) Are you really a Christian? An Honest-to-God Jesus Christ Christian?

XENOPHILUS: (*Coming down from the pulpit*) Baptized in the bay of Corinth. You know, I'm very lucky to be a Christian; not many pagans get into the church.

DEMETRIUS: (*Stretching his legs*) How did you have the misfortune to fall into this monstrous good luck?

XENOPHILUS: (*Sitting beside the sailor*) I dunno. I've been hungry most of my life—not so much in the stomach as in the heart.

DEMETRIUS: That's an ache you can't cure by roasting a rat on a stick. Stomach food can be salted, shipped, stored. *Soul* food is harder to come by. (*Xenophilus suddenly buries his face in his hands, weeping softly, bitterly. Surprised, the sailor stands—puts a hand on the young man's shoulder*) What's the matter with you, boy? You've got your hearing and your hair. More years ahead of you than behind, your nose is in a proper part of your face. And you're blessed with being a Christian—with guaranteed citizenship in the world to come. What more could a young man ask for?

XENOPHILUS: (*Struggling against tears*) But I—I'm wicked—!

DEMETRIUS: Who isn't! I'd shiver in my shoes to meet a perfect man; thank the gods, perfection hasn't been perfected.

XENOPHILUS: (*Gravely*) One man was perfect.

DEMETRIUS: Oh? That's bad news for the world. Your Jesus, is it?

XENOPHILUS: He was so good, people couldn't bear to look him in the face.

DEMETRIUS: And so they crucified him? (*The boy nods, sadly*) I'm in favor of flaws; *im*perfection is what keeps life going. Do you ever think about the cycle of the fishes?

XENOPHILUS: (*With little laugh*) Not often—!

DEMETRIUS: (*Expounding, mock-socratic*) Now *I'll* play the prophet for the time it takes to trim a sail. How does a fish fill his belly?

XENOPHILUS: By eating?

DEMETRIUS: By eating what?

XENOPHILUS: Other fish?

DEMETRIUS: Right. A guppy eats a tadpole, and a herring eats a guppy, and a flat-fish swallows a herring, and so on and so on and so on. Now suppose there were such a thing as perfection in this world. And every size of fish did a perfect job of swallowing up every fin of the next size smaller. What would we finally see in the sea . . . ?

XENOPHILUS: (*Thinking*) I guess there'd finally be just one great big fish.

DEMETRIUS: And how would that fish fill his belly—having perfectly devoured every smaller fish that swims? He'd starve to death, and cease to be! That's the end that perfection leads to. So cherish your blemishes, boy—not being perfect is what gives you work to do and sharpens your eye and your appetite. Perfection is standing still—a ship caught in irons. Avoid it, at all costs! My own good health comes from a lifetime of evading perfection. You do the same!

XENOPHILUS: But the Master says we should strive to be perfect—even as the Father in Heaven is perfect.

DEMETRIUS: Strive? Fine. Just be sure you don't make it!

XENOPHILUS: (*Morosely*) I'm the least perfect of all creatures on the flat platter of the Earth . . . !

DEMETRIUS: Oh, the Earth's not a platter. It's a *bowl!*

XENOPHILUS: A bowl? How do you know?

DEMETRIUS: It must have some kind of a *rim* around it. (*Shaping the edges of a bowl with his hands*) Otherwise all the water would run out. And we'd find ourselves walking around on a sea-bottom as dry as the sands of Ethiopia.

XENOPHILUS: I never thought of that . . . !

DEMETRIUS: When you want an answer to the difficult questions of this life, ask a sailor. You may not get the truth, but by Jupiter you'll get an answer.

XENOPHILUS: I'm not hungry for answers. What I care about is feeling. Before I was a Christian, I felt—dirty. Now I'm clean. Cleaner, anyhow. I'm afraid to understand too much. I just want to be saved.

DEMETRIUS: Saved? For what? And from what?

XENOPHILUS: I'm not sure. . . . If I could just know what I was saying when I prophesy—!

DEMETRIUS: You Christians are a curious sack of souls! I'd like to think one whisker of me is worth saving—good for something besides the stink of the bone-pile. (*Strokes his chin*) This last voyage out, I met a man who might've been a Christian. He was poor as a jailhouse mouse. Came aboard ship at Ephesus, a deck passenger, without so much as a copper coin to rent a hammock to sling himself to sleep in. I was on watch, from midnight to moonset. And I found him curled up in a coil of rope, wet from sea-spray. At first I thought he was asleep. But then the moon caught his eye, and I saw he was watching me . . . ! And his eyes spoke—as clear as if his throat had made a sound. "The God who crafted you puts high value on His handiwork. . . ." I swear to you, boy, that's what his eyes said to me: "You're good for more than dying . . . !" Right then, the prow of the ship dug into a mountain of a wave and threw a cold splash of the sea onto the poor devil of a saint curled up in the damp coil of the rope—and he shivered, and I drew a stretch of canvas over him to shield him from the wet—and he thanked me with his eyes . . . And I never spoke to him—nor he to me—but I think he was a Christian . . . He left ship when we came into harbor in Thessaly . . . (*Xenophilus has listened intently*) The gods willing . . . *God* willing . . . I'd like to meet that man again!

(*Both men are thoughtful as the lights slowly fade. In the black, Xenophilus and Demetrius clear. Again, the Cantor's melancholy chant, nearer and more sonorous. Then, the crash of brass, as before—the crunch of the crutch hitting the Roman helmet*)

BOY'S VOICE: (*Off*) Get the Roman—!

MONICA'S VOICE: (*Off*) Brat! I've got you—! (*In the dark, the Boy yowls in protest, screaming as the woman pours verbal vitriol at him*) Run off, will you? Little bastard of a bitch, son of a dog and a demon—!

BOY'S VOICE: (*Simultaneously*) Let go! Whad I do? Leggo my ear—!

MONICA'S VOICE: When I tell you to stay out of sight, off the streets, there's a reason—and you know what it is! Run off again, and I'll pound your bottom with that crutch so hard you won't be able to sit and you won't be able to stand. You're going to need that crutch, you shrunken little runt of a litter of mongrels—!

(*The voices of the angry Monica and the yowling Boy trail off in the distance as she drags him off, screaming. From the other direction, again the call of the Cantor. . . . Lights rise on the dining room of the house of Titius Justus within the chancel. Prisca enters with a cloth which she spreads on the communion table, center. Then she crosses to get a dozen brightly colored prayer-shawls, which she drapes in rainbow succession along the chancel rail. Prisca is in middle years—a fine, firm face—but with some bitterness in the set of her mouth. She pauses, looks toward the sound of the Cantor's prayer with a troubled reverence. Titius Justus enters from upstage right, watches her. He is the most patrician in a gathering of common Corinthians*)

TITIUS: Is everything ready for the service?

PRISCA: No. But it will be.

TITIUS: Who told you to dye the prayer shawls?

PRISCA: I told myself.

TITIUS: Would Paul approve?

PRISCA: I don't know. And I don't know that I care. (*Putting the last scarf in place, a bright scarlet*) There's enough bleak and black in the world.

TITIUS: Amen.

PRISCA: And if beauty and color have *any* place, it's in the worship of the Messiah.

TITIUS: (*A short laugh*) Dear Prisca! You sound like my wife!

PRISCA: God rest her.

TITIUS: She had a gift—*you* have it, too, Prisca—of—I don't know quite how to say it . . . ! Her faith was *sure.* You heard about Sosthenes . . . ?

PRISCA: (*Nods*) I heard.

TITIUS: My wife could have persuaded Sosthenes. *She* could have stopped him.

PRISCA: Or Paul.

TITIUS: Oh, yes, Paul—of course, Paul would have persuaded him. If Paul had been here . . . (*Again, the voice of the Cantor. Titius frowns*) I think the church should meet farther from the synagogue. How can we worship by the new covenant when we're within earshot of the old?

PRISCA: (*Wryly*) Do you plan to move your house to another part of Corinth?

TITIUS: (*With difficulty*) No . . . but I've been thinking that—it might be better if—

PRISCA: If the church stopped meeting at the house of Titius Justus . . . ?

TITIUS: I don't know what to believe. It used to be so clear . . . ! When we broke the bread and drank wine together, with Paul. It was a feast of beginnings. Now it's nothing but endings . . . (*He takes one of the scarves. There is respect and warmth between these two—even a sad kind of love*) What do you hear from your husband?

PRISCA: I don't think I have a husband. Paul has weaned him away from women. Now he's the bridegroom of the Christ—and to hell with his wife. We're adrift on the same raft, Titius: widow and widower. Your spouse is in heaven; mine is abroad in the world, saving everybody's soul but mine.

TITIUS: (*Gently*) Prisca . . .

PRISCA: (*Turning away, a little ashamed*) Forgive me, it's easy to be bitter.

TITIUS: (*He puts a comforting hand on her arm*) Don't you think Jesus was bitter—when he saw the Roman guards coming to arrest him?

PRISCA: (*Shaking her head*) Paul says that bitterness is a dry root that has no food or juice in it. If you swallow, it makes you sick. And even if you spit it out, the taste sticks to your tongue, makes wrinkles inside your mouth.

TITIUS: Do you ever wonder if Paul ever saw the Christ?

PRISCA: In the flesh? He could have. I think he knew more of the Christ than I know of my husband.

TITIUS: (*With a wry jubilation*) What if it's all some colossal hoax??? What if a man called Jesus never lived in our time? Never taught, never preached, wasn't crucified, never rose from the dead . . . ? What if the whole thing is just a delusion in the fevered head of a guilt-soaked Pharisee? What if Paul made it all up????

PRISCA: Jesus lived.

TITIUS: What a joke it would be! And how the gods must be laughing at us . . . !

PRISCA: No, no, Titius. My husband and I were in Rome when the good news came to us—bit-by-bit—from travelers who came from Judaea and the edges of Egypt. We knew the good news before we knew Paul. . . .

TITIUS: But how illogical it is—! (*Apollos enters the chancel from upstage right, carrying a staff with a banner which has the bold outline of a fish. He pauses to listen to Titius, who doesn't see him. Apollos is tall, imposing, authoritative*) Would a rational God send the Saviour of Mankind—His own Son, no less!—to the barren back-country of Galilee? Ridiculous! A wise God would have sent His saviour to the capital of the Caesars! Or at least to a place where there's some flow° of commerce, like Corinth—

APOLLOS: So you're giving advice to God—! (*Titius turns, sees Apollos*) Very generous of you. But you're a rich man, aren't you, Titius? Richer in silver, I think, than you are in wisdom. Who needs a logical *miracle*? What makes a miracle miraculous is that it couldn't possibly happen! (*He crosses down left and places the "Fish Banner" in a standard—inclines his head in a breath of reverence*)

TITIUS: Is that the kind of lackluster logic you used to stop Sosthenes from leaving the fellowship?

APOLLOS: I do not "stop" anybody. In Paul's absence, all I do is broadcast the good news. A man has ears? Let him hear.

PRISCA: A good shepherd doesn't let the lambs go astray.

APOLLOS: (*Exasperated*) What can I do? I can't *make* a man believe. The love of Christ Jesus enters the heart by Grace, by the Grace of God . . .

TITIUS: (*Throwing up his hands*) Not "Grace!" When you get off on the "Grace of God," I'm lost!

APOLLOS: A brother is free to worship with us, or he's free
to leave.

PRISCA: This church is so free it's almost worthless.

APOLLOS: If a man believes in the teachings of Jesus—

PRISCA: Sosthenes believed!

APOLLOS: If he'd believed, he wouldn't have gone back to
the synagogue.

PRISCA: He believed he believed.

APOLLOS: A man must be a *true* believer.

TITIUS: And what is truth?

APOLLOS: You sound like Pontius Pilate!

TITIUS: (*Angry*) Damn me for being rich—but don't brand
me a Roman official.

APOLLOS: You brand yourself as a wavering Christian!

TITIUS: (*Outraged*) I let the scum of Corinth into my house
for worship! I've given more for the Saints in Jerusalem than
everybody else in the church—

APOLLOS: You have more to give.

TITIUS: Well, I may be through with it.

APOLLOS: If your wife could hear you say that—

TITIUS: She does hear me! Jesus has given her eternal life!

APOLLOS: You ache for the flesh! How do you expect to
find heaven?

TITIUS: Can you lead me? You don't know the way!

APOLLOS: Heretic! Barbarian of no faith!

TITIUS: You call me a barbarian?

APOLLOS: I call you what you are!

(*They shout simultaneously*)

TITIUS: False priest! Fishmonger!

APOLLOS: Miser! Gold-worshiper!

PRISCA: (*Coming between them*) Stop it! You're calling each
other names like a couple of schoolboys! My God, it's a wilderness and we're all lost . . . !

(*A crash of pottery and glass from off, left. Voices in argument—the
drunken Plousio and the agitated Stultissimus. Prisca, Titius and
Apollos look at one another*)

APOLLOS: Who's in the kitchen?

PLOUSIO'S VOICE: Just a little blood! All I need is a little
blood—!

PRISCA: Plousio—! (*Prisca and Apollos hurry off left. Another
crash*)

TITIUS: (*Hopelessly*) Now I'm contributing crockery to the cause—!

(*Xenophilus and Demetrius enter the transept from right, walking along the street toward Titius' house*)

XENOPHILUS: Understand, our church welcomes strangers. But we do have enemies, so we have to be careful.

DEMETRIUS: Why don't I just say I'm an old friend? We *are* friends, aren't we? (*Xenophilus nods*) And I'm older than you are by enough winters to make it less than a lie. Oh, one favor, though. (*Apologetically*) Do you suppose your fellowship could find something solid—to silence the space below my ribs? I'd be a boor to disturb your prayers with a growling stomach.

XENOPHILUS: (*With a smile*) Eating is the way we worship! (*The sailor is puzzled*) It's all very peaceful and comforting. You'll see. Come on! (*He leads Demetrius into the chancel. Titius turns to face them*) Titius, I want you to meet an old, old friend of mine. His name is— (*Breaks off*) I don't know your name. (*Titius is skeptical*)

DEMETRIUS: What he means is that we are very *fast* friends. That is, we became friends very fast. They call me Demetrius.

TITIUS: You've come to worship with us?

DEMETRIUS: If you don't mind.

TITIUS: (*Shaking his head*) You don't know what you're getting into. (*He sorts the scarves on the chancel rail*) I used to know a silversmith in Ephesus named Demetrius.

DEMETRIUS: No relation. Silver and I are strangers.

TITIUS: What's your field?

DEMETRIUS: Wet. I'm a sailor.

TITIUS: I hope you haven't lost your sea legs. This deck has a pitch and roll to it—! (*He puts one of the bright scarves around the sailor's neck*)

XENOPHILUS: Are these new?

TITIUS: The colors are. In the Hebraic tradition, we like to wear prayer shawls for worship. Don't worry, it doesn't commit you to being a Christian. When we're through, if you're sufficiently disquieted, you can take the scarf home and hang yourself. (*Xenophilus is surprised at Titius' mood*) Since I'm already home it's a shorter trip for me.

DEMETRIUS: Are you a priest?

TITIUS: (*With a short laugh*) A priest!? Hardly! I'm more of a dispossessed sexton. A jester in the royal court of the King of Kings. (*Sadly*) Or maybe I'm just an unholy ghost haunting my own house . . . !

XENOPHILUS: I've never heard you talk like this—!

TITIUS: It may be the darkest hour just before dawn—but I think the brightest sky is at sunset—and then the world goes black! That's why Prisca arranged this rainbow for us . . .

DEMETRIUS: (*Warily, to Xenophilus*) I think I'll get out of here—!

XENOPHILUS: Wait—hear the Good News—!

DEMETRIUS: (*Glancing at the morose Titius*) Has he heard it? I don't know if I can stand it to be as happy as he is . . . !

(*There is a commotion left. Plousio bursts in followed by a distressed Apollos. Plousio is an intelligent slob—too smart to work, not lucky enough to come from a wealthy family*)

PLOUSIO: (*Thickly*) What's all the discombobulation? All I want is a little "Body!" And a little "Blood!" Bread and wine—that's the brick and mortar that holds a man together, isn't it?

APOLLOS: For God's sake, Plousio—!

PLOUSIO: That's right, Sir. For God's sake! When I was a pagan, this would just have been eating. (*He hiccups*) And drinking. But now that I'm a baptized Christian, I can feed my face and save my soul at the same time!

PRISCA: (*She goes in and out from the kitchen left, setting the table, placing the menorah. Disdainfully*) Pig!

APOLLOS: Plousio, you can't celebrate communion all by yourself!

PLOUSIO: Oh, is that a rule you just made up! Don't you know there *aren't* any rules any more? No rules—!

(*Stultissimus, gaunt and whimpering, enters from the kitchen. He stutters, always on the defensive*)

STULTISSIMUS: He-he broke into the k-k-kitchen, and s-s-s-started to eat and d-d-drink and I t-t-tried to s-stop him and he t-t-told me a b-b-big lie! About K-k-k-king David!

PLOUSIO: (*With drunken thunder*) Dolt! It is written that when King David was hungry, he demanded holy bread and the priests gave it to him, didn't you know that? Ha?

STULTISSIMUS: What business does a p-p-pagan have t-t-telling a J-j-jew about King D-d-david!?

PLOUSIO: Because you're *stupid*.

STULTISSIMUS: So I'm a little bit stupid. The Messiah d-d-didn't say: "You have to be smart in order to b-b-be s-s-saved!"

PRISCA: (*Gently*) Stultissimus, come help me in the kitchen.

STULTISSIMUS: D-d-do this, d-do that! Everybody orders me around!

(*He follows Prisca off left. Plousio weaves over toward Demetrius and flings an arm around the sailor's shoulder*)

PLOUSIO: But we're all brothers aren't we, Brother? Sons of God and Brothers in Jesus, isn't that great, old friend, old friend—? (*He looks into Demetrius' face. Stops dead*) Who are you? I never saw you around here before.

DEMETRIUS: Don't worry—I won't be staying long.

XENOPHILUS: He's an old friend of mine—

PLOUSIO: (*He flings a drunken arm around Xenophilus*) Hi, Xenophilus! How's old jibber-jabber these days? Ya know, I'm so full of blood I bet I could almost understand you! (*Laughs drunkenly, then turns to Titius*) Somebody's watering your wine, did ya know that, you old sourface?

TITIUS: (*To Apollos*) I think we should only admit Jews to the fellowship.

PLOUSIO: (*Wryly*) Jews like Sosthenes? You better watch out. Ya know what is going to happen? You're going to wind up without any Jews at all in your Messiah-Club. (*He staggers up toward the altar rail and looks at the remaining scarves*) OOOOOh! Pretty colors!

TITIUS: What has this boob of Bacchus ever given to the church or to the saints in Jerusalem?

PLOUSIO: (*Grandly*) I know it is more blessed to give than to receive. But *I'm not selfish* like *you* are, Titius. *Smaller* blessings are enough for me. The glory of giving is for greater than I; just let me receive a little—not much—just a little. That's all I ask.

(*Stultissimus and Prisca re-enter with the earthenware plates and wine cups*)

XENOPHILUS: (*To the sailor*) You will stay and break bread with us—?

DEMETRIUS: My good sense tells me to go. But my stomach says: why hurry?

APOLLOS: Where are the stools?

PRISCA: Stultissimus, go get the stools.

STULTISSIMUS: D-don't order me around!

TITIUS: (*Ironically*) Shall we celebrate the Lord's Supper standing up?

PLOUSIO: *I* did!

APOLLOS: (*He raises his voice above the bickering*) Let us gather in a reverent spirit! It is proper for us to share in the work, as we share in the joy of fellowship with the Son of God . . . ! (*They gather stools. Apollos is center—Prisca, Plousio and Stultissimus at his left, Titius, Xenophilus and Demetrius at his right. All have draped prayer shawls about their shoulders. Apollos lifts his arms, closes his eyes; his voice is sonorous*) Most esteemed Jehovah, our Father Which art in Heaven, we Thy unworthy children do humbly salute Thee, and give thanks for the bounties which Thou has showered upon us—

STULTISSIMUS: (*Interrupting*) I don't llike my shawl! (*Rustle of reaction; but Apollos continues*)

APOLLOS: —which thou hast showered upon us like a welcome summer rain . . .

STULTISSIMUS: Why can't I have a g-green one—like Xenophilus has—?

PRISCA: (*Throwing up her hands*) Why didn't I make them all the same color!?

APOLLOS: Why didn't God make men all the same color?

TITIUS: (*Scratching his chin*) It would have simplified things.

(*In a good spirit Xenophilus gets up, offers his scarf to Stultissimus*)

XENOPHILUS: You want this one? Here, we'll trade.

STULTISSIMUS: Sholom aleichem.

XENOPHILUS: Aleichem sholom. (*Xenophilus returns to his place*)

TITIUS: (*Puzzled*) How do you know that? You're not Jewish.

XENOPHILUS: (*Shrugs*) I don't know. The Holy Spirit must've whispered it to me . . . (*He sits, lowers his head*)

APOLLOS: (*Lighting the menorah*) As these candles bathe our lives with light, so let Thy wisdom illuminate our spirits. And may the goodness of Jesus fill our souls.

DEMETRIUS: (*He whispers to Xenophilus*) When do we fill our stomachs?

XENOPHILUS: (*Softly*) Shh—I'm praying.

DEMETRIUS: So am I. I'm praying that he'll stop praying so

we can get on to the eating. Oh, does the food have to be consecrated to the great god, Jesus Christ?

XENOPHILUS: The food *is* Jesus.

DEMETRIUS: (*Astonished*) And we *eat* it—?

XENOPHILUS: (*Nods*) By eating we're part of him, and he's part of us.

DEMETRIUS: Well, that's a switch! The pagan priests give the gods burnt offerings. I don't know if Dionysius would relish being served up as a meal for hungry worshipers!

APOLLOS: (*His voice is rich and resonant*) Two and twenty years ago, the anointed Son of God walked the hills and valleys of Judaea—even as did Isaiah and the prophets before him. But greater is He than they. Greater, too, than Socrates, the Wise, or eloquent Demosthenes of Corinth, greater is Jesus than Aristotle, setting the world in order from the leafy shadows of his Academy . . .

PRISCA: (*Standing, angry*) This is not Paul's teaching!

PLOUSIO: (*Suddenly wakened*) Is it time to eat?

PRISCA: How can you compare Socrates with the Christ?

STULTISSIMUS: Who's Socrates?

APOLLOS: Both are wise, both are teachers—

TITIUS: Pagan heresy!

APOLLOS: I didn't equate them—

(*Confusion is mounting*)

STULTISSIMUS: (*Accusing*) Why doesn't Prisca have her head covered?

PLOUSIO: A woman should cover her head.

PRISCA: (*Defiant*) Is that the law?

APOLLOS: That's the law.

XENOPHILUS: But Jesus set us free from the law— (*Now all are talking at once*)

PRISCA: Free from what law? Roman or Jewish?

STULTISSIMUS: We haven't even got a *minyan*.

PLOUSIO: I'm thirsty! Let's have a little blood!

APOLLOS: If Prisca feels in her heart that her head is covered—

PRISCA: Why should a woman's head be covered? In the new age, everybody's equal!

DEMETRIUS: Is your worship always like this?

XENOPHILUS: You hever know what to expect with Christians—

PRISCA: Maybe Sosthenes was right—

APOLLOS: Sosthenes renounced salvation, he'll go straight to Hell!

PLOUSIO: (*Affably*) I'll pray for him.

TITIUS: That'll do him in!

PLOUSIO: (*Offended*) I'm a pious man—

APOLLOS: Pious as an uncircumcised rabbi!

TITIUS: (*Despairing*) God's gone blind! How could He destroy Sodom and Gomorrah, and leave Corinth standing?

PRISCA: (*Angrily, she starts to blow out the candles*) This isn't worship, it's blasphemy!

(*All react, trying to stop her. Chaos. A Man enters from the back of the nave, walks slowly down the aisle toward the wrangling Corinthians. A spotlight burns on his back and throws his shadow long ahead of him. The Man is hunched, weary, has a burlap bag slung on his shoulder. Apollos struggles to relight the menorah. The approaching Man is unnoticed in the storm of argument. All voices come at once:*)

DEMETRIUS: God's not blind; he's bored with the world!

XENOPHILUS: The master is servant, the servant is master!

DEMETRIUS: My dear boy, that doesn't make any sense at all.

XENOPHILUS: When we admit our sins, the Jewish God forgives.

APOLLOS: Man must clothe his soul in the New Covenant—

TITIUS: How can he, if he's never worn the old?

APOLLOS: When we embrace as brothers—

TITIUS: We're all at each other's throats—and Satan's the schoolmaster!

STULTISSIMUS: You know what's wrong with the Christian Church? Not enough Jews!

PLOUSIO: The only sin is being sad. God has a good time, why shouldn't we?

PRISCA: Paul plants the seed, but leaves fools to do the watering—!

(*The wrangling continues. The Man, still unrecognized, comes closer. Xenophilus dashes toward the pulpit*)

XENOPHILUS: I've got to prophesy—! (*Shouting over the*

pandemonium) The Holy Spirit's moving through me. De eenescopholis! Egalopolis! Onnescalaba-labalis!

(*The Man comes through the doorway left into the chancel. One by one, the worshipers become aware of him, break off their wrangling. The urge to greet him is muted by a kind of shame—like children being caught by a parent in the midst of some mischief. The Man says nothing—moves slowly among them—looks into one face, then the next, then the next. All are silent now, except for Xenophilus who is still chanting nonsense from the pulpit. The Man crosses toward the boy in the pulpit, who looks down—breaks off. Silence*)

MAN: Shall I say "Amen" . . . ?

XENOPHILUS: (*Apprehensively*) If you wish—

MAN: You are the man who prophesies. The Holy Spirit sings through you, like wind through an Aeolian harp. Fine. But I speak many tongues, and I don't even know when to say "Amen" to your prayer . . . !

XENOPHILUS: Is it evil, what I'm doing—?

MAN: Can what the Holy Spirit tells you be evil? God forbid! (*He moves up into the pulpit beside the confused boy, puts an arm around his shoulder*) Is a flute evil because it doesn't speak words? Of course not. But if your ecstasy is gibberish, and nobody understands you, who gets any good out of it—except you? (*Xenophilus is awed. The Man looks down at the communion table, where half have risen—staring up toward the pulpit in a frozen shock*) For myself, I'd rather say five words that the congregation would understand—just five words!—rather than thousands of blabbering syllables of ecstasy. (*To the boy*) What do they call you?

XENOPHILUS: Xenophilus. . . I'm a new-caught fish in the net of the Messiah.

MAN: (*With warmth*) Try not to be childish, Xenophilus. Oh, it's good to be innocent as a new-born babe, untouched by evil. But try to be more grown-up in your thinking.

(*The boy is torn between the impulse to embrace this stranger, or to run from him. He suddenly flees toward the comfort of his companions*)

XENOPHILUS: (*Dropping to his knees*) You're Paul!

MAN: (PAUL. *Matter-of-factly*) What are you doing on your knees? I'm a man, not a saint. Kneel down when the Master comes; it will be soon! (*Tension charges the air. With a gentle irony*) Am I in the right place? Are these the children I left to carry out the word of Christ in Corinth? You *look* like Titius Justus—am I wrong, is this your house? Can this be Apollos? Does this frowning face belong to Prisca—my first dear friend on these shores—?

(*At this tenderness, Prisca breaks and runs to him. Paul quickly comes down from the pulpit and they embrace*)

PRISCA: Welcome, old friend!

PAUL: (*His arms around her*) Your husband sends his greetings.

PRISCA: (*A bitter echo*) His greetings!

TITIUS: I think we need you, Paul.

PAUL: (*Penetratingly*) And I need *you*, Titius. The Christ needs you!

APOLLOS: No one warned us you were coming—

PAUL: Obviously.

APOLLOS: I'm ashamed to have you find us in such disorder—

PAUL: (*Pointedly*) You might be more ashamed for trying to hide this disorder from me.

PLOUSIO: So you're the great Paul!

APOLLOS: This is a new convert, Plousio—

PLOUSIO: (*Fatuously*) May the great God in Heaven bless you in your mighty work.

PAUL: (*Drily*) I hope so. (*Seeing Demetrius*) I know you—!

DEMETRIUS: We crossed the Aegean in the same ship. I'm not a Christian.

PAUL: But you're breaking bread with Christians. . .

DEMETRIUS: I was hungry . . .

PAUL: (*Faint smile*) I know the feeling . . . !

STULTISSIMUS: Dddid you get my letter?

PAUL: (*Ignoring him, searching*) Where's Sosthenes? Our good and loyal friend—? (*A silence*) Is he ill—? (*No one moves or breathes*) Not dead—?

APOLLOS: (*With difficulty*) Sosthenes has left the church.

PAUL: (*Stunned*) Left—?!

PRISCA: He's gone back to the synagogue.

PAUL: Why?!

APOLLOS: Oh, I suppose we failed him. I told him he was free to follow his own conscience . . .

PAUL: Free to forfeit his own freedom . . .

STULTISSIMUS: D-d-do you remember me?

PAUL: Yes—Stultissimus. Your letter reached me.

TITIUS: How could you get a letter from Stultissimus
. . . ?

PLOUSIO: He can't write his name!

STULTISSIMUS: I know *how* to g-g-et a letter written . . .

APOLLOS: I would have helped you—

STULTISSIMUS: You w-w-w-would have *changed* everything.
I wanted Paul to know th-th-the *truth.*

PRISCA: (*To Stultissimus*) Troublemaker!

APOLLOS: Worse than a troublemaker. When there's already trouble, it's a crime to make it worse!

PAUL: (*Incisively*) When the body is sick, is it a crime to call
in a physician? (*They fall silent*) It was a cruel letter, Stultissimus. Vindictive and cruel. But God moved you to write it, so
I'd know there was truth in the rumors whispered to me in
Ephesus. And when I saw some of Prisca's letters—

PRISCA: I haven't written to you—

PAUL: Your letters to Aquila . . .

PRISCA: (*Indignant*) You read my letters to my husband—?

PAUL: He showed them to me.

PRISCA: (*Furious*) What I wrote was for *him*—for him
alone, not for you to see!

PAUL: I have no secrets . . .

TITIUS: We all have secrets, Paul.

PAUL: But from God!?? (*The voltage of hostility is building up
between the Apostle and his Congregation. Paul is not an imposing
figure. He lacks the grace and smoothness of Apollos. His body is
ill-proportioned, almost ugly. His prime characteristic is energy. His
gestures are in spurts and jerks. He is a fanatic with a fearful single-
ness of purpose. His restraint is more awesome than his anger. He is a
tightly coiled spring, packed with enormous latent force*) Is this the
Christian Church of Corinth? You sound more like a wrangling caucus of Roman politicians! How could any of you
hope to hear God's Voice? The tumult is so great you can't
even hear yourselves!!! (*Slowly, singly, the congregation sits—as
Paul berates them, striding restlessly and impatiently about the chancel*) Have you no fear? You are a Godmarked people—

TITIUS: (*Proudly*) We are Sons of Abraham—

PAUL: You are new men! No more Jew nor gentile, no
more Greek, barbarian, Scythian, bond nor free—you belong

to the Christ!!!! (*Softly*) So be thankful, Corinthians, not proud. (*Grimly*) God prostrates proud men, as surely as he has leveled the proud cities of the past. Why are you so pleased with yourselves? You're failing in your work for Christ. You do not *win* souls, you let them slither through your fingers! You cannot catch fish with bare hands! You need the hook of truth!!!! (*The Apostle scrutinizes the fat Plousio*) Who brought this man into the fellowship?

APOLLOS: *I* baptized him.

PAUL: And what happened to you, when you became a Christian?

PLOUSIO: I was set free.

PAUL: Free? Free from what?

PLOUSIO: From the law.

PAUL: What law?

STULTISSIMUS: N-n-not the law of Moses.

PLOUSIO: I'm no Israelite, I've never been under your law of Moses. (*He looks beatifically upward*) As the waters broke over my head, that released me from slavery to *any* law!

PAUL: (*Acidly*) So now you can do exactly as you please, is that what you think?

PLOUSIO: (*Blankly*) What other reason is there to become a Christian???

PAUL: (*He turns accusingly on Apollos*) Apollos! I blame *you* for this! Belief in the Messiah brings freedom, yes—we are all called to be free men—so we can be servants to one another.

PLOUSIO: That doesn't make sense. Servants have to do what they're told—

PAUL: You think God on High sent his Son to this earth— to die!—so you could wallow in gluttony? Self-indulgence? Jesus calls to you to lift yourself out of the appetites of the body. Shake yourself free from inpurity, indecency, the hungering for sex, drinking bouts, orgies and the like—oh, I've heard that you indulge in such things in Corinth! (*Plousio suppresses a hiccup. There is a general restlessness in response to this tirade*) The New Covenant gives freedom from law—so there can be a birth of *self-control!!!* But God does not give freedom to men or to nations—until they are *ready* to be free. (*Paul looks from one face to another*) Well? Do you think you're ready to be *free men* . . . ?

PRISCA: (*After a pause*) *I* would like to be a free *woman*.

PAUL: In the Kingdom of Heaven, there is neither male nor female.

PRISCA: How do you know, Paul? Have you been there?

PAUL: (*He is stunned by this insolence from Prisca*) Is this my dearest and oldest friend in Achaia . . . ? My Prisca . . . ?

PRISCA: I am not *your* Prisca. If I belong to anyone, I belong to my husband.

PAUL: You belong to Christ.

PRISCA: I belong to God the Father, who made me a woman. And if, some day, I am so blessed as to be welcomed in the Kingdom of Heaven, it will be as a woman that I enter—in the form in which God made me . . .

PAUL: When that day comes, the woman called Prisca will put on immortality. All that is corruptible in her will be cast off, to put on incorruption!

PRISCA: (*Eyes flashing*) Oh, does my womanhood make me something corrupt? Unclean? Has Paul decided that there will only be one sex in Heaven?

PAUL: You think I don't love you and your husband? I have tried to spare you the distractions of the flesh! When I asked your husband to come with me to Ephesus, it was to purify you both!

PRISCA: "*Purify* us"—!

PAUL: You think *I* am a stranger to animal desires—? *I* have appetites, which I put down so that I can give myself entirely to the building of churches—and spreading the Good News. I shake off the demands of my own flesh!—why? To glorify the Messiah! I try to make my body as insubstantial as air—so the breath of God may flow through me unimpeded by my own selfishness. Oh, I wish that all of you, all, could be as *I* am—!

DEMETRIUS: (*Arching an eyebrow, to Xenophilus*) Modest fellow, isn't he?

PAUL: Lose yourselves in the Gospel of Christ so that old hungers are barely remembered—only faint markings on a slate scraped clean!

PRISCA: (*Patiently*) Paul. Is it a sin to speak of love . . . ?

PAUL: God forbid.

PRISCA: When a man and wife touch, it isn't lust. It's a form of speech. A silent language which expresses love. And it leaps beyond the spoken word, higher than tongues of ecstasy, and sweeter than any words that can be written by a pen on parchment . . .

PAUL: Will it always be . . . ?

PRISCA: The love—yes . . .

PAUL: The body . . . ? The bodies, Prisca, which touch . . . ?

PRISCA: (*Looking down*) Will perish. You taught us, Paul, that the body is the temple of the Holy Spirit—

PAUL: And temples *fall*!!! But the Holy Spirit *endures*!!! (*Gently, to Prisca*) When I took your husband with me to Ephesus, I did it in a spirit of love for you both. Apart, each of you can come nearer to the perfection you will reach in the world to come. I wanted to spare you the ache of carnal longings . . . !

PRISCA: (*Marveling*) My God, I believe that you really believe that . . . !

PAUL: My God and your God knows that I do . . . !

PLOUSIO: (*He takes a deep drink of wine, tears off a lump of bread and waves it accusingly at Paul. A drunken accusation*) This man is interfering with the holy ceremony of communion! Behold, I am infused with the blood of the vine. (*Burps*) I am one with what I worship!!! (*He chaws at the bread*)

PAUL: (*Exploding*) You are nothing! Zero! A cipher! A nullity!

DEMETRIUS: (*Lifting an eyebrow*) Is it a sin to hunger?

PLOUSIO: Or to thirst?

APOLLOS: When satisfying these needs is an act of thanksgiving . . . ?

PAUL: To relieve a parched throat or an empty stomach, sharing the common meal as Jesus shared the last supper with his disciples—*that* is a blessed thing. Yes, the body is a temple, sacred to the Lord—a *temple,* not a public inn for carousing, wickedness, vice, drunkenness—

TITIUS: Paul, you do this church an injustice! We are not as bad as you want to think we are . . .

PAUL: I pray to Heaven that I'm wrong! At first, when word began to come to me in Ephesus . . . rumblings . . . "All is not well with the Church in Cornith"—why, I dismissed the stories. False gossip! A crumbling away of my Corinthians??? Impossible! Apollos would not let such a thing happen. Nor Prisca. Nor Titius Justus, in his own house. I want to

welcome only such things as are of good report. (*To Apollos*)
But then—more rumors.

APOLLOS: I preach freedom.

PAUL: Sexual freedom? Freedom to fornicate as you
please, without restraint?

DEMETRIUS: (*To Xenopilus*) The old boy's really hung up on
this, isn't he?! (*But Xenophilus' face is a mask of terror*)

APOLLOS: (*To Paul*) This is a church, not a court. I'm not a
judge. What a man does in private, or a man and a woman—

PRISCA: (*Narrowly*) Or a man and a man—?

PLOUSIO: (*Drunken*) Or a woman and a woman—

APOLLOS: Whatever. If both consent and are of legal age
under Roman law—

TITIUS: (*Itching his nose*) You *do* sound like a judge, Apollos. You should've been a magistrate.

APOLLOS: —and if no injury is done, is it my business? Or
yours? What happens between sheets in the uncandled night
. . . ?

(*Pause. Paul marvels*)

PAUL: God cannot see in the dark? Is that what you think?
Since Justice is blind, so is God? Oh, foolish Corinthians! You
think God doesn't know—or doesn't care—that you are committing acts of sexual immorality such as even pagans do not
tolerate? The union of a man with his father's wife!!!??? (*Dead
silence. All are motionless. Only Paul's eyes move from one immobile
face to the next. Then, suddenly, he lashes out*) Well? Why doesn't
somebody stand up and tell me: "It isn't true!"? Stultissimus
lied to you!

(*A few glances of contempt toward Stultissimus*)

PLOUSIO: (*Mutters*) You little stuttering spook—!

STULTISSIMUS: (*Eyes bright, righteous*) I-I-I-I only wrote
what I thought P-p-p-paul had a right to know—!

PAUL: (*Sadly*) It *is* true . . . ! (*Almost pleading*) Isn't one of
you going to cry out? Surely somebody in this congregation is
going to stand up and say: "Who is it? Who's committing such
an act? We will root him out of our company!!!" (*Silence. Paul's
calm is frightening*) You all *know* who he is . . . ?

STULTISSIMUS: (*Protesting*) I-I-I-I d-d-d—*I* don't know!
They don't t-t-t-tell me . . . !

PAUL: Apollos. Does the church of Jesus Christ *endorse incest*???

APOLLOS: (*Lamely*) Nothing has happened here which is against the law of Caesar. . . .

PAUL: (*Mock amazement*) Oh! You are pure! Because you have not broken the statutes of unbelievers!!! Make no mistake! No fornicator or idolator, none who are guilty of either adultery or homosexual perversion, no slanderer, no drunkard, no son who fornicates with his father's widow can possess the Kingdom of God. Am I too harsh, Titius? Can you say to me now: "Tch, tch, tch, you are too hard on us, Paul, we aren't really so bad—"

(*The sudden clang of weapons, the rattle of armor. From the back of the sanctuary a Girl screams*)

VOICES: (*Unseen, shouting*) She went between the buildings! I saw her! Come on! She'll get away! Bacchus pledges a flagon of ruby wine to the soldier who catches her—!

(*All the Corinthians rise, come forward to find out what's going on—all except Plousio, who takes the opportunity to stuff his mouth with food. A Girl creeps down the nave—crouching, frightened, looking back over her shoulder toward the clank and stomping of the unseen soldiers. She wears a crimson robe which is torn and dirty from an apparent struggle, and part of it is scorched from fire. The Girl would be beautiful, but her face is smudged, her hair disheveled, her eyes are wild with fear*)

PAUL: God, I hate the sound of soldiers—!

TITIUS: They keep the streets safe—

PAUL: Do they? Titius, you know there's only *one* shield . . . !

(*The Girl sees the flag of the fish, catches her breath—looks back to see if the soldiers have gone—then makes a dash toward the imagined door of Titius Justus' house. She tries to raise her right arm to knock for entrance, but winces from pain—pounds instead with the fist of her left hand.*)

GIRL: (*Pleading*) If there's any charity in you—? Let me in, please—! (*Paul looks at the Corinthians. But they are wary of harboring a fugitive*) Hide me, hide me.

(*Prisca starts toward the door*)

APOLLOS: Wait a minute—we might get in trouble with the authorities—

STULTISSIMUS: D-d-don't let her in!

PLOUSIO: The Romans are after her—it's none of our business—!

(*The Girl, whimpering, pounds at the doorway*)

DEMETRIUS: (*Snorts*) A fine crew of Good Samaritans *this is*—!

XENOPHILUS: (*Surprised*) How do you know about the Good Samaritan?

GIRL: Please—!

PAUL: (*With authority*) Let her in.

(*Prisca goes to unbolt the door in pantomime*)

TITIUS: At least ask her if she's Jewish.

GIRL: For the love of the gods—! For the love of God—!

PRISCA: (*To the Girl, through a crack in the door*) Are you Jewish?

GIRL: (*Distressed*) I don't know.

PRISCA: (*To the others*) She doesn't know.

TITIUS: Then she's a pagan. When you're Jewish, you *know* you're Jewish.

PAUL: (*Crisply*) What difference does it make? She's a human being! Let her in!

(*Prisca steps aside and the terrified Girl bursts into the gathering. Breathless, unsteady on her feet, she looks around . . . sees the prayer shawls, the menorah, the worshipers*)

GIRL: Gods save me! —it's a church!!!

(*She tries to escape—then reels, collapses. Prisca and Paul move to help her*)

PAUL: Wine—!

APOLLOS: (*Reluctant*) This is consecrated—

PAUL: For a holy purpose. Give it to me! (*He holds out a cup. Apollos fills it*)

GIRL: (*Protesting*) No, no, no—!

PAUL: Drink this! Why are the soldiers following you?

(*He gives the shaken Girl a sip. Xenophilus brings his stool for her to sit on, in front of the table*)

GIRL: (*Dazed looking around*) Where's the idol—that you worship—?

APOLLOS: We worship the unseen and all-knowing God!

XENOPHILUS: We're Christians.

GIRL: But Christians are all mad—!

PLOUSIO: It's madness to harbor a fugitive—!

GIRL: I've broken no law, no Roman law. But Bacchus is the god in Corinth. So the soldiers do whatever the priests ask them! Protect me—

APOLLOS: From what?

GIRL: (*Bitterly*) From the honor, the awful honor they want to give me! Oh, I'm the most fortunate daughter of Corinth, my father says: of all the virgins in Greece, I should be the happiest—because they chose *me* to celebrate the feast of Dionysius . . . ! They dragged me to the temple to lie with the high priest and sacrifice myself to the delight of the god of all delights! (*Xenophilus offers her another sip of wine*) The eunuchs held my arms, and laughed, while the priests tried to rape me! For the glory of the god of wine— (*The Girl— Ione—is taking another swallow from the goblet, then abruptly spits it out*) Wine! Then the fat one came at me, the beast-belly! Naked and wet with sweat, I lunged at him, clamped my teeth into his shoulder— (*Laughs bitterly*) Oh, it was good to see how he bled! I have sharp teeth! He groaned and rolled in the dust, blubbering with pain. Then— (*She pales*) they tried to make me into a *living* burnt offering—

TITIUS: That's against the law of Caesar!

IONE: Oh, they didn't have the courage to *kill* me. They tied my wrist to horns of the altar. Then they kindled a fire underneath my arm! I could smell my own roasting flesh!!! The priests went to get more wine and I managed to pull my wrist free from the altar and I ran—! And if you hadn't taken me in, they would have—I don't know *what* would've happened—! (*Gingerly she holds up her right arm, which is raw and blackened from fire*) At first I couldn't even feel my arm . . . it was like something that wasn't part of me, flopping from my shoulder—but I'm starting to feel it now—a throbbing . . .

PAUL: Oh, child, when there is so much pain in the world, how can anyone find joy in causing greater suffering . . . ?!

(*Prisca examines the girl's arm. Ione winces with pain*)

PRISCA: (*Softly, to Paul*) It's a bad burn—very deep—!

(*All press close to see the wound*)

TITIUS: Devils!

DEMETRIUS: (*Slowly*) It seems to me the time wouldn't be amiss . . . for a *miracle* . . .

APOLLOS: (*He is instantly on the defensive*) I'm not much good at miracles. Being Greek, I'm—I'm a very logical, you know . . .

(*All eyes shift to Paul*)

XENOPHILUS: (*Impulsively*) Paul can do it. He's an Apostle of the Lord—he'll perform a miracle, right now! (*Encouragingly, the boy bends over Ione*) He'll take all the pain out of your arm. He can make it well, quick as that— (*Snaps his fingers*) without even a scar—!

STULTISSIMUS: (*Nodding his head, excitedly*) I'd like to see him d-d-do it!

(*Paul is hesitant, uncertain*)

PLOUSIO: (*Amiably*) Go right ahead, Paul. Show us how you perform miracles.

PAUL: (*Sternly*) *I can do nothing*. It is only by the grace of our Lord, Jesus Christ, that a miracle is performed—

IONE: (*Suffering, pleading*) Is your God kind . . . ?

XENOPHILUS: Oh, yes!

IONE: Then pray to Him . . . to help me . . . !

PAUL: What do they call you?

IONE: Ione.

PAUL: Ione. Have you ever heard of the Messiah? Jesus of Nazareth . . . ?

IONE: No . . . All I know is that the Jews have a God named Jehovah—who doesn't live on Olympus . . .

PAUL: (*Swiftly*) There is only one God—the maker of Heaven and Earth. We are all his children. We are all brothers and sisters—because in the spirit we have the same Father. And this Father loves us so much that he gave His son—his only flesh-born son—to walk the world, just as we do, to feel pain, hunger, exhaustion, ecstasy—and to suffer the most cruel and disgraceful death . . .

IONE: Oh, He must be cruel. Why would this God let his only Son be killed—?

PAUL: In order to forgive us—the *rest* of us—for the wrongs *we* have done. So Jesus took the punishment for *us*—!

IONE: It's hard to believe—

PAUL: Ione, do you have faith???

IONE: I don't know what faith *is*. Is it like *hope*—?

PAUL: (*Gravely*) *Hope* is a vision of future good that you imagine for yourself. *Faith* is God's promise that what you hope can really happen! Ione, do you have faith that you are important in God's sight? That He wants you well, and whole, and strong . . . ?

IONE: (*Sadly, softly*) No . . . But if your God will give me faith . . .

PAUL: He can. He will . . . ! (*A pause—tense—silent. All watch Paul. The Apostle wets his lips, lowers his head, speaks swiftly, urgently*) Dear Father in Heaven . . . we pray, in the name of Thy blessed Son, Jesus Christ, our Lord, that the power of the Holy Spirit may relieve our sister Ione, of this wicked injury. By Your Grace, may she be healed—! (*Paul stretches out his hands, placing them on the wounded arm of Ione. Pause. Then Paul cries out:*) Let this insult to her flesh be cast out! Let her be made whole . . .!

(*Paul draws back his hands. He is weakened by the outpouring of his spirit . . . Very slowly, Prisca begins to lift the Girl's arm. Will the burn have vanished . . . ? Pause. All watch, expectantly*)

IONE: (*A shriek of pain*) Ahhhhhheeeeeeeeee . . . !

(*All see that the arm is still black and raw. An involuntary groan of disappointment. Paul turns away, disheartened*)

PRISCA: (*The practical*) I'll get her to a physician. Stultissimus, bring a blanket—so they won't recognize her in the street . . .

STULTISSIMUS: (*Disappointed*) Why wasn't there a miracle . . . ?

PLOUSIO: (*Mocking*) God doesn't seem to pay much attention to you, Apostle!

PAUL: It takes belief. Without faith—nothing!

APOLLOS: You blame the girl—?

PAUL: I blame you all! Because you're in love with your own skepticism! Our Lord Himself could perform no miracles in Nazareth, because they doubted Him.

(*Stultissimus brings a blanket, which they fling over Ione's ragged scarlet robe. Monica Maga enters from right along the transept— the street in front of Titius's house. The Boy-with-a-Crutch follows her. He is using the crutch now, limping on his right leg. Monica looks at the limping Boy*)

MONICA: Let me see you smile! (*The Boy-with-a-Crutch bares his teeth in a false grin. She hits him across the cheek*) Smile, brat! (*The Boy-with-a-Crutch reels from the slap, manages a more convincing smile*) Not *happy*, you little idiot! Just *loving*—! (*Within the house—the chancel area—Prisca is preparing to leave with Ione*)

PRISCA: I'll take her to a friend of Lucius, we can trust him. (*She glances back sympathetically at the frustrated Apostle*) Bless you—

(*Paul doesn't even look at her, just makes an aborted wave of his hand. The weight of heavy discouragement is on his shoulders. Prisca lifts the bar across the door, leads Ione past the fish-banner and out onto the street. At the sight of Monica Maga and the Boy-with-a-Crutch, Ione is startled, draws back. Monica lifts her arm in the stiff salute of a Roman Legionnaire*)

MONICA: Hail, Christians—! (*Prisca is wary*) This *is* the meeting place of the followers of Jesus, the Anointed Christ?

PRISCA: I don't know you—

MONICA: In your heart you do; I am a sister. May my little boy and I go directly in at the sign of the fish—? Oh, but of course we can! Christians are famous for their hospitality— though only a few of us have been admitted to the inner circle of knowledge! (*Unctuously, to the limping Boy*) Come, my little angel—

(*Monica and the Boy-with-a-Crutch enter the chancel. Prisca and Ione go off right along the transept. Apollos and Paul have been deep in a discussion*)

APOLLOS: (*Defensively*) I think you attack my ministry unjustly. Didn't they write you that we had collected *more* than you asked—for the Saints in Jerusalem?

PAUL: But I understand most of the money came from Titius.

APOLLOS: Well, what's wrong with that?

PAUL: A rich man can't really *give*. He can only *bestow*. A wealthy man never goes hungry—so how can he know the meaning of his own wealth?

(*Monica Maga demands attention. The Boy is leaning heavily on his crutch behind her*)

MONICA: (*In too loud a voice*) Blessings on all Christians in this room. Blessings in the name of the thrice blessed healer Jesus, the Divine Jew!

(*The Church members look curiously at one another. Who is this woman? Xenophilus hangs back, afraid of her*)

APOLLOS: Who are you?

MONICA: (*Mysteriously*) I know you, your *true* name. But don't worry, I won't mention it aloud, because I know there is a non-Christian in this room. (*She points a finger at Demetrius*) *That* man has not been baptized into the mysteries! (*Aside to Paul*) Be careful of him.

PAUL: What mysteries?

MONICA: Oh, you must be a newcomer to the faith . . . !
If you are interested in learning more about the mysterious
Jesus, I'll teach you—for a price. (*Claps her hands*) But
please—I need your help. Three—three of course is the
magic number. I need two more baptized Christians to join
with me in performing a holy act of mercy. (*Calls harshly*) Boy!!
Where are you? (*The Boy-with-a-Crutch has limped over to talk
with Xenophilus. But with a frightened start, he comes to Monica. Her
voice becomes honey-sweet*) This sweet little cripple—needs a
Christian healing.

STULTISSIMUS: (*Eagerly*) A m-m-miracle—???

MONICA: You'll see! Three Christians must join in a ring
about this boy, hands clasped. And by powerful incantations
known only to me, I will cast the devil out of his foot so he can
run again, and play like a normal child.

STULTISSIMUS: I-I-I'll help!

MONICA: (*To Plousio*) You—I can tell by your face that
you're a devout Christian!— (*Plousio, Stultissimus and Monica
join hands around the Boy-with-a-Crutch. Her voice is a barbaric cry*)
Ohhh, Jehovah on High! Eenescopholis! Egalopolis! Give us a
sign—in the name of Jesus Christ, mightiest of all magi-
cians—! Oon-esca-laba-labalis! (*She screams, flings back her arms,
breaking the ring*) You are cured! Throw away your crutch—!

(*Obediently the Boy tosses aside the crutch and scampers about the
room*)

PAUL: (*Outraged*) Witch! Sorceress! You befoul the ministry
of Jesus with heathen mysteries!

(*Demetrius smirks. Are they going to be taken in by this?*)

MONICA: (*Angrily*) What kind of a Christian are you? You
denounce a healing in the name of the Christ???

PAUL: You're a fraud, woman! A blasphemer! You use the
name of the Son of God in vain!

STULTISSIMUS: (*Smirking at Paul*) He's j-j-jealous—! He
t-t-t-tried to do a miracle—but it d-d-d-didn't work—!

(*The Corinthians have an air of approving curiosity toward
Monica. They marvel as the Boy cavorts freely, twirling the un-
needed crutch*)

PAUL: (*Pleading*) My children!—put no faith in this priest-
ess of ignorance—!

PLOUSIO: I felt the sting of a god in the palm of my hand—

PAUL: You were bewitched—

TITIUS: There's no doubt, the boy is cured—

DEMETRIUS: (*Wryly*) If he was ever sick.

MONICA: (*With an arrogant smile*) Blind men. I pity those who see, but won't believe. You've witnessed a demonstration of my power—

PAUL: Demons can demonstrate power. With Satan at his side, Jesus could have trampled Caesar—

APOLLOS: (*The eternal Greek*) We must discern between the mystical and the magical—

PAUL: Between black and white! Between the black magic of false prophets and the light of the Living God!

MONICA: Be careful—if you offend the great god Jesus, he might make this boy a cripple again. You want that on your head—!

XENOPHILUS: It's all a trick! I saw this boy this afternoon—

MONICA: Don't listen to him!

XENOPHILUS: He was running about—

MONICA: You saw another boy. All boys look alike—

XENOPHILUS: He's only *pretending* to be a cripple—

(*The Corinthians don't want to believe this; they want to be party to an authentic miracle*)

MONICA: (*Fast, firm*) Don't believe him. He lies, he's a sinner. He's committed a crime against the holiness of life itself!

DEMETRIUS: (*Sharply*) *How?*

MONICA: He has taken his mother as his wife! (*Xenophilus is pale. Silence. The secret is out. Paul frowns. Demetrius whistles softly through his teeth*)

TITIUS: (*Hushed*) How do you know this . . . ?

MONICA: (*Superior*) I am a Knower. A Gnostic. That is my professed profession. Half the soul is hidden. Like the back of the moon. But I have the gift to see what others hide—

PAUL: (*Almost a monotone*) Is this the man . . . ? (*None of the Corinthians speak. Some know, some only suspect. They look uncertainly toward Xenophilus, who lowers his head, ashamed*)

MONICA: Look at him! Of course he's the sinner! Will you believe the slander of his mouth . . . ?

PAUL: (*He ignores her as if she didn't exist. He is shocked and saddened that the personable Xenophilus might be guilty of this offense. To Xenophilus*) You, who presume to prophesy, have committed such an act . . . ? (*Xenophilus is shaken. Paul looks at the other members of the church*) You knew this man was the sinner . . . ? *All* of you . . . ? (*The Corinthians exchange nervous glances with one another. Paul's fury is mounting*) And you *condoned* this? *Ignored* it!? Continued, day after day, to worship with this creature you knew was guilty of the most flagrant immorality? Of sexual outrage which would doom him to hell-fire for all eternity—?

XENOPHILUS: (*He lets out a sad, soft protest*) No—no-o-o-o—!

PAUL: (*With growing fury*) You were party, every one of you, to this contamination of the Lord's Supper—! (*Monica starts to speak, but Paul overrides her*)

MONICA: Aren't you impressed with my miracle? See how he walks? Run—run for them, little one!

(*But the Boy isn't listening—he, too, is fascinated by the crescendo of Paul's anathema*)

PAUL: (*To Monica*) You are less of a Christian than Caesar's mule! (*Accusing each*) And you, Apollos! Titius, Plousio—and stupidest of the stupid, Stultissimus! You pay less heed to this abomination in your church than to a fly circling the butter! Is it only a speck in the wine that you sit next to a brother who has delivered himself to Satan??? Who lives by no law at all???

APOLLOS: We are free from law—

PAUL: Free? To put on the blindfold of indifference? The chains of fornicators? Adulterers! You quibble about whether a Christian must be circumcised. But morally you have gone the whole way: you are *eunuchs!* (*The thunder rises*) Who breaks in and steals your virtue? *You* do! You yourselves! You preen with pride, while you ignore this shameful canker which has planted itself among you—!

XENOPHILUS: (*In anguish*) I beg you—! Please—! In Jesus' name—

APOLLOS: (*Carefully*) Xenophilus is—

PAUL: Xenophilus is a sinner! Speak the truth, Apollos. He has no place here! But you must wait until *I* come before you cast him out of your company!!! Well? Is any voice raised on behalf of incest? Who speaks for the fornicator? (*A pause. He looks around*)

APOLLOS: (*Lamely*) I'm told she is *not* his natural mother—

PAUL: Is she his father's wife—???

XENOPHILUS: (*Faintly*) She *was* my father's wife . . .

PAUL: Is it not written that husband and wife are become

as one flesh? In the Last Judgment, which will you be? Son or husband? Wretched man, you'll never awaken at the trumpet's sound!

XENOPHILUS: (*In agony*) I'll change! I will! I'll change—!

PAUL: Unless—*unless*—you're delivered unto Satan for the destruction of the flesh! Then your spirit may be saved!

APOLLOS: Paul—

PAUL: (*Sternly*) Leave him to the mercy of Satan!

APOLLOS: Does Satan show mercy . . . ?

XENOPHILUS: (*Dazed, broken*) I thought I was lost before I found the Christ. (*Despairing*) Now I am doubly lost . . . !

(*Unsteadily, utterly despondent, he stumbles out of the group— steadies himself at the fish-flag—hesitates—then goes off left. Paul is weakened by his thundering tirade. The members of the church are silent but sullen. Monica watches, bright-eyed; though she has been spurned, she recognizes that something momentous is happening. The Boy sits on the floor, playing with his crutch*)

BOY: (*Puzzled, looking up at Paul*) What did he do that was so wrong . . . ?

(*Paul shakes his head, moves up toward the altar rail. Demetrius studies the Apostle thoughtfully*)

DEMETRIUS: I think I might have become a Christian. If Christians were a little more Christian . . . ! (*He crosses left to leave. All watch him*) Since my host in this gentle assembly has been consigned to hell-fire, I wonder if I've lost my welcome . . .

PAUL: Wait! (*Demetrius stops by the fish-flag. Paul confronts him*) What do you think it means—to be a Christian—?

DEMETRIUS: (*A little laugh*) That's what I hoped to learn— by coming here. But if *this* is a Christian Church, I'd rather worship the Pole Star. As a sailor, I know I can count on the "Northness" of the Heavens more than on the goodness of men . . .

TITIUS: (*He laughs bitterly, slaps the table*) Hear, hear! You're wasting your time, Paul, trying to save us! We're all evil—and I suspect that you're no better than the rest of us.

(*General laughter. Paul, upstage, is stunned to watch this precious church slipping through his fingers*)

PLOUSIO: He's worse. I feel a sacred responsibility to *enjoy* the blessings God has given me. If I keep turning sweet to sour, I'm corrupt.

APOLLOS: Sailor. What qualities do you look for in religion . . . ?

DEMETRIUS: You make it sound like shopping for a shirt . . . ! (*Demetrius thinks*) It seems to me that all a man wants is a God who is less *capricious* than a man . . . !

TITIUS: That eliminates Olympus.

STULTISSIMUS: And Sss-Caesar!

DEMETRIUS: Oh, I'll bow to the power of Rome—to keep the military from poking nails through my hands.

PAUL: But you'll crucify yourself on your own skepticism.

DEMETRIUS: (*Level*) I may be an unbeliever, but I'm honest. And that's better than being gulled by self-deception.

PAUL: You think I deceive myself . . . ?

DEMETRIUS: I don't know exactly *what* your trouble is. (*Turns away from Paul, then pauses, wistfully*) When I saw you, dank and drenched by spray on the wet ship's deck, curled up in a coil of rope, my heart leaped inside me . . . ! I was *sure*—and for no reasonable reason, I was *sure* I stood in the gaze of a saint . . . Now I have heard you preach, and I must go back to my own old god, to whom I pray for wisdom, on whose strength I rely, and to whom I pay solemn respects three times each day (if possible) with cooked rather than burnt offerings. Myself.

PAUL: Does this "god" content you . . . ?

(*A pause. The sailor looks down*)

DEMETRIUS: He is contemptible, unworthy of my worship, unresponsive to my prayers. I have no faith in my own Deity. So, I belong to the largest church in the world: that blithe and hopeless communion of men who don't believe in anything!

MONICA: (*Almost a shriek of damnation*) You'll go to *hell*—!!

DEMETRIUS: (*Politely*) Dear lady, I'm already there.

PLOUSIO: Has this worship service ended . . . ?

TITIUS: (*Wryly*) I didn't know it had begun.

(*Apollos has been scarred by Paul's slights. He begins to strike back, and the Corinthians band together, gradually, to join him. The Outsiders—Demetrius, Monica and the Boy, are intrigued to watch these gladiators grapple with the Lion of Judah*)

APOLLOS: You have been most generous, Brother Paul, in your criticism of us—of *me*, in particular—

PAUL: I didn't come to tear you down, but to build you up!

APOLLOS: It must be hard for Xenophilus to see that. You damn the boy for breaking a law, when he'd been taught there was no law.

PAUL: Does the Church condone sin?

APOLLOS: The Church is in a crisis of definitions. According to Peter, only a Jew can inherit the Kingdom of Heaven.

STULTISSIMUS: (*Eager to discredit Paul*) And he was a d-d-d-*disciple*.

PAUL: That's what Peter believes, he has a right to believe it. I disagree with him.

APOLLOS: And I disagree with you about Xenophilus!

PAUL: Are you a disciple?

APOLLOS: Are you?

(*Some disparaging laughter*)

PAUL: (*Shocked*) You question my authority? In a church which wouldn't be here, if it weren't for *me*—? You'd all be crawling about some heathen temple, cowering before idols—!

(*The voice of the Cantor is heard, offstage, wafted in momentarily by the wind*)

TITIUS: (*Almost wistfully*) I would be next door. In the synagogue, with Sosthenes.

PAUL: And cut off from the promise of the Messiah? What folly! I beg you, my brothers, my children—use wisdom—!

APOLLOS: You're inconsistent, Paul. Use wisdom, you say—yet you've told us that wisdom is foolishness. Help a brother who stumbles, you say. But did *you* help Xenophilus?

PAUL: You must strengthen your*selves*—

APOLLOS: In a proud voice, you condemn us for being proud—

PAUL: That is the Holy Spirit speaking through me—

APOLLOS: You have tricked us, lied to us—

PAUL: (*Aghast*) When? When have I lied to you—?

APOLLOS: About the birthday of the Christ— You said he was born on the Saturnalia—

PAUL: Who knows on what day Jesus was born? It was half a century ago! I told you to sing out a joyful Christ Mass on the greatest festival of the year—!

PLOUSIO: Should we imitate pagans?

PAUL: Do *any*thing which is Godward!!! To Romans I am a

Roman; to Jews, a Jew; to Greeks I will be a Greek. I will be inconsistent, play tricks on you, use any wiles to awaken you to the good news which has broken upon the world.

DEMETRIUS: But who awakened you—?

MONICA: (*Taunting him*) Who made you an Apostle!?

PAUL: (*Incensed*) You'd rather follow a sham-Christian, like this wicked woman? Oh, you'll find many masqueraders like this one. Satan disguises himself as an angel of light—so think how easy it is for his witches to pass themselves off as agents of good.

BOY: You're mean!

PAUL: (*Stung by the Boy's frankness*) Am I cruel? (*Wrenched with frustration*) Because I'm jealous of you with a divine jealousy? I promised this church to Christ as a chaste virgin, but I find you corrupted—!

APOLLOS: We find you presumptuous.

PLOUSIO: And insulting.

APOLLOS: We've been visited by other apostles—

STULTISSIMUS: Ttt-true apostles—!

PAUL: Who—?

TITIUS: Men who really *knew* the Master . . .

APOLLOS: Who heard him speak, while he was in the flesh.

PAUL: You doubt my credentials as a messenger of Christ? Why? Because I was the Pharisee, Saul of Tarsus? Through the grace and glory of God, I was changed! Instead of persecuting the saints, I became one of them! You want me to boast? All right, I'll boast! I CAN OUTDO ALL OTHER APOSTLES! (*Mounting the pulpit, fiercely*) How many times have I been in prison? Face to face with death? Five times they've given me thirty-nine strokes of the whip! Two—no, three times beaten with rods! Once I was stoned! Three times I was shipwrecked, and for twenty-four hours adrift in the open sea . . . !

TITIUS: Paul—

PAUL: Hear me out—! (*The words are a swift torrent*) How many journeys have I made? What dangers have I faced? From flooded rivers, from robbers, from foreigners—and danger from false friends—?! I've toiled, drudged, gone without sleep, without food or water, suffered from cold and exposure, I— (*Breaks off, looking at the cold faces*) Why do I tell you all this? I don't move you . . .

APOLLOS: (*A direct thrust*) How can you teach us about a man you never met—?

PAUL: Apollos. When will the world end?

APOLLOS: No one knows.

DEMETRIUS: I know. It's the end of the world when a man breaks the habit of breathing.

PAUL: It may be the world will end for all of us before the next breath. God knows. Or His world may last a thousand years. And a thousand years beyond that. (*Leaning over the pulpit*) How will men *then* know the teachings of Christ? From the mouths of those who walked with him? Simon Peter? Andrew? John? No, I give you a greater wonder! Generation upon generation unborn will know the living Jesus through Apostles chosen by the Holy Spirit . . . !

TITIUS: Such as Paul?

PAUL: (*With a nod*) Such as Paul. The Thirteenth Apostle. But first in the march of men who will spread the good news across the centuries—

(*A cry, far-off—a Man's voice—long, mournful, fading away*)

BOY: (*Standing*) Didja hear that?

STULTISSIMUS: W-w-what was it?

PLOUSIO: No concern of ours . . .

(*All look toward the sound, quizzically—except Paul, who doesn't seem to have heard it*)

PAUL: (*Sadly*) Why do I go on like this? You don't even listen to me . . . ! (*Almost trance-like; light narrows on him*) But I will tell you of a vision which came to a man on the road to Damascus. Upwards of fourteen years ago. Did it happen in the body? Out of it? I don't know. God knows. He was lifted up as far as the third heaven! And I know that this same man (whether in the body or out of it, I don't know, God knows!) this man was caught up into paradise—! And he heard words so unspeakable that human lips can't repeat them . . . (*Perturbed Figures begin to enter—Corinthians murmuring among themselves about some grisly news. By twos and threes they hurry to the choir stalls. Paul is unaware of them*) About such a man as that I'm ready to boast; and it would not be the boast of a fool, for I'd be speaking truth—!

(*Prisca bursts in from left*)

PRISCA: (*Breathless, distraught*) Is he here? I pray to God he's here, that my eyes lied to me in the torchlight— (*She looks*

around, then signs hopelessly) No . . . of course he's not here
. . . !

APOLLOS: Who—?

PRISCA: Xenophilus . . .

PAUL: (*Sternly*) Such a man does not exist!

PRISCA: (*Laughs at the irony*) Oh, you have great wisdom,
Brother Paul. You're right. Xenophilus no longer exists.

(*With a barely vocalized sigh in unison, the newly-arrived
Corinthians—the choir—sit in the choir stalls*)

DEMETRIUS: What happened to him . . . ?

PRISCA: Did you throw him out of the church?

(*Several reply at once:*)

APOLLOS: We didn't want to—

STULTISSIMUS: It was P-p-p-Paul's idea—

PLOUSIO: Paul made us do it—

PAUL: (*Coming down from the pulpit*) To purify the
fellowship—!

PRISCA: Did you damn him?

PAUL: He was a fornicator!

PRISCA: He was a confused, frightened boy! The fellowship of this church meant everything to him. He walked,
spoke, lived Jesus. The Master was more real to him, I think,
than to any of us. How he tried to prophesy, to spread the
Good News—! He was imperfect? So are we all! (*Confronts
Paul, witheringly*) Xenophilus cared! He cared about his step-
mother, pining for her husband, dead in the Lydian Wars. And
in her husband's son, she saw the figure of her lost lover,
young again . . . ! In all Christian goodness, he wanted to
give her some comfort. And so he lay with her! Is that wicked?
Vile? Lust? Surrendering to the flesh? Well, what if it is? How
many worse things happen in Corinth with every puff of wind,
every lap of the tide? Was anyone hurt by what he did? *I* know
what it's like to be cut off from a husband. Titius Justus can
tell you how it scars the soul when the warm body which has
slept close beside you in the wedding bed is cold and still. You
say God damns Xenophilus because he loved? Shared the joy
and comfort of a common bed with a woman who had lost
everything? He sinned, you say? Well, *I* say he was the best
kind of sinner! He sinned, not for himself, but in loving kindness to his dead father's wife!!!

PAUL: (*Dreading to hear*) What happened to him . . . ?

MONICA: (*With morbid eagerness*) Is he dead? He's dead, I know he's dead . . . !

PRISCA: I'd just left the physician's house. The girl's burn will heal, God willing. And I happened to look up, toward the cliffs . . . (*Imperceptibly, the choir voices enter*) A little grey moonlight had filtered through the clouds—and I saw a young man, a boy, standing high above me on the very brink of the Acrocorinth. I thought— "That's strange, it looks like Xenophilus—!" Then he let out a cry—! I felt the pain of it in my own breast—a wail that must've been heard as far as Athens! And then, as I watched, he hurled himself off the heights—and as he fell, a prayer shawl fluttered behind him like useless wings . . . ! (*A pause—she covers her face. Choir out*) I couldn't get to him on the pavement, there was too much of a crowd. Soldiers with their indifferent torches, and the push of those hideous death-lovers—! I got only one look at the face, so bloodied that I wasn't sure—But now I know—it was our gentle, sinful brother, Xenophilus.

(*One by one, they look toward Paul*)

APOLLOS: Jesus taught us to help those who stumble, not to damn them.

DEMETRIUS: (*A bitter burst of accusation*) You killed that boy! As surely as if you had pushed him off the cliff with your own hand—!

(*Paul is desperate. Everyone is against him*)

PAUL: (*Hoarse, lashing out at Demetrius*) How could you understand? You're not even a Christian—!

DEMETRIUS: (*Simply*) Only a human being.

PAUL: (*He looks about at the hostile faces, all staring at him coldly. He weaves unsteadily. Anguished*) I'm imperfect, I'm not a saint—! I–I make mistakes, *I'm* a human being, too—! You think I've failed you—? I'm a false apostle, worthy only of your reproach—? I swear to you, when I am weak— (*He breaks off. All watch, stunned. His head jerks to one side—a sound like a death rattle comes from his throat. He collapses, writhing—his left side twitching violently*)

MONICA: (*Gleefully*) A demon's got him—!

(*The Choir stands, as one man. A turmoil of reaction as the Corinthians crowd about the stricken Apostle. The next four speeches are simultaneous:*)

APOLLOS: Stand back, let him have air!

DEMETRIUS: It's the "King's Disease!"

TITIUS: Let Prisca take care of him.

PRISCA: Be sure he can breathe—!

(*She wads up a prayer shawl into a pillow, puts it under his head. The Boy, wide-eyed, clings to Monica. Stultissimus and Plousio are agape*)

APOLLOS: The thorn . . . the thorn in the flesh. . . .

PRISCA: Lie back, Paul. The worst is past. . . .

(*The seizure is subsiding. Apollos and Titius help the Apostle to his knees. He clasps his hands in supplication*)

PAUL: God in Heaven, have mercy—! (*His tone has urgency, without self-pity*) Have mercy on the boy whose tormented soul flies to you tonight—! And have mercy on me, his tormentor—! (*In dismayed self-anger*) Why is it??? The good that I would, I do not! And the evil which I would not, that I do—! Oh, wretched man that I am, who shall deliver me from the body of this death—? I've neglected the most precious gift your Son has brought to us . . . ! Though I speak with the tongues of men and angels, and have not love— (*Awed, the Choir sings—softly, wordlessly*) I am become as sounding brass, or a tinkling cymbal . . . ! (*Painfully, he comes to his feet*) I may have the gift of prophecy, understand all mysteries, possess all knowledge—but without love, I'm nothing! (*Looks toward Titius*) I may give all my goods to feed the poor . . . (*To Prisca*) and give my body to be burned, but if I have not *love,* what good does it do? (*Paul moves toward the fish-flag*) Love is patient. Kind. Envies no one. Is never boastful, conceited, rude . . . (*He laughs a little, thinking how boastful he has been*) Never selfish, nor quick to take offence. Love keeps no score of wrongs, does not gloat over other men's sins . . . (*Frowns, thinking of Xenophilus; then defiantly*) Love delights in the truth! Bears all things, believes all things, hopes all things, endures all things! Love never ends! (*With a gesture toward the pulpit*) Have prophets stood there? They'll pass away. Tongues of ecstasy? They'll cease. Knowledge? It will vanish. We don't know everything—only a part. But when that which is perfect is come, that which is partial shall be done away. (*To the Boy on the floor, his crutch across his lap*) When I was a child, I spoke as a child, I understood as a child, I thought as a child. But when I became a man, I put away childish things. For now we see through a glass, darkly—but then—FACE-TO-FACE! The

time will come when I shall know even as also I AM known
. . . ! (*This is a Second "Road to Damascus" experience for Paul, a
rediscovery of the centrality of love. Hostility toward him is subsiding*)
Three things will last forever: Faith. Hope. And Love. But the
greatest of these is Love! (*Music hovers, falls away into silence*)
You call me a weakling? An earthen vessel? Proud? Inconsistent, you say? The author of cruel judgments? And worst of
all—lacking in love—? I give you a mighty miracle,
Corinthians—and I am humbled by the wonder of it! Imperfect though I am, still GOD WORKS THROUGH ME—! For
when I am weak, THEN AM I STRONG!!! (*The pulsing beat of
a tympani. An incredible idea is rushing into Paul's mind. He seizes
the Boy's crutch—then strides swiftly to the fish-banner, rips it down!
He ties the crutch across the staff, a crude cross. The Corinthians are
shocked at this stark symbol*) No more will we be fishermen, trying
to ensnare souls in the net of Jesus. I preach Christ crucified,
and RISEN AGAIN!!! (*A clean trumpet figure sounds, the Choir
surges, the tympani beat resumes*) If God be FOR us, who can be
AGAINST us??? (*He lifts the cross. The Corinthians are spellbound
by this new vision of the Apostle*) He did not spare His own Son,
but let Him be crucified for us all—! So how can we be
worthless—mere sheep for the slaughter? NO! We are MORE
THAN CONQUERORS, through Him that loved us—! (*Paul
gazes up at the crude cross, held high in his hand*) For I am persuaded that neither death, nor life, nor angels—nor prin-
cipalities nor powers—nor things present nor things to
come—nor height, nor depth, nor any other creature shall be
able to separate us from the love of God which is in Christ
Jesus, our Lord—!!!
> (*All criticism is swept away in the tidal wave of Pauline charisma.
> The Choir, augmented by organ, tympani and trumpet, fills the
> sanctuary with exultation. Paul turns, holding aloft the cross, ad-
> vances toward the altar*)
> CHOIR: (*Sings*)
"Gone is the shame of the crucifixion—!
Hail to the Christ of the Cross of Glory—!
By loving—by forgiving—we are healed—!
By the holy act of love, we are made whole—!"
> (*Paul reaches toward the altar of this church, and seems to be
> lighting its crucifix with the first crude cross of Christendom. The
> cross above the altar seems to ignite with light. Paul kneels. One by

one, the Corinthians—facing upstage—kneel with Paul. Demetrius, however, remains standing. In a wave of agnosticism, he starts to go out left—but stops at the doorway, facing front. He hesitates—looks back—then Demetrius, too, drops to his knees. Music surges to a climax. The sanctuary reverberates in triumph)

Robert Patrick

MY CUP RANNETH OVER

Robert Patrick

After being showcased in several cities, Robert Patrick's *My Cup Ranneth Over* had its New York premiere at the Circle Repertory Theatre on June 8, 1978. The metropolitan critics found it "a funny and amiable teacup of a play" that "charmed its first night audience with its insightful wit and ironic humor on the theme of making it BIG in the Land of Hype and Money." As Michael Feingold reported in the *Village Voice*, "Nothing could be simpler than the situation, and nothing could be cleverer than the way Patrick keeps it moving, with an unending flow of reversals and laugh lines, all seeming to tumble quite by accident out of the characters and the event."

The play originally was published in *Dramatics* magazine and is included in an anthology for the first time in *The Best Short Plays 1980*.

In reply to a request for biographical information, Mr. Patrick has written: "I was born on September 27, 1937, in Kilgore, Texas, to working-class parents (oil field hand and waitress). We traveled extensively as Father looked for work in the Depression Southwest. In one year, I attended twelve schools. My only real, continuous environment was American Pop Culture which traveled from place to place with us.

"I hit New York in 1961 and wandered instantly into the Caffe Cino, the first Off-Off-Broadway theatre, and stayed there in every possible capacity until its closing in 1968.

"In 1964, I wrote my first play, *The Haunted Host.* That and *Camera Obscura,* also written for Caffe Cino, went on to Off-Broadway and, subsequently, world-wide production.

"I originated the comic book shows for Cino, and also worked at La Mama and innumerable other underground theatres."

Mr. Patrick later founded La Mama Hollywood, worked with Drama Shelter in Chicago, stage-managed for Tom O'Horgan, wrote a film for Ralph Nader, and television specials for Marlo Thomas and Lily Tomlin. The author of thirty-five published plays, he also has written articles and poems for *Playbill, Dramatics, Soho News, New York* magazine, and dozens of other publications.

Mr. Patrick's most noted stage work is *Kennedy's Children* which originated in New York in 1973 in a loft over a Y.W.C.A., went on to London (1974) where it received much acclaim, and finally found its way to Broadway where it opened at the John Golden Theatre on November 3, 1975. According to the author, "there have been literally thousands of productions of *Kennedy's Children* in forty languages."

A writer who keeps in close contact with his myriad productions, he admits that he travels whenever and wherever he can, and is "absurdly accessible."

PAULA
YUCCA

Scene:

The living room of Yucca and Paula's apartment, doors to bed-rooms, left; hallway and kitchen, right. On the walls are: a gradua-tion photo of Yucca and Paula, smiling in caps and gowns; a rock-concert poster advertising some huge names with "and other bands" at the bottom, with "And Yucca Concklin" added in magic marker; and along one wall, hundreds of rejection slips from Cos-mopolitan. *Under this wall is a desk with a typewriter. There is a telephone on a long cord. The desk also holds a clock radio. At the desk sits Paula Tissot, in her middle twenties, attractive and trim, wearing a long bathrobe. She is typing efficiently.*

PAULA: (*Reads from her manuscript*) "One Woman's Man-ifesto, by Paula Tissot." There. *Cosmopolitan* will print this one. They have to. They printed a dozen just like it last year. (*Reads*) "And so we must remember always to join in sister-hood, with respect for one another's talents and abilities, never to follow the loathsome male model of competitiveness . . ." (*The phone rings*) ". . . maintaining respect not only for one another but for ourselves" (*Phone rings*) "especially for our gentleness and kindness, our tenderness with one another." (*Phone rings. Paula screeches*) Yucca! Yucca! (*She listens. Phone rings*) Yucca! Yucca! Yuck! (*Phone continues ringing*)

YUCCA: (*Sleepy, off*) Whaaaaaat?

PAULA: Get up and take off your sleep mask and put on your robe and stagger in here and answer the phone! (*Off, a long, incoherent mumble. Paula, sharply*) You don't want to get up and take off your sleep mask and put on your robe and stag-ger in here and answer the *what*?

YUCCA: (*Staggers in in robe, sleep mask on her head. She's funny and awkward*) I forget why you can't answer the phone.

PAULA: (*Making corrections on her manuscript*) Because it's for you.

YUCCA: I forget how you know that.

PAULA: Because my friends know I write in the mornings and they do not call before noon.

YUCCA: Right. I remember now. (*Answers into phone*) Hello?

PAULA: (*Reading to Yucca with relish*) "We must recognize one another."

YUCCA: Lola who?

PAULA: "We must communicate."

YUCCA: There's no one here named Lola.

PAULA: "We must revere one another."

YUCCA: We have a Paula.

PAULA: "We must encourage one another."

YUCCA: (*Still into phone*) Paula.

PAULA: She writes. "We must be without ego."

YUCCA: She writes.

PAULA: Brilliantly.

YUCCA: And me, Yucca, I sing. Pretty well. No Lola.

PAULA: I'm not in except to the Pulitzer Prize Committee.

YUCCA: (*As Paula returns to work with a pencil*) Oh, you're Lola? You're an old friend of mine? I remember you? Look, I was up very late last night. I had to go across the street and fill in for somebody. (*To Paula*) Hey, I had to go across the street to The Bitter End, I mean The Other End. It used to be The Bitter End.

PAULA: It's not across the street.

YUCCA: It was across the street from where I was. Anyway, I had to go over there last night and fill in for Tod Mitchell, no less. He had a throat.

PAULA: Useful for a singer.

YUCCA: Sore.

PAULA: No, I'm just trying to write.

YUCCA: No, he had a sore throat and I had to fill in for him. And the people actually stayed.

PAULA: Did they like you as well as *Cosmopolitan* is going to like this article which I will finish writing as soon as you stop bothering me?

YUCCA: They loved me. They always love me. I am their spiritual selves delivering a rueful rigadoon from the depths of poverty and obscurity. Also, I'm better than a sore throat. (*Into phone*) Oh, were you there? Did you enjoy yourself? Me, I mean.

PAULA: No, I wasn't there. I was home working. I write.

YUCCA: Not you. Some person called Lola who insists she is

an old friend. (*Into phone*) You weren't there? How could you like me, then? Huh? You want to read to me? No, don't. My roommate reads to me. I can read, I just don't. She reads. She writes.

PAULA: (*Grimly*) She tries.

YUCCA: (*Into phone*) Read it to her. (*Hands phone to Paula*) It must be some writer-friend of yours. She wants to read something.

PAULA: Oh, really, Yucca! (*Yucca exits to kitchen*) Hello? What? The time? Yes, I have the time, it's eleven-thirty and I don't take calls before—The *Times*? What times? The *Times*? The *New York Times*? (*Yells*) Yucca, you got reviewed in the *New York Times*! (*Into phone*) Wait, read it to me slowly!

YUCCA: (*Re-enters with banana. She has not understood*) You got a rejection slip from the *New York Times*? (*Pats Paula consolingly*)

PAULA: (*Brushing Yucca away. Into phone*) Wait, start that over.

YUCCA: (*Indicating* Cosmo *rejection slips*) You'll have to start a whole new wall.

PAULA: (*With ever-mounting excitement*) Yucca, hush! Hold on, Lily. All right, "Lola!" Yucca, you're in the *Times!*

YUCCA: I never sent anything to the *Times*. They don't print songs.

PAULA: There was a reviewer there last night.

YUCCA: The *Times* reviews folk-rock?

PAULA: Listen. (*She repeats what Lola is reading to her*) Funky Punk Subs for Tod Mitchell . . .

YUCCA: Oh, no!

PAULA: With her tousled hair . . .

YUCCA: Oh, God, you told me to comb my hair!

PAULA: In a sweat-stained T-shirt . . .

YUCCA: You told me to dress better!

PAULA: A scrawny street punk lumbered onto the stage at The Other End last night . . .

YUCCA: (*The pits*) Since freshman year you've tried to teach me to walk.

PAULA: (*To Yucca*) Well, it's a hard way to learn, dear, but maybe you'll listen in the future. Go ahead, Lola.

YUCCA: (*Trying to grab phone*) No, don't.

PAULA: (*Expression of shock. Into phone*) And what?

YUCCA: Made a goddamn fool of herself and didn't even get paid!

PAULA: Yucca!

YUCCA: (*Strangling herself with phone-cord*) Paula, how does a lady kill herself?

PAULA: Yucca, listen. (*Hands phone to Yucca*)

YUCCA: Oh, God. (*Listen and repeats what Lola reads*) And proved to be the most exciting and original new pop talent in years. How many years?

PAULA: Well, what do you know?

YUCCA: (*Staring at phone*) I remember her now. Some incredible bore that used to hang around the coffee-houses and knock folk-rock.

PAULA: (*Grabs phone, listens and repeats*) She's obviously bled on the streets she sings about so winningly.

YUCCA: Lola has?

PAULA: You have!

YUCCA: Oh, I have not.

PAULA: (*Repeating Lola*) A remarkable lyric style backed by profound musical expertise. The next thing is going to come from this T-shirted essence of the post-Watergate street punk.

YUCCA: (*Grabs phone*) Lola, does anybody read the *Times*? I've got to wash and hang up my face. I'll call you back. (*Hangs up*) I can't call her back. I don't know her number.

PAULA: Yucca, how fantastic!

YUCCA: (*Beginning to realize*) They must have been there to see Tod Mitchell. The *Times* never saw me in their life.

PAULA: Well, they sure 'nuff saw you now. Congratulations, kid.

YUCCA: Congratulations, "punk."

PAULA: (*Rising and exiting*) This would seem the time to break out a certain bottle of champagne.

YUCCA: (*To phone*) Post-Watergate street punk? I was a street punk early in '68. Champagne? (*Pulls sleep mask over her eyes*)

PAULA: (*Runs back on with champagne and two glasses*) Champagne it is!

YUCCA: Paula. I'm interrupting your rigid schedule.

PAULA: (*Opening and pouring champagne*) Once can't hurt. This is an event.

YUCCA: The *Times* can't be of any importance in rock.

PAULA: Darling, enjoy it, have fun.

YUCCA: It's probably some twelfth-string hack. Everybody thinks they're a rock reviewer if they know Helen Reddy from Phoebe Snow.

PAULA: (*Very party-mood*) *Is* Helen Reddy from Phoebe Snow?

YUCCA: I have a confession to make. I have no faith in myself. I drank the champagne Tuesday.

PAULA: Well, I had faith in you. I bought some more Wednesday.

YUCCA: (*Removes sleep mask*) Oh, you shouldn't have. (*Giggles*) Well, as it turns out, you should have.

PAULA: In fact, I bought two—I have faith in me, too. (*Offers glass*)

YUCCA: (*Takes glass*) Oh, you should. This will happen to you before it does to me.

PAULA: Maybe when Germaine Greer gets a sore throat. But it *has* happened to you, and it's wonderful.

YUCCA: It's only one review.

PAULA: It's only your first.

YUCCA: But that champagne was for my first gold record!

PAULA: We'll just drink a little and keep the rest in a quart jar.

YUCCA: They came for Tod Mitchell.

PAULA: They stayed for you.

YUCCA: They probably thought I was Tod Mitchell.

PAULA: It's those T-shirts. Drink up, darling. Here's to a fantastic fluke. It couldn't happen to a sweeter punk. (*Paula drinks. Yucca won't*) Oh, enjoy it, darling. It may never happen again. (*Phone rings*) Oh, bicentennial bucket of buttered popcorn!

YUCCA: I'll get it, I'll get it. Hello! Oh, hi, Brad. (*Hands phone to Paula*) It's your boyfriend from the *Village Voice*.

PAULA: Oh, come on, he's not my boyfriend (*Into phone*) Brad, you brute. You know I never take calls before noon. But you're forgiven, this is your lucky day, we're having a little celebration. My little roommate, Yucca? She sings a little? Well she got a sweet little review of all things in the *Times* of all places, and we were just—Oh, certainly. (*Hands phone to Yucca*) He wants you.

YUCCA: Of all little people. (*Into phone*) Hi, Brad. You what? No, no, you want Tod Mitchell. You've had Tod Mitchell? You were? I was? You do? (*To Paula*) He wants to interview me over the phone.

PAULA: He is. (*She sits at typewriter*)

YUCCA: Right. (*Into phone*) Oh, sure, I understand. I understand about deadlines. It's all right, really. (*To Paula*) This is just a short interview to fill in. He'll do a great big longer one next week.

PAULA: Of course.

YUCCA: (*Into phone*) I guess that's all right. Shoot. Huh? Why do I call myself Yucca? (*Paula types answer and hands it to her*) Because it's the state flower of New Mexico. (*Paula continues typing. Yucca reads from Paula's typewriter*) No, I'm from Nebraska but I couldn't very well call myself Goldenrod Concklin, could I? Concklin? (*Paula types. Yucca reads*) It's your name, stupid. I mean, it's my name. My inspiration? (*Reads as Paula types*) I've bled on those streets. Where did I get the idea for the T-shirt? (*Paula does not type*) Uh, I'll tell you next week. No, I've certainly never had a shorter interview. Bye Brad. (*Hangs up*)

PAULA: (*Philosophically*) Bye, Brad.

YUCCA: Imagine the *Village Voice* interviewing me.

PAULA: I think I am.

YUCCA: Maybe they'll make a movie of my life.

PAULA: I think they have.

YUCCA: They liked the same song you like! (*Sings*) "Folks Get Up At Nine in California, Because They Know It's Noon in Alabam'."

PAULA: Is that what I like?

YUCCA: (*Going to Paula's desk with champagne and glasses*) Sure, you love that one. Oh, Paula, you're always right. It's just like you said a few minutes ago. "This may never happen again." Oh, well, I guess as it turns out you were wrong, but you know what I mean. (*Drinks her champagne, pours more*)

PAULA: Well, I'm an unpublished writer, not an unpublished prophet. And speaking of unpublished writing, (*Phone rings*)—I'm going to kill myself.

YUCCA: Hey, what's wrong? You sound sad.

PAULA: I'm not sad.

YUCCA: But you don't usually look like this until the mailman brings you your rejection slips. Woops!

PAULA: I think your best move right about now would be to answer the phone.

YUCCA: Sure. (*Answers phone*) Hello? Lola who? Oh, Lola. The *New York Post*? No, I'm not listening to the *New York Post*. It's a newspaper, isn't it? Oh, I see. (*To Paula*) Have we got a radio that gets WNEW-FM?

PAULA: On my desk. Where I once wrote. (*She turns on radio. It comes on instantly*)

RADIO: ". . . and she makes so improbable a garment as a T-shirt into a uniform of deliberate despair. This is a debut not to be forgotten. Her talent stunned an audience that came to hear glitter rock and stayed to relish street poetry from a lovable, shaggy-haired punk."

YUCCA: (*Spaced throughout the above speech, into phone*) Uh-huh. The *Post*, too? Talent . . . T-shirt . . . Tousled hair . . . Top star . . . Terrific . . .

RADIO: (*Clearly*) "Look out, world. Here comes Yucca Concklin! And now, late weather and news."

YUCCA: Oh, leave it on.

PAULA: You're not weather yet, Yucca.

YUCCA: Thanks, Lola. Sure, I can get together sometime. He liked which? What? (*To Paula*) He liked, the *Post* especially liked (*Sings*) "The Bar is Closin', It's Quarter to Two, Isn't There Somethin' You Can Do To Make Me Fall in Love With You."

PAULA: Late weather and news especially liked your T-shirt.

YUCCA: Holy Moses, it's a plain white T-shirt! Oh, why didn't we record it?

PAULA: We were busy. Once.

YUCCA: Look, Lola, I have to set up my roommate's tape recorder. I'll call you back someday. No, I guess I don't have your number, do I? It's what? Paula, will you take Lola's phone number? (*Puts phone to Paula's ear*)

PAULA: Sure, why wouldn't I? (*Types phone number as Lola speaks*)

YUCCA: (*To Lola*) Thanks loads.

PAULA: (*Whisking number out of typewriter to Yucca*) You're welcome.

YUCCA: (*Crumples phone number and throws it away idly*) Bye. (*Hangs up, goes for tape recorder*) Who *is* she?

PAULA: Incredible bore. Hung around coffee-houses. Knocked folk-rock.

YUCCA: (*Taking tape recorder from desk*) Oh, do you *know* her? (*Phone rings*) Can you get that? I've got to get this thing hooked up in case . . .

PAULA: I'll fit it into my schedule. (*Answers*) Hello? Yes, this is Yucca Concklin's apartment. Yucca— (*Holds out phone*)

YUCCA: (*Oblivious, entangled with wires and jacks*) We should hook it up to the TV, too, just in case they say anything about me on Today today or Tomorrow tonight.

PAULA: (*Imitating Yucca into phone*) This is Yucca Concklin, in fact. Yes, I'm joyed over. Because it's the state flower of New Mexico. No, I'm from Montana but I couldn't very well call myself Bitter Root Concklin, could I? T-shirt?

YUCCA: (*Mutters while working*) T-shirts are a major American industry for God's sake.

PAULA: (*Still into phone*) Because the T-shirt is the sartorial symbol of the lost, the hopeless, the helpless, all who wish to escape the treadmill of media-dictated fashion and simplify their lives and take a wider-eyed view of the hung-up world we're living in. A quotable quip? You want a quotable quip? Okay. How about this? I don't believe in foods without preservatives, because: they'll never last. Thank you. (*Hangs up*) You just gave an exclusive interview to Earl Wilson.

YUCCA: Maybe they'll put out Yucca Concklin plain white T-shirts. It'll be cheap.

PAULA: That won't stop you.

YUCCA: (*Realizing*) Earl Wilson? He's *real!* Why didn't we record it?

PAULA: He doesn't make records. He writes. I write too, Bruté. (*She starts cleaning up champagne glasses, etc.*)

YUCCA: Paula, is there any way to leave the radio on all the stations sameltimeously?

PAULA: If there is, you'll find it.

YUCCA: Wish me well.

PAULA: I wish you were.

YUCCA: (*Following behind Paula as Paula cleans up*) Paula, are you okay?

PAULA: I'm okay, you're okay, I read it in a real book.

YUCCA: Your face looks like a fig.

PAULA: Thanks.

YUCCA: Did I do something wrong?

PAULA: Ask Celebrity Service.

YUCCA: I washed the dishes and our socks last night, didn't I?

PAULA: Yes.

YUCCA: I didn't wash 'em together, did I?

PAULA: No.

YUCCA: Did I leave water spots on the champagne glasses?

PAULA: No.

YUCCA: Did I leave my electric guitar plugged in all night?

PAULA: You can afford it, Yucca; just do an endorsement ad for Con Ed.

YUCCA: Well, then, why are you uptight?

PAULA: I'm not uptight; don't project your anxieties on me.

YUCCA: Oh, am I doing that again? I'm sorry. I never know I'm doing that until you tell me. Thank you.

PAULA: What are friends for? She asked herself. Profoundly. Returning to work. (*She has cleared champagne, etc., off her desk and sits down to work*)

YUCCA: But you do seem upset. Is it possible *you're* anxious and projecting *your* anxieties onto me and then projecting your projecting them onto *me* onto *my* projecting them onto *you*?

PAULA: Yucca, I have to keep *Cosmopolitan* supplied with rejection material. I can't spend the morning playing anxiety-pong.

YUCCA: Well, gee, couldn't we take the morning off to celebrate? How often does one of us have this happen?

(*Phone rings*)

PAULA: Yucca, did you not hear me? I have to work on my article.

YUCCA: Aw, come on, Paula, it can't be that urgent, they just shoot 'em right back, anyway.

PAULA: (*Evil glare*) Yucca!

YUCCA: Probably my best move now would be to answer the phone, right?

PAULA: I'm going to change into my mailbox clothes. (*Starts off with champagne, etc.*)

YUCCA: (*Answers phone*) Hello. (*Stops Paula*) Don't take that away, I want some more. (*Paula leaves champagne and one glass and exits*) Hello again. Why, thank you. I'm just as surprised as I can be. That wasn't coy. Yes, I was filling in for Tod Mitchell. No, we're not lovers. No, he didn't deliberately fake sick to get me on. (*Angry*) Well, I don't care what Joan Baez did for Bobby Dylan at Newport in nineteen sixty——. (*Rebuffed*) I'm sorry, sir, I didn't mean to be curt. Have you got some right to talk to me that way? I'm only asking. I'm new in the business part of this business. You are? Why, I've never talked to one before. An agent, huh? Hey, what exactly do you people do? That wasn't smart. You represent people? Okay. Let's hear you do Burt Lancaster. You want to represent me? (*Elated*) Fantastic—wait, I want to drink to that. (*She starts pouring, eventually overruns her glass*) I am? You do? Oh, you read my reviews, huh? Well, sure, it feels fabulous, it just—I don't know how to express it.

PAULA: (*Enters, dressed*) Yucca, your cup runneth over!

YUCCA: That's it. Oh! (*Scrambles for a dirty T-shirt to wipe up champagne*) Oh, God! Paula, I'm sorry. (*Paula seats herself and types. Yucca speaks into phone*) Huh? You do? Sure, use it. Hey, Paula, he loves that as a quote, "My Cup Runneth Over." (*Into phone again*) Oh, of course, use it. (*Paula types louder and faster*) Well, no, I just love talking to big-time, important agents who make people into universal stars. It's your nickel. Where are you calling from? Los Angeles? It's your bankroll, then, talk. Oh, sure, you can call me here anytime.

PAULA: (*Without stopping typing*) Not anytime, Yucca.

YUCCA: What? Oh, yeah. (*Into phone*) Listen, just not before noon anymore, okay? Noon New York time. It's because of my roommate. She's a terribly disciplined and talented person. She writes. She—Paula, could you cut out the racket? (*Paula stops cold*) She writes. Yes. Thanks. (*She hangs up. Paula gets up and heads for Yucca to kill her. The phone rings. Yucca answers gracefully, sipping champagne*) Hello?

PAULA: (*Wheeling and returning to her chair*) Thank God!

YUCCA: Yes, this is she. You're very kind. You're very kind. Were you there? Your friends are very kind. You can get other opinions in the papers. All the papers. *Daily Variety* you read? Isn't that charming of them, and me a mere unknown. No, it's a sweat-stained T-shirt, not a tea-stained sweatshirt! No, I don't have an agent. He just called me, though. Oh, you are, too? Are there two agents? That doesn't really help me, I don't know any agents' names. I'm sure you are. I'm sure I do. I'm sure we could. You're very kind. You're very kind. You're very fast. Well, who is someone you represent, then? (*Awed*) John Denver? You're very kidding. How do I know that? Look, could we possibly handle this this way? If you put me in touch with John Denver and he says you are you, and you are good, then I'll think about it, provided I think. I hope that's reasonable and I hope I can remember it. His number? John Denver's home phone number? Shoot. 303-236-8790? (*Paula types each digit separately with one finger and hands it to Yucca. Still into phone*) You're very kind. Thank you.

PAULA: You're very welcome.

YUCCA: Thank you, Paula. (*To agent*) Goodbye. (*Hangs up*)

PAULA: I'm not going anywhere.

YUCCA: (*Dreamily dialing*) *Daily Variety* said I had American eyes: red, white and blue. (*Door buzzer buzzes. Into phone*) Hello. I haven't finished dialing.

PAULA: It's the door, Yucca. (*Presses talk switch*) Hello?

MAILMAN: (*Over speaker*) It's the mailman with some more of them heavy envelopes from *Cosmopolitan*.

PAULA: I'll be right down.

MAILMAN: Hurry it up, lady. These streets ain't safe.

PAULA: Right down! (*Goes to desk, turns on tape recorder*) Yucca?

YUCCA: (*Into phone*) Hello. Please hold. What, Paula, darling?

PAULA: My white knight is below with my daily fix of rejection slips. Whoever you talk to, remember you gave an exclusive on your clothes philosophy to Earl Wilson. (*Pause*) You've got John Denver on hold. (*She exits*)

YUCCA: Right. (*Into phone*) Hello? Oh, God, I'm sorry. Listen, you don't know me, but for various reasons I call myself Yucca Concklin, and—you do? You did? That's very kind, especially from you, especially if you are—you are? Well, why

I called is this man said—he represented himself as representing you and—funny, that's the name he gave, isn't that a coincidence? And anyway he said he wanted you to be my agent. His. Mine. Him to be mine. Yes. You think I should? Well, I never doubted it, only my senses. Probably I will. House seats? I don't know. No, I know what house seats are, I just don't know if I get any. The subject just never came up before. If you say so. You're very kind. You're very kind. (*Awed*) You would? Why sure. Uh—look. I don't want to seem paranoid, but I've always had the intense conviction that worldwide conspiracies were working against my happiness, so could you please just say "Country Road?" (*Pause*) You're very John Denver. (*Paula reenters in great disarray with two or three big envelopes. Yucca hangs up*) John Denver wants me to go on the road.

PAULA: I couldn't have put it better myself.

YUCCA: And am I free after the show tonight.

PAULA: As far as I'm concerned. (*Paula hands her the cassette out of the recorder*)

YUCCA: Paula. How sweet! You recorded my whole first conversation with John Denver.

PAULA: I thought you might like to frame it in your new house.

YUCCA: New house?

PAULA: Or perhaps you'll move to a hotel. Where you can call room service. When you want more room.

YUCCA: (*Sees envelopes*) Are those your rejections?

PAULA: All I've thought up so far.

YUCCA: Papers! I've got to go out and get the papers.

PAULA: You can't.

YUCCA: Sure. I'll put on shoes. And an official Yucca Concklin white T-shirt.

(*Phone rings*)

PAULA: Yucca, you can't go out on the street.

YUCCA: Sure I can. I've bled on those streets.

PAULA: Not yet you haven't. Listen. (*She drags Yucca to door and presses listen button*)

YUCCA: That isn't the door ringing, it's the phone.

PAULA: Yucca, listen.

VOICES OVER BOX: Yucca! Yucca! This is her house. This ain't her house. Yes, it is! Whose house? Yucca Concklin. The big new singer. The one that wears the T-shirts. Yeah, this is her house.

YUCCA: They're talking about me.

PAULA: They're talking about you.

YUCCA: They're bandying my name about on the streets.

VOICES: She lives here? Yucca Concklin? Yeah, this is her house. This is where she lives. The one that they were talking about on TV!

YUCCA: (*Into squawk-box*) TV! What channel?

PAULA: (*Dragging her away*) Yucca!

VOICES: That is it. Three thirty-three. Just like in the song. See there's her name. Hey, Yucca!

YUCCA: Hey, yourselves!

VOICES: That's her mailbox. There's her name. Hey, let's take her mailbox!

(*Hideous wrenching sound, then silence. Phone is still ringing*)

PAULA: Yucca, what song are they talking about?

YUCCA: It must be the new one I put into the act last night.

PAULA: What's it called?

YUCCA: "I'm just a street punk, just like you, from three thirty-three First Avenue." I'll take it out of the act.

PAULA: No. Just take the act out!

YUCCA: What are you trying to say?

PAULA: I'm trying to say I want you to move!

YUCCA: Because you think I'm going commercial?

PAULA: Because I know I'm going crackers! This is impossible.

YUCCA: But it can't last. (*Answers phone*) Hello? *People Magazine?* Can you call back in five minutes? (*Aghast*) You can? (*Hangs up*) Okay, it can last. (*Phone rings immediately*)

PAULA: But I can't. I want you to find another place.

YUCCA: It may not be real. (*Answers*) Hello? *Playboy?* (*Pause*) Really? Can you call back in ten minutes? Thank you. (*Hangs up*) They want to photograph me without my T-shirt. It's real. (*Phone rings at once*)

PAULA: It's real, Yucca. You have made the jump. Turned the corner. Gone over the rainbow. Through the looking-glass. Round the bend. Taken the veil. Hit the parade. Made the grade. Started school. Crossed the street by yourself. You're late weather and news.

YUCCA: (*Runs to hall door*) No, I haven't. Look, it's over

already. (*Presses listen button*) See, they've stopped talking about me.

PAULA: No, they stole the squawk-box for a souvenir.

YUCCA: But I don't want to move. Where would I move?

PAULA: Maybe John Denver needs a roommate.

YUCCA: We've always stuck together.

PAULA: Stick it yourself, Yucca.

YUCCA: But I'm a success now. I'll be surrounded by false friends.

PAULA: You won't know they're false after a while, Yucca, they'll be the only friends you've got.

YUCCA: Maybe I'm not a success. You can never be sure.

PAULA: (*With a harsh laugh*) Answer the phone.

YUCCA: (*Does*) Hello? (*Curt*) *Time Magazine?* Call back in fifteen minutes. (*Hangs up. Phone rings. To Paula*) I can be sure.

PAULA: You can be sure.

YUCCA: All right, I can be sure. But I owe it all to you.

PAULA: And three months back rent.

YUCCA: Oh, I know, Paula, but I can pay it all back now. I can help you now. Look what all I've got out of our relationship. What do you want out of our relationship?

PAULA: Out of our relationship!

YUCCA: You can't mean that. I owe so much to you. Every time I'd start to give up, I'd think of you over there, clawing away at that machine, writing articles no one wants, collecting rejection slips, people returning your stuff without buying it, without reading it, editors begging you not to waste your time, and no matter how many of them told you to go into social work or home economics, you kept on! Without hope or promise, all your friends laughing behind your back, editors taking sexual advantage of you, love and life and youth passing you by, and I'd say, Golly. If she can take all that and still believe in herself, who am I to flag? That's what I owe you!

PAULA: Well, and here it comes back with interest. That's beautiful. That's some of your best work! Now would you like to hear the flip side? You've changed, Yucca, you've changed, success has changed you!

YUCCA: Me? (*Answers phone*) *Newsweek?* Later! (*Hangs up*) Me? (*Phone rings.*)

PAULA: Anybody else in this house had success? You've

changed overnight. You all of a sudden expect me to get the phone for you, pour your champagne, give your interviews, sacrifice my writing time!

YUCCA: I haven't changed.

PAULA: You have. You used to do everything for me and now you won't even move!

YUCCA: I haven't changed, I haven't had time.

PAULA: And on top of everything else, you insult my work!

YUCCA: I didn't insult it, I just said nobody wants it.

PAULA: Is that your concept of a rave?

YUCCA: I was just being honest.

PAULA: Well, that's a change.

YUCCA: I'm always honest. You just never listen.

PAULA: I listened to you practicing on your twelve-string torture instrument night and day for five years grinding out dime-a-dozen despair. (*Imitates Yucca singing*) "Oh, you may be goin' to Buffalo, but you ain't goin' to Buffalo me!"

YUCCA: Well, I listened to you on your (*Quick glance at typewriter*) forty-two key racket-package and I listened to all those fumble-fingered rewrites of *Sexual Politics* and I never said anything.

PAULA: You never say anything! What's too silly to be said can be sung!

(*Phone is still ringing*)

YUCCA: I thought you liked my music!

PAULA: I do, I love your stupid music, and now you've got me insulting it. You've changed, Yucca, you've changed!

YUCCA: I've changed? Honestly, Paula. You do a few simple things for me at a time of extreme crisis, things you never do for me, by the way, and which most friends would do for each other without even asking, you scream at me because I've had success, which you all of a sudden act like you never thought I'd have, and after we've struggled and starved together ever since matriculation, you try to throw me out on the streets!

PAULA: (*Running to hall door*) You've bled on 'em, now live on 'em! (*Into squawk-box*) Look out, world, here comes Yucca Concklin!

(*Phone is still ringing*)

YUCCA: I haven't changed: you've changed.

PAULA: You just hung up on *Playboy, People, Time* and *Newsweek!* You never did that before.

YUCCA: I only did it so I could beg you not to throw me out.

PAULA: Don't do me any favors.

YUCCA: Watch out or I won't!

PAULA: Just answer the phone!

YUCCA: It's afternoon now, it's your turn. If you don't want things to have changed, you answer it!

PAULA: All right, I'll keep up the empty shallow, hollow . . . (*Answers phone*) Hello! (*She listens, pales*) —Yucca, it's for you.

YUCCA: Paula, I'm obviously in hysterics. Can you take it?

PAULA: I can take a lot but not this.

YUCCA: Oh, God, who is it, *National Geographic?*

PAULA: It's Cosmo-Fucking-politan.

YUCCA: It *can't* be! I guess it can. What does *Cosmopolitan* want with me?

PAULA: Margaux Hemingway broke an eyebrow.

YUCCA: (*Takes phone*) Look, can you hold? (*Not into phone*) Oh, my God. (*Grabs Paula by arm*)

PAULA: What is it? What did they say?

YUCCA: They said for me they'd hold anything. I'm sorry, Paula.

PAULA: I'm thrilled for you, Yucca. I'm tickled, I'm delighted, but will you please let go of my arm, give *Cosmopolitan* your fiftieth exclusive interview of the day, then bundle up your banjo picks and move!

YUCCA: I don't wanna move. I'll never be here anyway. I'll be on the road with John Denver.

PAULA: Oh, rub it in!

YUCCA: Paula, you're jealous!

PAULA: Gee, that would explain so many things.

YUCCA: You're jealous of me!

PAULA: I'm ecstatic for you, Yucca, but my cup ranneth over about two minutes ago!

YUCCA: I don't want you to be jealous.

PAULA: Then let go of my wrist so I can cut it. That's the alternative.

YUCCA: We've always had this very special feeling of trust

between us, respect for one another's talents and abilities. We've always believed in each other, haven't we? Haven't we? We haven't? All right, I never believed in myself but I always knew you did and that's what pulled me through. Has that feeling just gone?

PAULA: Yucca, this is embarrassing.

YUCCA: But has it?

PAULA: It's just too humiliating to live together, Yucca. I'm jealous—and for Christ's sake, of *you!*

YUCCA: What do you mean, of *you?* What's wrong with you? Me, I mean? What's not to be jealous of?

PAULA: I don't want to fight, Yucca.

YUCCA: Okay, but has the feeling gone?

PAULA: Only from my left hand! (*Yucca releases her*) Thank you, Yucca. I'm very glad for you.

YUCCA: You're being unreasonable.

PAULA: It isn't unreasonable to be glad for a friend.

YUCCA: All right.

PAULA: I just cannot spend the rest of my life thinking up clever quotes for your interviews, Cora Sue Concklin.

YUCCA: You what?

PAULA: I said . . .

YUCCA: I heard you! (*Into phone with great and growing style*) Hey, Cosmo? Shoot. I want to be a star because I'm lazy, and stars only come out at night. I thought Yucca was my full name because my folks always looked at me and said, "Yuck." I wear T-shirts because I've always liked getting into men's underwear. Overnight success? I just hope it's not over tonight. My ambition? I want to go gold before I go grey. You want to print a cover story on me? Won't that hurt? But seriously, I'd love it . . . on one condition. It must be written by my roommate, Paula Tissot. She writes. I believe you are familiar with her work. That's the one. Now, come on, be fair—give the kid a chance. She knows me better than anyone. In fact, she used to be my best friend. Here—I'll give her to you . . . (*She extends the phone to Paula, who sits looking at it*)

Curtain

Elyse Nass

SECOND CHANCE

Elyse Nass

Elyse Nass' *Second Chance* is a tender and humorous look at a near-septuagenarian who wants to spark a renewal of her life and fulfill a long-time ambition. It was initially performed at the Off-Off-Broadway Quaigh Theatre and is published for the first time in *The Best Short Plays 1980*.

Miss Nass has written the following of herself: "I was born on February 14, 1947 in New York City and grew up on the Lower East Side. I was a very precocious child and remember reading all the time. I started to write poetry and short stories at the age of fourteen, and at eighteen completed two novels. My interest in theatre was encouraged at the age of sixteen by a teacher at Washington Irving High School. She suggested that I write a play for a contest. I did, but lost. However, my excitement for the theatre was born and I continued to write plays.

"I attended Hofstra University for a year and a half but left to become totally involved in theatre. I became a 'theatre addict' and went to every play I could and got an all-around theatrical education from 1966–1970 by taking various jobs such as summer stock apprentice, stage manager and publicist for Off-Off-Broadway shows, 'Gal Friday' for small theatres and, most importantly, playreader for the Chelsea Theatre Center and Lincoln Center Repertory Theatre.

"I started to get my own plays produced Off-Off-Broadway at the age of eighteen. One early work, *Avenue of Dream*, which was produced, subsequently was broadcast on radio in New York as well as in several other major cities and abroad in foreign translations. My first full-length play, *The Marriage Museum*, was a winner of a national playwriting competition sponsored by Brooklyn College and produced as part of their New American Playwrights series in the summer of 1970.

"In 1971, I decided to finish college and attended Richmond College of the City University of New York. Two years later, I received a B.A. in Psychology–Women Studies *summa cum laude*. After that, it was back to my writing and an odd assortment of jobs: writer of industrial training films, ghostwriter for a Senator, and researcher-writer in the social sciences.

"In the summer of 1977, I was a Fellow at The Virginia Center for the Creative Arts at Sweet Briar where I completed another full-length play entitled *In Between*. From 1978–79, I was a Literary Artist for The Cultural Council Foundation where I worked as a drama teacher with the elderly, a dramaturge for an Off-Off-Broadway theatre, and a scriptwriter and playwright for social service agencies.

"To date, fifteen of my plays have been produced Off-Off-Broadway, in summer stock, at colleges and on radio. Additionally, I have published a number of articles in various publications and literary journals. I have recently completed a novella and am now dividing my energies between plays and fiction."

Characters:

RITA, *late sixties. Vivacious, trying to appear buoyant.*
EVELYN, *mid-sixties. But she looks tired and is letting things take their course.*

Scene:

A small, nicely furnished apartment in New York City.
Old movie posters and theatrical memorabilia are on the wall, as well as family photographs.
The time is the present.
As the curtain rises, Rita is pacing around in a full-length caftan.
Finally, Evelyn knocks on the door.

RITA: (*In a British accent*) Hurry up and enter! (*Evelyn walks in. She is wearing a plain housedress*) I never thought you'd get here.

EVELYN: Why? I live right next door. What's the matter?

RITA: Please sit down.

EVELYN: Why?

RITA: You're all out of breath, so take a seat quickly. (*She pushes her down in a chair*)

EVELYN: I am not out of breath. What's going on?

RITA: Now just relax. (*She begins massaging Evelyn's temples*)

EVELYN: Just what are you doing to my head?

RITA: Just massaging your temples to give you a sense of calmness.

EVELYN: I am calm. What's happening?

RITA: Breathe deeply—

EVELYN: Look, Rita. You better tell me what this is all about.

RITA: A calcium tablet is good for the nerves. Let me get—

EVELYN: No, I'm not taking anything. I want an explanation. Right now!

RITA: I only wanted to prepare you for the surprise.

EVELYN: Surprise?

RITA: Yes, the big surprise . . . the revelation . . . but you won't sit still for a minute . . . So here we go . . . But first close your eyes . . . (*Evelyn does so reluctantly. Now Rita takes off caftan and is wearing a flesh color leotard with matching tights*) Now open them slowly—very slowly . . . (*She does so*) Ta-ta!

EVELYN: (*Rises, doing a doubletake*) Oh, my God! What are you wearing?

RITA: It's my costume for the play.

EVELYN: That's your costume?

RITA: Yes, this is what I wear.

EVELYN: But it's so—so revealing.

RITA: It is not.

EVELYN: Oh, let me sit down. (*She does*) I can't believe it. So that was the surprise?

RITA: I didn't realize you'd be so shocked.

EVELYN: Well, you told me about the play. I didn't expect you to look like that. You said you were a strange British grandmother who sits around blowing bubbles and eating Barricini chocolates.

RITA: Yes, and my whole family is all around me. My grandson believes he's a frog. My daughter goes back and forth to Mars.

EVELYN: And the people around you—how are they dressed?

RITA: In various ways. Some are clothed, some are—

EVELYN: I don't want to hear anymore! I'm living next door to a weirdo for twenty-five years and didn't know it till now.

RITA: Don't be such a prude. This is a different generation we're living in. It's the "now" generation.

EVELYN: Maybe for you, Rita. (*Pause*) I don't think we'll be at the play. I mean, George and I. He might have a heart attack seeing . . . (*Pause*) Is that what you made me rush in here for? To see you like this, like a—a woman of ill-repute?

RITA: I had no idea you'd be so shocked. I thought you were more up on the times. Evelyn, you better sit down for the second part.

EVELYN: Oh, no! Don't tell me you have to take that off?

RITA: No, it's nothing like that. (*Pause*) It's serious business, Evelyn. (*Pause*) They're coming.

EVELYN: Who?

RITA: My children.

EVELYN: Your children?

RITA: Yes, they're coming to see me.

EVELYN: To see you?

RITA: Yes.

EVELYN: In the play?

RITA: No, not exactly. They're coming to spend the weekend with me. A year ago, Charlie died. So they don't want me to be alone. Now here I am opening in this play in the Village. My first part in a play—my acting debut!

EVELYN: And what a debut! You can't let them see you. Why, it's a sin that you're doing this. Now I always thought you shouldn't be acting. But no, you insisted. So I thought, all right, you'll keep busy. Maybe it's for the best. But look what you're going to be in. You could be arrested wearing that . . . and on this of all weekends!

RITA: No, I won't be arrested. There's nothing wrong with how I look or with what I'm doing. It's a perfectly good avant-garde play.

EVELYN: But it's outrageous! To do it, on the first anniversary of your husband's death.

RITA: Let's not keep going over that, Evelyn. I've made up my mind to go through with this. And we've got to think of what to do.

EVELYN: What did you tell your children?

RITA: I told them they didn't have to come here. I said I would have company, I wouldn't be alone. But they insisted. What could I say?

EVELYN: Nothing. And you'll have to stay home with them, right here where you belong.

RITA: Evelyn!

EVELYN: That's right.

RITA: But I'm going to be busy—with run-throughs during the day. I won't have much time to spend with them.

EVELYN: This is a solemn time, Rita. How can you think of that play? The play doesn't matter. Lots of times, those things never go on.

RITA: Oh, but this will. The show must go on even if it's in a loft.

EVELYN: But what about Charlie's memory?

RITA: I've mourned him long enough. The days I spent crying—the endless nights—empty. It's a year.

EVELYN: That's too soon, Rita.

RITA: Only I can decide that, Evelyn. (*Pause*) You're old-fashioned.

EVELYN: Maybe, but you're crazy to be doing this at all . . . After Charlie died, you went wacko . . . Took up acting . . . You're nearly seventy!

RITA: I only do it as a hobby. I don't want to be a star. What's wrong with doing it for enjoyment?

EVELYN: It's crazy!

RITA: I always wanted to be an actress. (*Pause*) In high school I played in all the shows . . . Oh, you should have seen me . . . Then what did I do afterwards? Get married. Isn't that what everybody did then? Take care of a husband, raise children, take care of a house . . . be a caretaker . . . My dream died . . . slowly . . . Now my children are grown—my husband is dead . . . But I'm alive . . . My dream is coming back.

EVELYN: But so are your children this weekend. Don't you think you have a responsibility towards them?

RITA: To them?

EVELYN: Yes, they want to be with you on the anniversary of your husband's death . . . And you're going to be prancing around on a stage in that.

RITA: I have my own life to lead now.

EVELYN: But they're coming to see you, be with you.

RITA: Yes, but I don't want them to. I don't need them now. I have my own life and they have theirs.

EVELYN: You act like you're disowned or something. They send you things, cheeses, baskets of fruits, from time to time. And look at the interest they're showing.

RITA: Yes, now.

EVELYN: In a way, it's more than my children. I *still* don't know why they moved so far away—to Iceland. It's like another planet. If I hear from them twice a year, I'm lucky. Sometimes I think my children are senile.

RITA: That may very well be, Evelyn. But it's more than that. Our grown children have gone their own ways.

EVELYN: But your children—

RITA: All I'm saying is that I feel separate from my children now.

EVELYN: What a selfish woman you've become.

RITA: Maybe. But my problem all my life has been that

I've been too giving—to everyone—my children, my husband. Now I want time for myself.

EVELYN: But not this weekend. Call up the theater, I mean the loft. Have somebody else do your part. Look, you're not getting any money for it.

RITA: I don't know if I can tell them that.

EVELYN: If you're not taking my advice, Rita, how can I help you?

RITA: You can help me by calling my children.

EVELYN: What?

RITA: Yes, calling them and telling them that you and George will be with me this weekend. If they hear it from you, maybe they'll change their minds.

EVELYN: No, no! I'm not going to lie, especially on the first anniversary of your husband's death.

RITA: Don't be so moralistic, Evelyn. Surely you can do me this favor.

EVELYN: Why don't I call that loft—tell them the situation?

RITA: No, call my children, Evelyn.

EVELYN: I can't.

RITA: For me, for our friendship of twenty-five years.

EVELYN: I just don't want to be involved in this. You'll just have to invite them to see the play when they're here.

RITA: But I can't let them see the play. Not that there's anything vulgar about it—there isn't. It's just the idea, Evelyn . . . I'm sure they'll be hurt and won't understand.

EVELYN: I don't blame them. They have a right to be. (*Pause*) No, I won't do it.

RITA: (*Whirling around; British accent*) I am sixty-eight years young. I eat Barricini chocolates. (*Begins blowing bubbles*)

EVELYN: I can't bear it!

RITA: What I can't bear is your attitude. After all these years, I find out that I have no friends. (*Pause*) Not one who comes through when you really need her.

(*Pause*)

EVELYN: I suppose a good friend would do it for another good friend. After all, we've been friends for ages.

RITA: Oh, thank you. I knew you'd come through. Good old Evelyn. I knew I could count on you.

(*Pause*)

EVELYN: (*Sniffing*) I never thought you'd come to this, Rita. (*Pause*) Because I am your real and best friend, I'm going to save you the embarrassment, the shame. . . . Give me Carolyn's number.

RITA: (*Hands it to her*) Here.

EVELYN: (*Dialing*) Your daughter first . . . All right . . . (*Pause*) Hello. . . Carolyn. . . This is Mrs. Kane. . . Evelyn Kane . . . Yes, your mother's next door neighbor . . . Yes, I'm fine . . . Everything is all right . . . Listen, Carolyn . . . Your mother doesn't know I'm calling you—but she mentioned you were thinking of coming this weekend . . . I mean, planning . . . yes . . . Well, George and I were going to be with her . . . You see, we had it all planned. A visit to the cemetery . . . A quiet weekend . . . I'm just saying that she won't be alone . . . Oh, I see . . . Everything is packed? It's not necessary really . . . I understand . . . The memory of your father is sacred . . . And you should all be together at home quietly. (*Begins to sniff*) Just a cold, Carolyn . . . All right. Don't mention my call, please. I hope I see you . . . Good-bye. (*She hangs up*) Such a wonderful daughter—you should count your blessings.

RITA: A beautiful try, Evelyn, but it failed.

EVELYN: You really should be ashamed of yourself.

RITA: Please try Mark's number now . . . Maybe if you could convince him not to come, he can call Carolyn . . .

EVELYN: The whole thing is confusing.

RITA: No, please, Evelyn. Finish the job. (*Hands her the number*)

EVELYN: (*Dials the number; long pause*) No answer . . . (*Waits*)

RITA: Oh, hang up already. You can try later.

(*Evelyn puts phone back on hook*)

EVELYN: No, it's all settled. They're coming. And you're going to be with them.

RITA: Who are you to tell me what to do?

EVELYN: How dare you speak to me that way? After doing you that big favor . . . By phoning I told a terrible lie.

RITA: Thanks for the favor. Don't worry, you'll still go to heaven even after that terrible lie.

EVELYN: I don't know what's wrong with you. Why don't

you stop all this nonsense? First it was the part-time job, when your husband left you so well provided for. But it turned out that even that job wasn't enough.

RITA: It keeps me busy, but it's so unfulfilling. For it's only a job. I want to do something that matters. Why can't a woman do that? How many years do we have left to do what we want? Why dream of what we once wanted? Let's just do it!

EVELYN: Instead of taking up acting, you should take life easy, like George and I. We're happy.

RITA: Sitting like zombies in front of the television set?

EVELYN: We enjoy it.

RITA: When I come to your house and ask him what's happening in the news, he looks at me like I'm crazy. He doesn't know.

EVELYN: The news and TV make him sleepy.

RITA: It's not a very productive kind of life.

EVELYN: He worked hard all his life. Doesn't he have the right to relax the way he wants to?

RITA: Yes, I suppose he does.

EVELYN: We take vacations—a week or two in the country, take in the sunshine—fresh air—what else is there? When you're old. After a lifetime of working, just breathe the clean air—enjoy the pleasures of retirement.

RITA: It makes me sad to think of the way Charlie killed himself to make a living—working, working, working, no enjoyment . . . Always planning for the day when he'd retire. Oh, he had great dreams . . . A farm house with a horse or two . . . ducks, geese, sheep, chickens . . . and we'd sit on the porch . . . in the clear air . . . But then he died before he had a chance to make it happen . . . Ironic, isn't it? But that wasn't *my* dream . . . (*Pause*) Now it's time for myself. I want to fulfill myself—my own being. (*Pause*) You can't help it if your life is so ungratifying.

EVELYN: Ungratifying? I go with George for walks. He loves the parks. Even though they're all filthy now and covered with dog—you know what. And then he loves to listen to Barry Gray so I stay up at night and hear him call in and talk with him. Every time Barry Gray gives him fifteen minutes. George loves to reminisce about the good old days. Then we go to Roseland because we met there and our names are on those plaques on the wall. George loves to see it.

RITA: Why live through him? Everything for him. Do you stop to think of what makes *you* happy? What *you* want to do?

EVELYN: I want to make him happy, so I'll be happy.

RITA: But surely you have interests?

EVELYN: Interests?

RITA: Interests. Things you enjoy doing. Hobbies, pastimes.

EVELYN: Oh, one time I wanted to be an artist. Go to Paris, live a Bohemian life. But didn't every woman want to be something at one time?

RITA: Who says you can't paint now?

EVELYN: Now? Paint? Are you crazy?

RITA: You have the time. Just buy the paints.

EVELYN: George is allergic to paints. He sneezes.

RITA: Come and paint in my house.

EVELYN: I can't. My hands are arthritic . . . I'm happy with my life, Rita. I'm taking it easy . . . What are you trying to stir up?

RITA: I'm just trying to make you realize that you're not fulfilled. You're not doing anything.

EVELYN: There's nothing I want to do.

RITA: So you're going to sit around till you die? (*Pause*) Now we have some time. How much, we don't know. That's why we've got to seize it now. Don't let it rush by us. (*She begins jogging slowly around the room*)

EVELYN: Do you think you're having a breakdown?

RITA: No.

EVELYN: I do . . . look at you . . . and this whole thing about your children and you not wanting to see them. (*Pause*) And you do the strangest things lately.

RITA: Like what? (*She is now doing simple calisthenics*)

EVELYN: Like thinking you're an athlete.

RITA: I'm exercising. It's good for me. (*She continues exercises*)

EVELYN: And you even ride a bicycle!

RITA: That's even better exercise.

EVELYN: An old woman on a bicycle?

RITA: I want to keep in shape. I'm sixty-eight years young! (*She stretches on toes and stretches her arms in the air*)

EVELYN: Ha!

RITA: I had to get in shape physically for acting.

EVELYN: And then all those vitamins with that horrible-looking granola. I don't understand it.

RITA: I want to be healthy. It all helped me prepare for the stage. (*She does breathing exercises*)

EVELYN: You're really bit by this acting bug only it seems to have stung your brain.

RITA: (*Relaxed, in a meditative position*) Do you know the moment I love best? When everybody is seated, the house is dark. And then slowly the lights go up. Like magic time. And it's a whole new world.

EVELYN: But to be at that world at your age—

RITA: I know I can do it now. I want it. (*Pause*) I remember when Charlie and I used to reminisce about our childhood, to see how far we could remember. He could remember colors, the color of his crib, his underwear. And do you know what I remembered—pictures in books of ladies with pinafores, gentlemen with high-buttoned shoes, singing, dancing . . . And I remembered what I wanted to be. . . . Once Charlie said, "Do you really think you would have been an actress if you didn't get married, raise a family?"

EVELYN: And what did you say?

RITA: I said, I don't know. How does anybody know? If such and such was—if this was that way—why think about it?—torment yourself about it? I spent the major portion of my life as a housewife. Fifty years.

EVELYN: That's half a century.

RITA: Yes. Half a century of doing for others.

EVELYN: I've put in close to half a century.

RITA: All the years . . . They pass so quickly. (*Pause*) Sometimes I think about the people who grew old with me. . . . They retired to warm climates, the Southeast, the Southwest. . . . I get postcards every so often. . . . The husband with a golf stick in his hand smiling, his wife waving . . . surrounded by green grass . . . then the ones in mobile homes in the West, living out their lives . . . the ones who are dead and buried somewhere . . .

EVELYN: Yes.

RITA: That's why you have to spend the rest of your life doing what you want. It's my last chance to fulfill the dream of a lifetime.

(*Pause*)

EVELYN: Look in the mirror. What do you see?

RITA: I see a woman—an older woman trying to begin her life again.

EVELYN: No. Let me tell you what I see. An old woman thinking she's sweet sixteen.

RITA: Don't make fun of me. Inside I still feel sweet sixteen.

EVELYN: Rita, I know you for twenty-five years. I know what's good for you. This isn't. (*Pause*) What you need is a man.

RITA: No. Men are not my answer right now.

EVELYN: You joined a women's lib group? I heard they have them for old women now.

RITA: I have not joined a women's lib group! I've come to my senses—my feelings.

EVELYN: But isn't it lonely without a steady man around? Admit it.

RITA: Sometimes, but I've gone with other men since Charlie died. To this social, that social. They talk about their security, their pensions, their men's clubs—when they chased bears down mountains—

EVELYN: You don't want to give to them. You're shut off in your own world.

RITA: Evelyn, maybe you should go back to your apartment. You're making me nervous.

EVELYN: Well, George is reading the newspaper and watching TV. He doesn't talk much when he does that.

RITA: So why don't you start to do something? For yourself. You always said you liked working with your hands.

EVELYN: My hands?

RITA: Yes.

EVELYN: I always did like working with my hands. (*She begins arranging Rita's flower bowl*)

RITA: You always arrange them so well. Flower arranging is an art. Maybe you should start doing that.

EVELYN: Oh, look, Rita. I'm not about to start *anything* now. I don't think much of this old age. It's something that happens. You get pains, here and there, this hurts, that hurts. You don't know when it's going to be over . . .

RITA: We have opportunities, but you don't see them. Look how long we've lived. We have knowledge, wisdom,

those things youth can never have . . . You make us sound like we're all invalids to be cast aside. We have strengths.

EVELYN: Strengths. What strengths?

(*Pause*)

RITA: I'll tell you a story about strength. A ninety-year-old woman learned wood carving.

EVELYN: Ninety years old? She should be resting at her age.

RITA: According to you. Evelyn, that woman is alive and so are we!

EVELYN: , Alive?

RITA: Yes, alive! Why does everybody think of old age as a time to freeze, a time to die? To be dumped like scrap iron? People in beds, motionless, waiting for their eyes to finally close? No, this is a time for our freedom!

EVELYN: Those vitamins you take must have dope in them.

RITA: You should take some. They'll pep you up.

EVELYN: Vitamins at my age? I've never taken any. No reason to start now.

RITA: That's your problem. Your whole life is set. A routine, the same pattern, it never changes. Never try anything new—even if it's a small thing like a vitamin.

EVELYN: I can't wait for your children to get here and pull you back to your senses.

RITA: I'm fine. I'm just trying to get through to you. (*Pause*) Sometimes I see you walking with George. Following him. You go where *he* goes.

EVELYN: So?

RITA: So? Can't you understand? Don't you want to explore for yourself?

EVELYN: Explore, Rita? Please! This conversation is going in circles. I'm getting dizzy. (*Pause*) Why not forget about this play? Why don't we go out tonight? Look, we'll have a good time . . . I'll drag him away from the paper and the TV. We'll have dinner and then go to Roseland. We'll have fun, a lot of laughs. George-is a riot when he wants to be. When he talks about the way the streets used to be paved . . . a place where he used to work where waiters sang and danced Irish jigs . . .

RITA: What do *you* remember, Evelyn?

EVELYN: Me?

RITA: Yes.

(*Pause*)

EVELYN: ⌈Well, I never gave it much thought, but . . . let's see . . . (*Pause*) On every Sunday in June, God, it was years ago, they were such bright Sundays . . . there would be lots of cars going by . . . They had posters which said, "Just Married." And old beat-up shoes and tin cans were tied to the cars. And the tin cans made so much noise as they rode along. I think all the young women picked a Sunday in June to get married⌉. . . (*Pause*) Come on, Rita, we'll all go out and reminisce . . .

RITA: No, I can't. I want to go over the script again.

EVELYN: So you really intend to go through with it?⌉Not caring about anyone but yourself?⌉ (*Pause*) Did you ever stop to think that you're about to make a fool of yourself?

RITA: A fool of myself?

EVELYN: Yes. Your first time on the stage in over forty years, no fifty years, right? It's been ages.

RITA: Yes, but I'm confident that everything will be all right. Nothing will happen.

EVELYN: What if you forget your lines?

RITA: My part is mostly pantomime.

EVELYN: How will it feel to be the laughingstock in front of a lot of people?

⌈RITA: Why should I be the laughingstock?⌉

EVELYN: I can just hear everybody asking, who does she think she is, somebody so old thinking they can act and wearing that leotard . . . Let's face it, your figure isn't what it used to be.

RITA: That may be true. But people aren't that cruel. I'm old, but I'm still a person and deserve to be treated with respect.

EVELYN: The way old people are treated? They're laughed at or pitied.

RITA: No, Evelyn.

EVELYN: Yes, Rita. I'm telling you for your own good. ⌈Come on, take that off. Put on a dress. Throw away that script.⌉ (*Pause*) Besides you were probably cast because that director felt sorry for you.

⌈RITA: No, the director liked me very much. He said, "For a woman your age, you certainly have a magnetism."

EVELYN: Sure, it's like people giving old people seats on trains and buses, they feel sorry for them, because they feel they might die any second.⌉

RITA: Why do you think he pitied me?

EVELYN: Well, it just seems funny to me that he'd pick someone with no experience for the part. He's not paying you, is he?

RITA: No, as a matter of fact I offered to make a contribution to the theater group for . . . (*She stops, she has slipped*)

EVELYN: Now I see everything, old girl!

RITA: I don't know what you're talking about!

EVELYN: Come on, Rita, I'm not a fool and neither are you.

RITA: I won't listen to your nonsense, Evelyn! My small donation to the theater was only—only a gesture—a gesture of goodwill.

EVELYN: Well, I'm sure it meant a great deal. Those crazy theatres have nothing. They were probably very grateful for your "goodwill." Face it, Rita. They needed your money!

RITA: (*After a long moment*) Maybe you're right. Give the old hag a chance, he thought, out of pity . . . out of a need for my money.

EVELYN: You finally see the light?

RITA: The cast probably talked about me. Who's that crazy old woman? (*She takes script and throws it on the floor*)

EVELYN: That's where it belongs.

RITA: Take a look at me! You're right. The audience will howl. (*Puts caftan back on*) Every audition I've gone to, they've all been young. I stuck out like a sore thumb. Old women don't take up acting.

EVELYN: Oh, honey, don't torment yourself now.

RITA: He cast me for the *money*, Evelyn! I've been such a fool!

EVELYN: Oh, Rita, just think of having a good time tonight. Look, I've got to start talking George into—

RITA: Going? Dragging him away from his routine?

EVELYN: Oh, he'll love it. He likes you.

RITA: He hardly says a word to me. Just nods.

EVELYN: George is a wonderful dancer.

RITA: He never dances. Just stands around looking into space as though he were remembering something he lost fifty years ago.

EVELYN: Come on, don't take it out on George. Think of the great time we'll all have tonight. In a few days, the mourning begins, silence . . . remembrance . . . with your children.

RITA: Yes . . . You're right . . .

EVELYN: At last you've come around to my way of thinking. I knew I could talk some sense into you. Well, I'm going to give George a buzz. (*Dials phone*) Hello . . . George . . . Yes, Evelyn, who else? George, let's all go to Roseland tonight with Rita . . . All three of us . . . It'll be such fun . . . Her children are coming this weekend . . . Yes, her children . . . Carolyn and Mark . . . To commemorate Charlie's death . . . Charlie . . . her husband . . . Dead one year . . . They'll all be staying at home . . . to be with her . . . So I thought why not go out tonight . . . a few days before . . . cheer her up a bit . . . Oh, don't be that way . . . Think of— Oh, all right . . . Look, when Carolyn and Mark come . . . Rita's children . . . Carolyn and Mark . . . we'll all get together for coffee and discuss things—current events. (*Slowly hangs up*) He's watching the news and reading the paper. I suppose I should be in there with him.

RITA: I don't know why he watches the news and reads the paper at the same time. He just stares at them both . . . like sleeping with his eyes open.

EVELYN: I know. He doesn't want to go to Roseland tonight but maybe some other night, Rita?

RITA: We'll see.

EVELYN: Oh, I wish you'd say yes. You wanted to tonight. Look, we'll make it up to you. (*Pause*) I better go in now . . . Or he gets mad . . . He doesn't talk to me as it is . . . Oh, well, you know how men are . . . But he was excited to hear that your children were coming. And he thought it was only proper that you spend the weekend quietly with them.

RITA: Did he say that?

EVELYN: Well, not exactly in those words, but he meant it anyway.

RITA: I got the feeling that he didn't know who my children were. You had to keep repeating their names.

EVELYN: Oh, no. He knew who they were. Well, when Carolyn and Mark come we'll all get together . . .

RITA: I don't know how much time I'll have. It's so limited this weekend.

EVELYN: But you won't be in the play . . .

RITA: I don't know . . .

EVELYN: Rita, this get-together with your children on this

sacred occasion is the only thing that matters this weekend
. . . Don't you want to share Charlie's memory with them?
Think of what it's going to feel like to be with them again.

RITA: But then what? What about all the silences? So much
distance and time between us . . .

EVELYN: But this weekend you'll be reunited! That's the
way it should be. What kind of mother thinks only of herself?

RITA: I suppose my time should be theirs this weekend.
(*Pause*) So my life has to stop for them.

EVELYN: You act like it's the end of the world. You have
nothing to do.

RITA: How can you say that? I have something important
to do, something *very* important to me!

EVELYN: Are you still talking about that play? You're not
going on in that play . . .

RITA: (*Suddenly picking up script from floor*) Yes! Yes, I am!
(*Takes off caftan*) I guess I let all the old fears take over! I was
cast because the director thought *I could do it.* He believed in
me . . .

EVELYN: But what you said before—?

RITA: You were forcing me to say it! It doesn't matter *how* I
got the part. The most important thing is that *I can handle it!*

EVELYN: But what about your children?

(*Pause*)

RITA: I won't tell them about the play.

EVELYN: Thank God for that!

RITA: When they call I'll just tell them that I'm going to be
busy this weekend. But there'll be time for us to go to the
cemetery. Put flowers on his grave. Lilacs. He loved lilacs.

EVELYN: That's the least you could do.

RITA: And we'll all cry. . . . He really was a wonderful
man. I think he'd be happy to know that I was acting in a play.
(*Pause*) And then on with the course of living . . . We'll all
have lunch . . . Then the rest of the time is my own.

EVELYN: Think it over. You may lose your children
forever. If they find out, they won't forgive you.

RITA: You might be right. But how can I hide it? I guess
I'll have to find the courage to tell them and pray they understand.

(*Pause*)

EVELYN: Well, I've tried my best. (*She is about to start*) Good luck, Rita, you'll need it!

RITA: Thanks, Evelyn. (*But Evelyn lingers on, looks at the flowers, then rearranges one or two*) That looks nice.

EVELYN: I guess I *do* have a knack with my hands.

RITA: Yes, you do.

EVELYN: Crazy at this age to have a knack with your hands. Oh, well, what are you going to do? I've got to go in and watch the news with him.

RITA: And I guess I'll practice my part. (*Pause*) You will come to the play, won't you, Evelyn?

EVELYN: Rita, I wouldn't miss it for the world!

(*They hug warmly*)

Curtain